W9-CSP-001

West's Law School
Advisory Board

_____

JESSE H. CHOPER
Professor of Law,
University of California, Berkeley

JOSHUA DRESSLER
Professor of Law, Michael E. Moritz College of Law,
The Ohio State University

YALE KAMISAR
Professor of Law, University of San Diego
Professor of Law, University of Michigan

MARY KAY KANE
Professor of Law, Chancellor and Dean Emeritus,
University of California,
Hastings College of the Law

LARRY D. KRAMER
Dean and Professor of Law, Stanford Law School

JONATHAN R. MACEY
Professor of Law, Yale Law School

ARTHUR R. MILLER
University Professor, New York University
Professor of Law Emeritus, Harvard University

GRANT S. NELSON
Professor of Law, Pepperdine University
Professor of Law Emeritus, University of California, Los Angeles

A. BENJAMIN SPENCER
Associate Professor of Law,
Washington & Lee University School of Law

JAMES J. WHITE
Professor of Law, University of Michigan

MAXIMIZE YOUR LAWYER POTENTIAL

PROFESSIONALISM AND BUSINESS ETIQUETTE FOR LAW STUDENTS AND LAWYERS

By

Amee R. McKim

Mat # 40743609

Thomson/Reuters have created this publication to provide you with accurate and authoritative information concerning the subject matter covered. However, this publication was not necessarily prepared by persons licensed to practice law in a particular jurisdiction. Thomson/Reuters are not
engaged in rendering legal or other professional advice, and this publication is not a substitute for
the advice of an attorney. If you require legal or other expert advice, you should seek the services of
a competent attorney or other professional.

The views expressed in this book are those of the author alone, and do not represent the views of
Hunton & Williams LLP.

© 2009 Thomson/Reuters
  610 Opperman Drive
  St. Paul, MN 55123
  1–800–313–9378

ISBN: 978–0–314–19403–9

*TEXT IS PRINTED ON 10% POST
CONSUMER RECYCLED PAPER*

This book is dedicated to law students and lawyers who work so hard every day to infuse professionalism into all they do. It is equally dedicated to all the law school faculty, law school administrators, and the legal employers who spend countless hours teaching and modeling professionalism to the newest members of the legal profession.

*

Acknowledgements

There are many people who merit my gratitude in the writing of this book. My family deserves many thanks and my endless appreciation. I'm grateful to my parents, Rahlo and Erna Buehler, for beginning my education about life and believing in me, and to my sons, Joe, Jake, and Josh, for continuing that education (particularly during their teenage years) and being all-around remarkable young men. My sister, Lisa Spalding, has always encouraged my professional pursuits and provided a good ear when frustrations run high. Last, but not least, my husband, Robert, has been unfailingly loving, supportive, flexible, and good-natured throughout my career—specifically, every time I take on another project that will eat up my "copious spare time" (aka, our time together). He has sacrificed much for my career and I am so grateful to have his encouragement, creativity, love and support. He challenges me and inspires me to achieve. But, Robert continually reminds me not to take myself, or life, too seriously. His uncanny ability to break my gridlock or irritation with a one-liner that makes me laugh out loud is one of the many things I love so much about him, and why I'm so lucky to have him as my best friend and partner in life.

I also want to acknowledge all of the teachers, colleagues, friends, and mentors I have had the pleasure of knowing—all of you have contributed to this work in some way, and your sharing of stories, research, challenges, and initiatives over the years has enhanced my knowledge and work. I owe a special thanks to the many contributors—some of whom I met during the process of writing this book—who took the time to provide their knowledge and wisdom in the quotes published throughout this text. All were unfailingly helpful, supportive, and knowledgeable. The team at NALP, now and over the years, merits my thanks as well. The team at Thomson West was extraordinary, specifically Bonnie Karlen, Staci Herr, Laura Holle and Roxanne Birkel. Julie Coleman also deserves my gratitude for working with me on this project. Everyone has been very helpful and has answered many questions with patience and knowledge throughout this process.

In a sea of wonderful people who are dedicated to improving the legal profession, two stand out for me and deserve special mention. First, Cybele Smith took special pains to edit and provide comments on my initial thoughts for this book. She has been a dear friend for many years, and provided me with my oft-used phrase, "copious spare time". Cybele is dedicated to making careers in public service and public interest a reality for many law students.

Finally, immeasurable thanks go to my own highly-valued mentor, Nancy B. Rapoport. In August 1991 I was a new and petrified law student, and Nancy was a new law teacher, fresh from law practice. (She later confessed that she was petrified, too.) She quickly mastered teaching, I quickly mastered contracts, and her role expanded to de facto advisor on issues big and small for many of us first-year students at Ohio State. I have often thanked whatever lucky star, deity, or fate put me in Nancy's first-year contracts class, because it really did change the course of my professional life. Nancy modeled a caring attentiveness that was the basis for my own career in counseling and development. Throughout the years, her devotion to students has not faltered one bit, and I'm sure that hundreds of law students and lawyers feel the same way about Nancy as I do. It is not an exaggeration to say that Nancy has had a hand in every career success I have had. May everyone have a Nancy in their lives.

Table of Contents

vii

MAXIMIZE YOUR LAWYER POTENTIAL

PROFESSIONALISM AND BUSINESS ETIQUETTE FOR LAW STUDENTS AND LAWYERS

*

Chapter One
Legal Skills Are Only One–Third of What You Need to Succeed in Law

Tom's Story

Tom sighed heavily as he eyed his large pile of mail. Flipping through the many envelopes, he said out loud, "Rejection...rejection...rejection...rejection." In all, there were six rejection letters in today's take. Although Tom knew good news didn't normally come in the mail, he couldn't help but feel let down. He was a third-year law student in the top ten percent of his law school class with no immediate job prospects. How had he gotten to this point?

Tom's version: Tom had worked hard as an undergraduate and thought that law school would be the easiest way to land a six-figure job. However, he quickly learned that, despite his school's reported ninety percent placement rate, the jobs at large firms went to those second-year students who finished at the top of the class. Tom had borrowed the most he could in student loans each year to go to law school (on top of his college loans), and he maxed out his credit cards to make ends meet.

To land a large firm job after law school, Tom had focused on getting high grades in every class he took. He finished his first year in the top ten percent of his class and landed a job at a small firm his first summer. He graded on to the law review and had his pick of law firms during the fall interviewing season of his second year. After selecting the large firm that paid the highest summer and associate salary, Tom breathed a sigh of relief. It was time to reap the rewards of all his hard work.

Tom thought the summer went well. He thoroughly enjoyed partaking in the firm's events, particularly when high-end food and drinks were involved. He spent time schmoozing with the important partners of the firm—after all, it was important to see and be seen. He felt that he fit right in. Unfortunately, much to Tom's surprise and dismay, he did not receive an associate offer to join the firm upon graduation. He assumed it was a "numbers" issue and felt that he was being punished because the firm had over hired for the summer program.

Despite Tom's stellar grades, the career services office in his law school offered no help in finding him another job. They told him that jobs at large firms were few and far between for third-year law students and perhaps he should consider something else. Tom was angry. He wanted to make a lot of money—partly to pay off his massive debt—and he felt he deserved a job at a large firm. After all, he was smarter and had better grades than ninety percent of his classmates.

Tom had heard through the grapevine that the large firm of X, Y, and Z was in need of a few third-year students to join its associate ranks the next fall. Although the firm wasn't as prestigious and wouldn't pay as much as his other job would have, Tom was certain he'd be able to land that job—they had made him an offer the previous fall for their summer program. He figured this was his ace in the hole. The rejection letters slid out of his hands as he began dreaming about his future office in the corner of the twentieth floor. . . .

Assistant Dean Sue Smith's version: Sue also sighed heavily as she considered Tom's latest pile of rejection letters. She tried to convince him to re-assess his options. Although she wasn't exactly sure why Tom had not received an associate job offer after the summer, she couldn't exactly say she was surprised.

Tom had been a bit "difficult" since his first year of law school. He was always one of the students who signed up for events and then failed to attend. He complained about the policies of the office, particularly those that required mandatory attendance at certain programs. During fall on-campus interviewing, he was a no-show for several interviews with smaller firms. Sue knew that after Tom had obtained a few job offers from the larger firms, he "blew off" anything that was not comparable in terms of size and money. After landing his summer job, he didn't attend any career service–sponsored events for the rest of the year, including the panel about having a successful summer clerkship. Sue figured the lack of an offer was probably appropriate based on Tom's attitude of entitlement.

Summer firm's version: On paper, Tom was everything they could ask for in a summer associate. He had law review membership, grades that placed him in the top ten percent of his class, and superb research and writing skills. Although he had seemed a bit arrogant in the previous fall's interviews, Tom was too promising to ignore. Clearly other firms thought so, as well—Tom received offers to join various summer programs. However, during the summer it soon became apparent that Tom was struggling on a number of fronts. He lacked maturity and social graces. He not only drank heavily at most of the firm's functions, he also discussed inappropriate topics. He showed a lack of good judgment almost all of the time.

Despite Tom's strong legal skills (he turned in excellent work throughout the summer), the firm reluctantly decided that he posed too much of a risk for the firm—he could not be trusted with clients, and they didn't need that kind of liability. Although the firm prided itself on working with new lawyers to develop their skills and abilities, they just didn't feel comfortable with Tom's potential downsides. They reluctantly concluded that they could not make him an associate offer.

X, Y, and Z Law Firm's version: X, Y, and Z lawyers realized they had under hired for their summer program. Based on the large amount of new work coming into the firm, they wanted to beef up their associate ranks with a few additional third-year hires. As the recruiters and lawyers reviewed incoming resumes, they checked their database to see if any of the students had applied previously.

When X, Y, and Z's recruiter came across Tom's application, she recalled having made him an offer for the summer program the year before. She pulled his file and saw that Tom had not responded to any of the lawyers or staff who followed up after making him an offer. In fact, not only had Tom failed to respond to their outreach, he had not even bothered to respond to their offer for employment (which had been made early in the recruiting season the previous fall). When the NALP deadline for acceptances and responses rolled around and the firm still hadn't received a response, they wrote to Tom and said they were interpreting his lack of response as a declination of their offer. The recruiter pulled this information, attached it to Tom's resumé and cover letter, and forwarded it to the hiring partner. The next day, the recruiter received it back with a single word scribbled across the top: "CUT."

The Gap Between Law School and the Practice of Law

Tom and other students like him will, unfortunately, learn the hard way what it takes to be successful in the legal profession. As you have no doubt discovered, law school teaches aspiring lawyers many useful skills—how to analyze and synthesize large amounts of data; how to read and understand case law, statutes, and regulations; how to write legal documents; and how to present cogent arguments. In short, you learn how to think like a lawyer, act like a lawyer, and talk like a lawyer, but not necessarily how to *be* a lawyer. In recent years, schools and bar associations have taken steps to bridge the gap between legal education and the legal profession. Clinical education, bar association–sponsored seminars, and a host of new law school courses have been added to the mix to address the challenges that new law graduates face and to give them more practical experience during law school.

However, even with these positive changes in legal education, few newly minted and barred lawyers are ready to fly solo in the practice of law, and all can benefit from several years working alongside more experienced lawyers. Of those few new graduates who do hang out their own shingle when they graduate, they have likely engaged in special preparation, research, and mentoring relationships throughout their time in law school to ready themselves for a solo endeavor.

The term "practicing law" is not really that far off—practice doesn't make perfect, but experience and seasoning do make you a better lawyer.

Part of the challenge for new lawyers is that, aside from clinical offerings, most law school courses simply do not prepare you for the day-to-day necessities of law practice, such as meeting with clients, dealing with opposing counsel, filing papers in court, managing a case or deal from beginning to end, interacting at a business lunch or cocktail party, and developing new legal business for those in private practice. Unlike law courses, a client seeking help does not come neatly labeled as a contracts client or a torts issue. But the area of legal skills development has received a lot of attention, so most law students know that they need to supplement their education with practical experience—whether it be a summer or part-time job, an externship, or volunteer experience. It behooves every law student to fill in those knowledge gaps and ensure that you have experienced lawyers and other resources to whom you can turn as you learn the ropes, regardless of your first job in law.

So far, we've identified two important spheres of knowledge for law students: 1) honing your legal skills, which law school is very adept at teaching you, and 2) learning the day-to-day practice of law through experience. Don't relax too much, however; there actually is a third area of professional development that is equally critical to your success. Although it does not receive nearly as much attention, training, or acknowledgement as the other two, it is no less important. The skills comprising this critical third sphere are sometimes referred to as "soft skills."

The Necessary "Soft" Skills

In addition to the legal skills and knowledge you need to succeed, and the practical skills you will develop, your ultimate success as a lawyer depends upon a host of other skills, sometimes referred to as "soft" skills because they are more difficult to quantify or are more subjective in nature than those in the other two spheres. Unlike your other credentials, such as your GPA, your class rank, your membership on a law journal, and the rank of the law school you attend, these other skills often fall under the "I know it when I see it" category of assessment.

Although "soft" implies that such skills are optional extras in the legal profession, most legal employers assume that they are, or should be, part of the "standard package" that comes with a new lawyer. Because it can be difficult to quantify these skills during a series of interviews, employers sometimes do not discover deficiencies until after the initial hire, leaving the summer associate or new lawyer vulnerable. So what are the soft skills that comprise the essential third sphere of development?

In broad terms, these soft skills fall under the large umbrella of "professionalism." Respect, courtesy, etiquette, strong communication, leadership, debt management, good judgment, maturity, management aptitude, networking, ethical standards, timekeeping, and organizational ability are all part of the hard-to-measure, but vitally important, skill set that can mean the difference between a high-performing new lawyer and one who is soon forced out the door.

In fact, some law school faculty, administrators, and legal employers are concerned about the narrowing set of candidates who possess these crucial professional skills. Stories, theories, and descriptions abound about the downsides and challenges, as well as the positive traits, of the newest crop of "up-and-coming" lawyers. Because this new generation seems so different from those before it, law firms and other employers have spent large amounts of money on consultants and seminars in their eagerness to learn about them—their wants and needs, and their strengths and weaknesses. Employers are not only aiming to understand this generation of lawyers but also making better efforts to recruit and retain these newest additions to their ranks.

Professionalism Is the Infrastructure of Career Success

Law students and newer lawyers must learn about and cultivate the *critical* link to success in the legal profession and beyond, that third sphere of development after legal skills and practical experience: professionalism. Please note, it is a *profession* you are entering into if you plan to practice law or otherwise work in the legal arena. Whether you are a Millennial, a Gen Xer, or a member of some other generation, professionalism is really the infrastructure of your career success, and that is exactly how you should approach it.

Without mastering the cornerstones of professionalism, as broadly defined in the previous section, your carefully built legal career could come tumbling down around you, even if you have a brilliant legal mind, conducted a thorough job search, and carefully mastered the legal skills you were taught in law school. These professionalism skills are not options—they are part of what employers demand in the "standard package." There are too many people like Tom, whose story began this chapter, who blow a promising career before it even gets started. Worse, they walk away from the experience with little, if any, understanding about how their own lack of professionalism skills led to their downfall. Without this knowledge, they may be destined to repeat the same mistakes, leading to a tumultuous and troubled career path. Listen to the valuable advice of one attorney who directs the character and fitness portion of admission to the bar for his state:

> The most satisfying aspect of my professional life is my involvement in the character and fitness process for applicants to the bar. I know this process has saved lives and helped students get back on track, and that is very rewarding. Everyone makes mistakes, and many of us have done things in the past that we are not proud of. But law students must exercise responsibility and honor their commitments—a failure to do so can affect their ability to become admitted to the bar.
>
> If you are a law student or new lawyer, you must learn to govern your behavior and show respect for others. Take your responsibilities seriously. There is a higher standard for lawyers, and graduating law school just means you are minimally academically qualified to practice law, not that you are fit to practice law. The practice of law is a privilege, not a right. One professor I had in law school, who taught us the code of professional responsibility, gave us a piece of advice that has served me well for more than thirty five years. He said, "If in doubt, don't do it."
>
> **Stephen A. Isaacs, Attorney at Law**
> **Director of Character and Fitness, the Virginia Board of Bar Examiners**

If you are already a practicing lawyer, it's not too late to begin or continue the development of professionalism, including business etiquette, professional courtesies, best practices, leadership, and strong ethics. These skills can be challenging in today's world of information overload, electronic social networking sites, the blurring of public and private domains, and your need to land—or keep—the legal job for which you've worked so hard and in which you've invested so much.

In addition to building your paper credentials, solid career planning must include professionalism, and applicants who embrace and demonstrate it will far outshine those who do not. Professionalism is a reality that today's law students and new lawyers cannot afford to ignore, but it need not take the exact same feel and shape of the professionalism of earlier generations. Today's quickly changing legal landscape and diverse world calls for a new professionalism that does not ignore current realities such as technology on demand, a diverse and global workforce, growing demands on your time and attention, and increasing expectations for efficiency and specialization. You can enhance your career prospects by growing and honing these professionalism skills, regardless of your starting point. Only by improving and sharpening the broad skills under the umbrella of professionalism will you truly be able to maximize your lawyer potential.

Chelsea's Story

Chelsea, a second-year law student, picked up the phone on the second ring. It was the State Department of Health and Human Services offering her a summer job. Chelsea was thrilled. Although she had a few employment options already, this was her top-choice employer for the summer, and she couldn't believe her good fortune. This agency rarely hired summer law clerks, and she really wanted to work there upon graduation. Getting her foot in the door was a critical first step. She had to call Assistant Dean Sue Smith and share the great news!

Assistant Dean Smith was thrilled for Chelsea. She knew firsthand how much effort had gone into landing this summer job, and she couldn't think of a more deserving student. Since Chelsea's first year of law school, she'd been working to develop her contacts at this agency and others through networking. Dean Smith knew that Chelsea had learned as an undergraduate how helpful making the right contacts can be, through her involvement in a variety of student groups and experience in several leadership positions. Dean Smith had suggested that Chelsea do some informational interviewing in a few agencies to see what work might appeal to her upon graduation. Chelsea spent many hours researching and learning everything she could about a number of government agencies, and she'd been preparing her job-search and interview skills. She hadn't put all her eggs in this one basket—she knew this opportunity was a long shot, and she had been working different angles to get the necessary experience to set her up for a great job when she graduates from law school. Dean Smith knew that Chelsea would impress the lawyers at her summer job, and if there were any openings upon graduation, she suspected that Chelsea would be their first choice.

Why Worry About Professionalism?

- Uncorrected issues in law school will plague you in your profession. Correct them now!

- The results of a lack of professionalism can range from minor social consequences from your colleagues for less serious infractions to ethical violations and illegal behavior that affect your ability to sit for the bar or practice law.

- Strong professionalism skills will enhance your ability to find and keep a job.

- Many employers are now conducting extensive background checks and asking for full references. Your professionalism will ensure that these have a positive impact on your employability.

- Professional behavior contributes to a higher-quality work life for you and your colleagues.

- Regardless of your title or role, professionalism IS part of the job.

- Breaches of professionalism don't stop with you—they can impact your fellow students or colleagues. Your professionalism, or lack thereof, is a reflection on your school, employer, and/or family.

- Professionalism contributes positively to the image of the legal profession and helps counteract negative lawyer stereotypes.
- Lapses in professionalism can create risk for you, your school, and your employer.
- By developing strong professionalism skills now, you can maximize your lawyer potential!

Chapter Two
Using Law School Opportunities to Help You Succeed

Tasha's Story

The first day on a new job is always exciting and nerve-wracking, and today was no exception for Tasha Wilson. She looked around her new office with a sense of disbelief, still in awe of her new title, new position, and new salary. Currently in between orientation sessions, Tasha began to unpack some of the boxes she had shipped over from her previous employer. She thought of the former law school professor who had alerted her to this potential career opportunity and recommended her for the job. Professor Dalton—who had taught Tasha's first-year contracts course—had been, by far, Tasha's favorite professor in law school. Because Tasha had enjoyed that course so much, she applied to work as Professor Dalton's research assistant in the summer between her first and second years of law school—a job that she landed and loved. She took one other class from him during law school, and she always stayed in touch with him, even when she wasn't working directly with him.

Professor Dalton served as an informal mentor and advisor for Tasha throughout law school, listening to her doubts and concerns, encouraging her when she applied for jobs, and

11

helping her with her law review note topic. Professor Dalton eagerly served as a reference when Tasha applied for internships, scholarships, and career positions.

After law school, Tasha accepted a legal job in another state, but she had sent Professor Dalton periodic updates on her life and career in the five years since she graduated. She also took the time to talk with any current law students with whom Professor Dalton was working and had even helped one secure an internship with her employer. She enjoyed working with law students and sharing her experiences in law with them. However, she knew she was one of many law students over the years that Professor Dalton had mentored, and she held no illusions about the number of talented students he had met throughout his years of teaching.

Thus, it was a huge surprise when Professor Dalton called her about six weeks ago to tell her about this career opportunity and ask if she was interested. Tasha's new employer had actually contacted Professor Dalton to see if he could recommend any alumni for the position they were trying to fill, and Professor Dalton told Tasha that she had come to mind immediately as a strong match for the job. Although Tasha was not in the job market at the time, she was intrigued about a job that Professor Dalton thought worthy of consideration. She researched the position thoroughly and ultimately applied for the position.

Tasha was excited about this career opportunity, but she knew she wasn't experienced enough to land a position of this caliber on her own at this fairly early stage in her career. It was Professor Dalton's strong recommendation that put her on top of the candidate list earlier in her career than she had expected, and she knew the best way to repay him was to work hard and be successful in the position for which he had recommended her. She was still amazed that a relationship she had formed in one of her first-year classes in law school more than seven years ago led to such an amazing opportunity.

Law School Is Short—Make the Most of It!

Although your three years in law school may seem like they will never end—and especially during your first year of school—they actually go by quickly for most students. Your time in law school provides a unique opportunity to build your legal skills, obtain practical experience, and focus on critical professionalism skills: respect, courtesy, etiquette, strong communication, leadership, debt management, good judgment, maturity, management aptitude, networking, ethical standards, timekeeping, and organizational ability. You should chart your academic courses carefully, and you should also learn as much as you can about the myriad opportunities available to you while you are a law student. You will only be a law student for three short years, so you really should work to make the most of your time. Both your curricular selections and extracurricular activities in law school should be viewed as a chance to build your cache of professionalism skills and forge professional relationships that could last throughout your lifetime. Making and keeping strong professional relationships can only benefit you, as it did Tasha.

Chart Your Academic Coursework

Since you only have six semesters of law school to learn how to become a lawyer, it is up to you to make the most of your time there. In most cases, since the first two semesters of coursework are selected for you, you effectively have four semesters in which to chart your academic path. The moral is: Choose wisely.

Belly Up to the Bar?

Although law schools are not supposed to be solely focused on "teaching to the bar" that is, focusing on bar exam material to the exclusion of other important legal theory and education, most law students quickly realize that in order to practice law, they must pass at least one bar exam to become licensed after graduation. Therefore, most law schools have recommended courses that dovetail bar exam subjects, as well as other curricular graduation requirements that vary a bit from school to school. It is pertinent to question whether you should plan your legal coursework around those subjects over which you will be tested on the bar exam for your jurisdiction. Experts in the field have differing viewpoints on this issue. As Bill Chamberlain, Assistant Dean at Northwestern University School of Law, says, *"I think it is important to take as many bar classes in law school as you can. First, most contain the basic things that every lawyer should know and, second, you will not have enough time in a bar review course to learn much from scratch—especially since you will be learning a lot of state law."*

Dr. Karen Britton, Director of Admissions, Financial Aid, and Career Services at the University of Tennessee College of Law, adds this, *"If there is a strong likelihood that you will sit for a bar in a particular state, I would know the topics covered on the exam and use this as one of several factors you use when selecting elective classes."*

So, what should you do about your academic plan? The answer, like any good law school answer, is "it depends." Law school is your chance to explore a variety of areas in which you might have a career interest. A clinical law practicum may be your only opportunity to experience a real client and case under close supervision—you will receive far more instruction and oversight in a clinic than in most work situations. Advanced legal writing courses offer the opportunity to hone your legal writing skills. Few new lawyers have really mastered the art of legal writing, and this is a marketable skill to have during your job search and throughout your time in practice.

Additionally, seminars offer you the chance to explore a subject more in-depth. Typically such courses feature a wider variety of reading materials, the opportunity to explore an individualized topic of interest through researching and writing a paper, and small-group discussions during class that leave the Socratic method at the door. Many students find seminar courses to be more similar to other graduate degree programs, and a welcome reprieve from the typical law school course. Negotiation skills courses will help you hone your ability to persuade in a variety of situations, even beyond law practice. The opportunities to cultivate your legal and related skills through your coursework in law school are broad—in fact, many graduating students bemoan the fact that there wasn't enough time to take all the classes that interested them.

You should weigh a variety of factors in planning your law school course selection. Your personal and career interests—and how definite those interests are—will be relevant to course selection. Your ability to grasp subjects quickly is also something to consider—if you are confident you can learn the bar material during the bar review course, it may free you up for more elective courses. Areas you know to be challenges for you should be addressed while in law school. For example, if legal writing is not your strength, you will want to hone that skill before entering the job market. Although it might be tempting, selecting courses in order to have Fridays off will not help you get the most out of your legal education.

Many law schools that are part of a larger university will allow you to take a course or two in other colleges or disciplines that will count toward your graduation credits. If you hope to be a corporate lawyer but you don't have a strong business background, for example, you may want to consider a business course or two to supplement your knowledge. If you have a strong interest in representing abused and neglected children, you may do well to complement your legal education with some offerings from the school of social work. Check carefully with your school to determine what your options may be and exactly how credits earned in other colleges of the university will count toward your law degree.

Take advantage of the resources within your law school to help you plan your coursework. Faculty members, your dean of academic advising, and your career services dean are all excellent resources, among many that exist within your law school, who can assist you in making wise choices for your future. Take advantage of those resources while you are in law school—you are, after all, paying for these services through tuition and associated fees.

Joint Degrees: A Double–Edged Sword?

If you are extremely interested in a particular field or career opportunity, or you want to enhance your marketability in the career sector, you may want to consider a joint degree program as a way to expand both your education and professionalism skills. This is another method to enhance the cache of skills you obtain in law school, and one that supplies you with additional credentials when you are done. Many law schools that are part of a larger university offer law students the opportunity to earn a master's degree in some other subject area alongside the J.D. By combining the law program with another degree program and by attending one additional year of school (four years of combined study to earn two degrees, rather than three years of law school to earn your law degree), you can finish with two advanced degrees. This can be a cost-effective method of earning an additional degree by shaving off a year of schooling that would be required if the degrees were pursued separately.

Before committing to a joint degree program, however, it is important that you carefully examine your motivations for obtaining an additional degree. You will want to ensure that it will help your plans and not hinder them, or at least be a neutral, no-loss, no-gain investment. Students who have not fully thought through their plans are sometimes frustrated with the return on their joint degree investment. There are both challenges and benefits to obtaining a joint degree, and these vary based on the person, his or her career goals, and the potential employers involved. Bill Chamberlain, Assistant Dean at Northwestern University School of Law, has counseled many law students who are deciding whether or not to pursue a joint degree. He has this to say:

My first question to students deciding whether to pursue a joint degree is always, "why?" followed quickly by: "What are you hoping to do with the added degree? What does it give you in terms of the market? Is it worth an extra year of school (debt)? Do you really need it?" Be prepared for employers who may doubt your interest in law if you are also going for an M.B.A., for example. Explore what others with your joint degree have done with their careers. Finally, if that's where your passion lies, go for it! Think about how the joint degree will make you a better job candidate. J.D./M.B.A.s, for example, know how the business client thinks, and other specialized master's degrees may make you more of an expert in a certain area such as public health. If you are a joint degree candidate, you need to be proactive—make sure you are working with the career centers in both schools.

If you are pretty sure you don't want to practice law either immediately upon graduation, or at some point down the road (but you would like legal training), a joint degree may be an excellent option for you to pursue. On the other hand, if you are committed to law practice, you should ensure that the joint degree actually enhances your marketability to potential legal employers—although some look favorably upon the extra education, others will question your commitment to a legal career path.

Convincing potential legal employers that you are committed to the practice of law while pursuing a joint degree can sometimes be a challenge. (The converse can also be true: Some corporate employers will question why you pursued a law degree in addition to an M.B.A. if you really want to work in business!) Some legal employers see a joint degree as a lack of dedication to the long-term practice of law, and it can be an uphill battle to convince them otherwise. Other employers will value the knowledge of another discipline that a joint degree brings to the table, and it will set you apart from the thousands of other J.D. candidates. For example, an M.B.A. might really enhance the work of a transactional lawyer, and some firms will even offer bonuses to qualifying M.B.A. recruits. But an M.B.A. may not be as valued in an area of law like environmental, for example, and it could actually work against landing a job in that field. It really pays to know as much as possible about your potential employers.

Beyond the marketability of the additional credentials a joint degree provides you, it is also helpful to consider other benefits and challenges to pursuing a joint degree program. Fulfilling the requirements for a second degree will potentially broaden your network of connections while in school and provide you with experiences and coursework you otherwise may not have had the opportunity to explore. Further, it could lead to additional job opportunities, more faculty and staff references and assistance, and new and different options for student involvement. Courses that you take will expand your knowledge and enhance your skills in many ways.

On the other hand, a joint degree means an additional year of your time and the added expense of an extra year of school, and it delays for a full year the point at which you become a full-time member of the workforce (thus likely accumulating more debt as you remain in school). A joint degree can make scheduling classes more complicated and difficult, and, depending on the academic calendars of each program, it can be difficult to be successful in the standard recruitment cycles for either program. Additionally, dividing your attention between two programs brings the risk that you will not work up to your potential in either case.

Pursuing a joint degree can be an excellent way to expand your repertoire of skills—including professionalism skills—but the decision to enroll in a joint degree program should be explored from all angles and researched carefully, taking into account your individual needs, career path desires, short-and long-term goals, skills, interests, and abilities.

Nancy B. Rapoport, Gordon & Silver, Ltd. Professor of Law at the William S. Boyd School of Law, UNLV, wishes she had pursued a joint degree in law school. Professor Rapoport notes: *"One mistake I made in law school was in not going for a dual degree: either an M.B.A. or a Ph.D. I wouldn't have added appreciably more time to my law degree, and I could have really improved my understanding of law and a social science field (psychology, in my case) with a doctorate, or my understanding of the business world with an M.B.A. It's much more difficult to go back for another degree later. What was I thinking?"*

Judicial Clerkships: To Pursue or Not to Pursue?

You will likely hear a lot about judicial clerkships in law school—these are unique post-graduate opportunities to work closely with a judge as his or her "right-hand person," assisting him or her in the administration of justice. These coveted positions give clerks an opportunity to learn about legal professionalism from an entirely different angle—that of the bench. Judicial clerks assist their judges with a variety of research and draft-opinion writing, analysis of precedent and arguments, discussions with counsel, and other tasks. Depending on the type of clerkship, the day-to-day work may involve trials or oral arguments. Many clerks observe both the written work and the in-person performance of lawyers of differing skill levels and varying commitments to professionalism. It is a potential bird's-eye view of the best (and the worst) the profession of law has to offer. Here's what one former federal judicial clerk has to say about his clerkship:

My first legal job after law school was working for a federal judge as a judicial clerk. A clerkship is truly one of the best legal jobs you can have. It's the only job in which, while you work extremely hard, you do not have the same set of pressures that exist in other legal environments. You only have to please your judge and meet his or her deadlines, unlike other environments in which deadlines are driven by clients or the Court. If you are thinking about practicing in litigation at all (and there are benefits to clerkships, even if you aren't) a judicial clerkship is one of the most valuable insights you can obtain. You will learn how a judge works, the thought processes that go into decisions, and, administratively, how the clerk's office works. You will observe fantastic and really bad attorneys in action. You will be exposed to a large variety of areas of law, and, most importantly, you will likely have a strong mentor. My judge was extremely influential to my life, and it's a relationship I value greatly. Finally, a judicial clerkship can be a way to boost your credentials if you are not at the top of your law school class. It's a prestigious position that will give you the flexibility to do what you want in your career—it helps remove barriers to many career options, and although clerkships can be competitive to land, with some research, effort, and work to build your resume in a variety of ways, you can land one.

Christopher A. Snyder, Prosecutor, Montgomery, AL, former Judicial Clerk to Judge Jose A. Gonzalez, Jr., U.S. District Judge, Southern District of Florida, and Judge Lavenski R. Smith, U.S. Circuit Court Judge, Eighth Circuit Court of Appeals

Clerkships usually last for a year or two after graduation from law school, and they require time and effort—and sometimes great expense—to land. But a clerkship provides a unique opportunity for law students to work closely with a judge and mentor and to see the profession and the administration of justice from an insider's vantage point. Clerkships are definitely not for everyone, so research and information are key to wise decision-making.

The good news is that there are a variety of clerkship opportunities at the federal, state, and municipal levels, including trial, appellate, Supreme Court, administrative, and even career clerk or judicial staff attorney positions. Non-traditional clerkship opportunities serving multiple judges, as well as clerkships that are not federal trial or appellate-level, are on the rise and becoming easier to locate and land by students from all law schools. These opportunities can range from highly competitive to hardly competitive at all—the compensation and benefits, as well as the resume value, will also vary. Traditionally, the time to land a clerkship was during the second year of law school for a clerkship position beginning upon graduation. Now, the federal clerkship application period is at the beginning of the third year of law school.

The other good news regarding clerkships is that there is a growing trend for lawyers to pursue clerkships a year or two after graduating, rather than immediately after law school. For prestigious clerkships, many law firm employers will grant a leave of absence for clerking. Although students should not rely on the chance that they will be able to land a clerkship several years after graduation, this trend does provide hope for students who simply miss the clerkship train while in law school, who find that their career interests and opportunities change dramatically after graduation, or who were not able to land a clerkship while in law school.

Whether or not to pursue a judicial clerkship is an intensely personal decision. Although some clerkships will enhance anyone's resume, others will not add value to certain career paths, and some may be out of reach for the average law student. If a clerkship is your destiny, however, rest assured that there are ample opportunities to pursue such an experience, and sometimes serial clerkships (two or more different clerkships in row) will allow you to "trade up" on the type and prestige of the clerkship you first land. Having a judge at any level serve as an advisor, mentor, and advocate for you in your career is usually a positive career move (as with anything, there are certainly judges who are exceptions to this rule), and a clerkship will help you develop a host of marketable skills and abilities for your career. You may not have the opportunity for such a unique experience at any other point in your career.

To make an informed decision about whether or not to pursue a judicial clerkship, you should attend as many sessions as are offered at your law school to learn about these opportunities, and you should research the variety of clerkship resources available in print and on the Internet. Even if you are inclined to dismiss this unique opportunity, you should at least do some preliminary exploration. If you ask, your career services office may track current and former judicial clerks, and those alumni may be happy to talk to you about the pros and cons of clerking. It's fine not to pursue a judicial clerkship—they are not for everyone—but please ensure that your decision to pursue or not to pursue is an informed one.

Other Law School Curriculum Options

Other curriculum options available vary somewhat by law school. These may include one or more study abroad program options, which allow you to spend a summer or semester in another country, learn about a different system of law, and earn course credits. Many study-abroad programs sponsored by law schools will accept students from other law schools.

This can be an excellent opportunity to broaden your horizons, polish up previously obtained language skills, and form relationships across the globe, all while earning credits toward your degree. These programs aren't free, however, and the desire to participate should be balanced against the cost and practical work experiences you may be foregoing.

Certificate programs are another option offered by law schools. Certificate programs or concentrations allow students to focus much of their elective coursework on a particular subject, such as environmental law, children's law, or alternative dispute resolution, among many others. Students earn these specialty certificates by completing a core set of courses and a number of advanced level elective offerings in the specific subject matter area. Students generally earn the privilege of denoting the successful completion of a certificate or concentration on their resume. Some employers will appreciate a concentration or specialization in the area for which you are applying; others may not see the value, particularly if it is in an unrelated area.

Other curricular options include specialty clinical offerings (a children's rights clinic, for example) and other internships that allow you to combine course credit with work opportunities to help you gain hands-on experience (such as legislative internships or a summer program in Washington, DC). You should learn what opportunities exist at your own law school and what might be available to you at other law schools, perhaps as a visitor for a summer or semester. It is impossible to fit every available opportunity into three years of law school, so learn your options early; research their availability, cost, and benefits; and wisely select those that will help you most for your career goals.

Using Law School Extracurricular Options to Build Your Repertoire of Skills

Your time in law school, like your undergraduate education, offers you a variety of opportunities to become involved in student life. In many respects, the options and opportunities in law school parallel those that will be available to you in your professional life. These post-graduate opportunities take the form of special-interest organizations, community service, board positions, service organizations, hobby groups, and sports options, among many others. It is important that you choose wisely and spend your limited time both pursuing personal interests and passions, and developing helpful and necessary career skills and relationships. Simply joining a variety of "clubs" does not a leader make, but by selecting extracurricular activities that complement your personal and career interests, you can add valuable skills to your catalog of abilities. Building your resume is another advantage—you should highlight these unique talents and experiences in your cover letters and during interview discussions.

From highly competitive and coveted positions (such as a spot on your school's premier law review) to positions that no one really wants to take on, and everything in between, opportunities abound during law school to get involved in campus life and community service. Examples include political and special-interest groups, pro bono opportunities, Street Law, Inc. programs, domestic abuse volunteering, assisting with income tax preparation, journal and research opportunities, and student organizations that range from affinity groups (BLSA, Law Student Parents, etc.) to interest groups (such as Law Students for Animal Safety) and the Student Bar Association. Getting involved and connected through activities and taking the time to form relationships with your peers, faculty, and staff administrators will help you make the most of the time and money you are spending on your legal education.

Advantages of school involvement include the development of long-lasting friendships (and future business contacts), learning skills like how to plan a large event, and effecting necessary change for students who follow after you. Involvement in leadership positions that allow for creative and strategic planning requires you to use a different side of your brain than the traditional law school course—and stretching your skills in all directions will make you more well-rounded and attractive to potential employers.

If you work with other law students or lawyers in your community, you will have the opportunity to give of yourself and learn firsthand about the professionalism skills that employers value so much—and develop them in yourself. Any law student can read about organizational skills or tell an employer that he or she has good management aptitude. It's much more persuasive to actually describe your leadership of an organization and the accomplishments you oversaw, or to explain in detail the prioritizing and organizational skills that planning and implementing the first-ever alumni/law student golf tournament took while balancing that with coursework and exams. There is no doubt about it: Extracurricular options in law school are ready-made opportunities to hone the necessary and sought-after professionalism skills that law school coursework does not necessarily teach you—respect and courtesy, strong communication, leadership, debt management, good judgment, maturity, management aptitude, networking, ethical standards, and organizational ability.

Relationships to Build

Your time in law school provides a unique opportunity to cultivate and build relationships that will serve you over the course of your professional career, along whatever path you find yourself in the future. One career counselor advises the creation of your own personal "career advisory board":

> *Whether comprised of parents, friends, professors, or fellow alumni, all of us need what I call a "career advisory board" to bounce ideas off of when we are at a career crossroads. Regardless of how well we claim to know ourselves, it is helpful to complement that self-knowledge with insights from those who see us in another light. Some members of our career advisory board will love us unconditionally and serve as cheerleaders. Others, such as career advisors, will help us take an objective look at our talents, our goals, and our options. Both of these board members play essential roles as we navigate our professional journeys.*

> *Our career advisory board does not dissolve when we land the dream job. Its members should be in place when we consider our next move, grieve a lost promotion, or celebrate a professional accomplishment. Think about who serves on your career advisory board, and if you don't have one, consider creating one. Have their addresses, phone numbers, and e-mails handy, and keep them apprised of your employment status. They may not always be able to open doors for you, but they may help you test your decisions and examine your career from another perspective.*

Andrew T. Ceperley, Director, Career Services Center, University of California, San Diego

Your "career advisory board" will be an important subset of your wider network. (Exactly how to go about building your network will be covered in Chapter Five.) For now, your law school classmates, faculty, and administrators are all rich sources of referrals, references, career opportunities, and

potential business. Take the time to get to know your fellow
law students, faculty, and staff, and don't be afraid to step
out of your comfort zone a bit. You'll get more out of law
school if you actively participate in all aspects of it. Participating in class discussions is one way to become engaged and
connected. Nancy B. Rapoport, Gordon & Silver, Ltd. Professor of Law at the William S. Boyd School of Law, UNLV,
notes:

> *One of the biggest mistakes I made in law school was not
> talking in class, ever, on the theory that I never had anything
> original to say. That was probably true, but that fact never
> bothered a lot of my fellow classmates, who ended up being a
> lot more comfortable talking in public in school, which trans-
> lated into being more comfortable talking in public at the law
> firm. I don't know if women tend to put more brakes on their
> in-class speaking than men do—I've read some studies sug-
> gesting that's true—or if I was just too intimidated by how
> smart everyone else was in school, but that self-regulation of
> my speaking didn't hurt anyone else but me. I doubt that I
> would've been the center square in anyone's Gunner Bingo
> game, but I could've been more engaged in my classes if I'd
> just swallowed my fear and tried to talk more in class.*

You should also reach out to people outside the walls of
your law school. Community service, a part-time job, and/or
participation in career-services programs such as mentoring
and mock-interviews are all fertile ground for establishing
relationships. Although it is tempting to focus on the demands of law school to the exclusion of other aspects of your
life, you will be well-served to resist that temptation.

In addition to developing new relationships while you are
in law school, it is important to maintain the relationships
you built prior to your matriculation to law school. Your
undergraduate relationships with your classmates, faculty,
and staff should be nurtured, as should friendships, family,
and other parts of your network (church, clubs, sports, etc.).
Although you may not have the same amount of time to give
that you did prior to law school, quick e-mails or phone calls
to stay in touch will be appreciated and will guarantee that
your network will be twice as strong when you graduate from
law school.

The Biggest Mistake of My Life?

At some point, many law students—and even lawyers—
have felt that going to law school was a mistake. For most

people, the feeling that you've made a very expensive faux pas passes. Although some students love law school and enjoy their time there very much, for others it is a challenging, anxiety-inducing, and overwhelming experience. The time commitment is extraordinary (as is the time commitment for most careers in the practice of law) and for many students, it is the first time that they are not at the very top of the academic heap. Even those that have excelled academically often feel overwhelmed and experience constant worry about losing their academic standing. There are a variety of resources available for students who are struggling. Be sure to explore the Humanizing Law School website, available at: http://www.law.fsu.edu/academic_programs/humanizing_law school/humanizing_lawschool.html for a variety of resources and vital information for law students.

It is important to recognize that law school is challenging, and feelings of doubt are normal. Not everyone who attends law school thoroughly researched their options beforehand or fully understood what studying law would entail. It is common for students to enter law school with false assumptions about their earning potential with a law degree, the ease of landing a large firm job if that is their goal, the day-to-day life of a lawyer, the amount of research and writing involved in law school and law practice, the timing of job offers, and many other aspects of legal careers.

If you've already taken the plunge into law school but don't actually want to practice law, know that there are a variety of career options available to those who earn a Juris Doctor. With a bit of elbow grease and endurance, many students who are initially disillusioned about their prospects become excited about the opportunities available to them in government, public interest, politics, the courts, and in other areas of which they weren't aware prior to law school. So if you are one of the students who did not research law school and legal careers as carefully as you might have before entering law school, remember: Better late than never. Focus your anxiety, and learn exactly what unique and non-traditional opportunities are out there. Set your goals, and begin working toward them.

Going through the challenging law school experience with others instead of alone can also be a big help—yet another

reason to take the time and make the effort to form relationships in law school. It is also vital to have a support system in
law school, so you can share your concerns and get advice and
reassurance, which is often very useful and eye-opening. Talk
with upperclass students about their experiences in law
school, and find out how they navigated the hurdles they
encountered. Faculty and staff can also reassure you that you
are not alone and that many law students experience doubts,
but most are able to successfully overcome them. Career
counselor Dave Diamond shares a success story about one of
his former students:

> *I once had a student who enjoyed law school but was very
> distressed because she felt out of sync with everyone else. Her
> classmates wanted to work in law firms, but she was not
> interested in a career in private practice. When she first came
> to talk to me, I convinced her that she was not the only one
> out there interested in a career in social justice, and I sent her
> to the Equal Justice Works Career Fair. There, she met a lot
> of people who had similar career goals, which was very
> encouraging. This opportunity really re-invigorated her feel-
> ings about obtaining her law degree, and she became excited
> about her career. I worked with her until she found her post-
> graduate job in public interest. When I last spoke with her,
> she was still at her job and still loving it. If you feel like law
> school might have been a mistake, start talking to people—
> practicing attorneys, alumni, career counselors. You will
> quickly find that you are not alone and will likely discover
> something that reminds you why you wanted to be a lawyer.*

**David M. Diamond, J.D., M.A., Director, Center for
Career Strategy and Advancement, Northwestern University School of Law**

If you have the opportunity to talk with practicing lawyers, it's always enlightening to ask them about their lowest
point in law school. You will probably be surprised to hear
stories from these highly successful practitioners that are not
all that different from your own.

Finally, break out of your doubts by keeping busy—but
not just with law school. Make sure that the people and
pastimes that were important to you before you started law
school don't go totally by the wayside once you're mired in
contracts, torts, outlines, and exams. Your well-being will be
well-served by setting aside some time in your life for people
and pastimes outside of law school.

Chapter Three
Addressing the Debt Dilemma

Jason's Story

Jason was nervous—it was the day of his character and fitness interview, a standard part of the registration process for the bar exam. He hadn't thought twice about this being a potential hurdle to his career plans until he attended a Q & A session about registering for the bar exam last year, and suddenly, his world turned upside down. He already knew that prior problems with the law, such as drug use, posed potential hurdles for some students. What he hadn't known was that his debt load and credit issues could raise red flags during the character and fitness investigation and possibly delay or even prevent him from sitting for the bar exam.

In addition to a healthy amount of undergraduate and law school loans, Jason had a car loan, a personal loan, and large amounts of credit card debt, which he had accumulated throughout his undergraduate years and during the two years he worked in human resources before starting law school. Not only did Jason have a lot of debt, his payment record up until that fateful Q & A session a year ago was abysmal. He hadn't realized the potential long-term consequences of his lackluster attention to bill payment besides a few collection letters and calls each week, and now he was paying the price. Since realizing the impact his debt could have regarding his admission to the bar, Jason had followed up to learn as many details as he could, and how he might mitigate the impact of his poor credit record. He made arrangements with his creditors, and he'd been paying faithfully on all of his bills for the last year. He even obtained a part-time job during his second year of law school to help pay down some of his balances. He had carefully documented his finances, and he hoped he was ready for the scrutiny and questions he was sure to be asked. He hoped his attempts to turn his debt issues around happened in time—at this point, his future was up in the air.

Relevance, Your Honor?

Why should anyone care about your financial condition as a law student, lawyer-to-be, or newly admitted or even seasoned lawyer? You might think that such personal aspects of your life should be off-limits to the governing bodies of your profession, potential employers, and possible clients. However, personal financial responsibility—or lack thereof—shows a lot about your character and your trustworthiness to handle delicate client matters, cases where large sums of money or personal freedom may be at stake, and escrow funds that are entrusted to your oversight. Your ability to handle your personal finances is extremely relevant to your professionalism and to your character and fitness to practice law. As such, it is particularly important that if you do not already understand the basic concepts of credit, credit reporting, debt management, and loan repayment, you become well versed in them sooner rather than later.

It is a rare law student who graduates from both undergraduate and law school without accumulating student loan debt and/or some credit card debt. If you are one of those rare students, count yourself very fortunate, but don't excuse yourself from knowing and understanding the same concepts about credit and debt management that law school borrowers need to know. If you are like most law students and your student loans approach six figures, it is imperative that you take stock, understand these concepts, and learn how to minimize your growing loan balances. The cost of your legal education is an investment in your future—hopefully a strong investment that, with careful planning and hard work, will yield a positive return.

The Basics: What Is a Credit Report?

Whenever you borrow money, pay for something with a credit card, or purchase a new car on payments, you are using credit to obtain something now that you will actually pay for in the future. This ability to buy now and pay later is not free—it usually comes with interest charged and sometimes additional fees. (You will pay some percentage of interest on your student loans, and many credit cards charge an annual fee just to have the card). Your use of credit (or lack thereof) is tracked and reported on your credit report. A credit report has information about the debts you have accumulated, the available credit you have at your disposal (for example, if you have a credit card with a $5,000 limit and you are carrying a $2,000 balance, you have $3,000 of available credit on that card), inquiries from potential lenders about your credit and debt, and your payment record on your open accounts and loans. A credit report gives you a "score" based on all of these factors. Your credit score is used by potential lenders to evaluate your credit-worthiness, which determines if they will give you a loan and, if so, what the interest rate might be.

It's important to learn about the various types of debt. Education loans and home mortgages that are within your means are examples of what is generally considered "good debt," or debt that is positive to carry. Other kinds of debt are not necessarily positive—credit card debt or other "revolving credit" accounts are generally considered to be "bad debt" if you carry a balance on the account each month. It is best to avoid carrying balances on credit cards. Credit cards are easy to obtain, generally at high interest rates, and it's easy for your debt to accumulate if you do not make a practice of paying off your balance in full each month.

Consider the practice of using a credit card to pay monthly bills, such as a utility, cell phone bill or another credit card bill, or to buy merchandise. If you do not pay the balance in full when your credit card bill comes, you will likely end up paying much more than the actual cost for the bill or merchandise when all of the interest you pay over time is taken into account—even if you bought clearance or sale-priced merchandise. Remember, a bargain on credit is not always a bargain! Many times the merchandise is worn out or discarded by the time the balance on the credit card is paid off.

Many an unwary student has obtained a credit card for buying merchandise, dining out, and even paying bills. Once the credit card limit is reached, the student discovers how long it takes to pay off a credit card that has accumulated a large balance, and the clearance merchandise that seemed like such a good buy at the time actually ends up costing more than double the original retail price!

There are a variety of excellent resources available to help you understand credit reporting, what determines credit scores and how they are used, and how to maximize your credit score. Generally, your goal in law school should be to keep your loans, credit card balances, and other borrowing to a minimum and to pay all your bills on time each and every month. Beyond that, you should consult with the professional resources available to you (your financial aid office, your education loan lender, financial advisors, and consumer credit counseling services) for in-depth information about your personal debt management, credit situation and score, and how to maximize the return on your law school investment.

It is also important that you periodically examine your credit report. It's a good way for you to learn about what your potential lenders see when they examine your credit-worthiness. It is also important for you to ensure periodically that your credit report is accurate. With identity theft becoming more common, regular assessments of your report will guarantee that someone else isn't using (and ruining) your credit-worthiness. Finally, when you examine your report, you should look for old accounts that you aren't using anymore, then close them so they don't add to your available credit. The more you understand your credit report and your credit rating, the more you'll be equipped to make wise credit choices.

Although you can pay for various credit report monitoring services, you are entitled to one free credit report a year from each of the three major credit reporting companies—Equifax, Experian, and TransUnion—by virtue of the Fair and Accurate Credit Transactions Act (FACTA Act) of 2003, which is an amendment to the Fair Credit Reporting Act.[1] You should take advantage of this free access every year—you can either request one report from a different company at different intervals, or you can obtain all three reports at once and

---

1. 15 U.S.C. § 1681j

compare the information and scores. There are also a variety of credit-monitoring services you can use for a fee. To obtain information about accessing your free credit reports, go to the following Web site: https://www.annualcreditreport.com/cra/index.jsp.

Avoid Living Like a Lawyer in Law School

Before you explore the first law school Web page, conduct a serious self-analysis of your long-term life and career goals. Learn about typical jobs for J.D.'s, and identify some careers and job settings that appeal to you. Investigate what attorneys who are working in those job settings (and in the city or area where you want to live) currently earn right out of law school. If possible, have an informational interview with an attorney in this career, or speak to someone in law school or legal recruitment who can provide some insight on the job market and anticipated earnings. Ask how many hours a week someone in this position can expect to work. How does this compare with your expectations?

Research law schools on these points:

1) Where do their graduates typically work—both job settings and locations?

2) If you enroll there and perform at a high level academically, what is the likelihood that the law school can help you position yourself to be hired in the employment setting you seek?

3) How much will it cost to attend that law school for three years—tuition, fees, and living expenses? What is the average indebtedness for recent graduates?

4) What is the range of starting salaries for graduates of that school? For the type of job you seek?

5) Using readily available consumer information, evaluate the likelihood of admission to schools that interest you. Evaluate the likelihood of scholarship assistance from these schools.

6) Armed with this information, choose the law school that should afford the best long-term return on your investment given the anticipated cost of attendance and expected earnings.

Dr. Karen Reagan Britton, Director of Admissions, Financial Aid, and Career Services, University of Tennessee College of Law

It's easy to get caught up in living on borrowed money—student loan money, that is. Full-time law students who find it necessary to finance their education also quickly discover that, per American Bar Association guidelines, first-year law students are not permitted to work while law school is in session. (Evening students at law schools with this option are an exception.) And even if students can find the time to work during their second and third years of law school, while school is in session they are limited to twenty hours of work per week during those years. Because so few students come to law school with a year of living expenses in the bank, most find it necessary to borrow living expenses for that first year, on top of loans for tuition, fees, books, and other educational expenses. Although the initial loan sums are often shocking and mind-boggling, over time law students become de-sensitized to the amount of debt they are accumulating. They often form an attitude that goes something like this: "I've already borrowed more than fifty thousand dollars, so I might as well borrow the maximum this year and enjoy the extra five grand."

Furthermore, because loan checks come all at once at the beginning of the semester, many law students are flush for the first month or so and then find that they've overspent their funds without carefully budgeting to make their loan money last as long as a single semester. The solution, for many, is to ask for more student loans, borrow from someone else, or use a credit card to cover expenses toward the end of the semester. None of these are great options. Some students use their loan money for purchases such as engagement rings, vacations, new cars, and flat-screen televisions, and even as funds for gambling. These are not appropriate uses of student loan funds, but many students assume that they will be earning a lot of money once they graduate and start practicing law, so it's fine to enjoy a few luxuries now. That attitude has landed many law students in over their heads in debt.

Budgeting is a crucial step in financing your legal education. A loan check should last for the duration of that loan period, barring any unusual circumstances, and it should only be used for the intended purposes of student loans. Do not always take the easy way out when you are considering a purchase—think about the professional approach to debt management. For example, if you need transportation, force yourself to consider first whether you really need a personal car or if you can make do with public transportation. If the answer is that you really need a car, then consider a reasonably priced, dependable used car, for example, rather than buying a brand-new one. Explore the costs of insuring various makes and models of cars, as well as the costs of maintenance and gas mileage, before making your decision. Thorough research and knowledge of total costs when making a large purchase will pay off greatly in terms of good debt management.

It is equally important that you borrow only what you need for your living expenses and explore all options for minimizing the amounts you must borrow. One option at some law schools that students often overlook is the Federal Work Study Program for law students. This program allows law students to work in law-related jobs, on and off campus, to earn money toward their education. Check to see if this option is available to you at your law school (it isn't available at all schools), and find out what you need to do to apply. Some students pass over this option because it lessens the amount that can be borrowed through student loans, but that is actually the idea—lowering your indebtedness upon graduation! And as a bonus, you might be able to get some valuable hands-on legal experience while earning what would have been loan money. Everything you borrow will need to be paid back—with interest. Even though the interest rates on student loans are generally pretty low, the interest does add up, particularly if you repay your loans over a longer period of time. As such, every dollar you do not have to borrow is money you save in the long run.

To avoid getting de-sensitized to your loan amounts, regardless of how large they are, and to really understand what your repayment obligations will be, you should calculate your projected loan amounts and monthly repayment amount *every semester*. That way, as you adjust your loan amounts (for example, if you take out an unexpected emergency loan, or you don't need to borrow as much as planned because you were able to obtain a job or a work-study award) you can track what your monthly repayment amounts are likely to be once you are working.

Calculating your repayment amounts also allows you to see the impact of borrowing. Here's a great example of how minimizing your borrowing will save you money in the future. If you are able to take out even $1,000 less each semester in student loans, you will owe $6,000 less upon graduation. If your total loan amount would have been $50,000 and you manage to minimize your borrowing to a total of $44,000 upon graduation, you will save significantly. Assuming a 6.75 percent interest rate and a ten-year repayment plan for $44,000 in loans, you will save almost $70 per month on your loan payments and more than $2,200 in interest paid over the life of the loan. The more you don't borrow while in law school, the less future income you will have to commit to monthly payments and interest.

Loan repayment calculators are available on the Internet to help you determine your possible monthly repayment obligations. You can access one such calculator at http://www.finaid.org/calculators/loanpayments.phtml. Even if you are already well into your law school curriculum, you can still work to minimize your loan debt.

One great source of information about credit and debt management for graduate students is The Access Group, a non-profit graduate loan specialist (www.accessgroup.org). The Access Group Web site has information that is extremely pertinent to law student borrowers. Online tutorials about credit, debt management, and budgeting, in-school and out-of-school budget calculators, ideas for minimizing what you spend while in school, repayment and consolidation options, and a host of other useful information will help you determine the best way to pay for your law school education.

The Impact of Poor Credit and High Debt

By now, you should be convinced that there are many reasons to understand credit, maintain good credit, keep your debt under control, and live within your means (and if you are a full-time law student, your "means" is not very much at all—you should be as frugal as possible)! Credit-worthiness and debt management are issues of professionalism, and you should understand the potential impact of poor credit and high debt. Debt problems can raise red flags for those who are deciding whether you have the appropriate character and fitness to be admitted to the bar. The *Comprehensive Guide to Bar Admission Requirements 2008,* published by the National Conference of Bar Examiners and the ABA Section of Legal Education and Admissions to the Bar, lists "neglect of financial obligations" in the list of conduct that should be "treated as cause for further inquiry" when such conduct is discovered.[2] Many factors are taken into account when making decisions about character and fitness, and it's impossible to predict how your particular situation may play out. Do yourself a favor, and don't give the bar authority any reason to inquire further.

Stephen Isaacs, a practicing lawyer and Director of Character and Fitness for the Virginia Board of Bar Examiners, has this to say:

> *Delinquent payments on debt are definitely a concern for the character and fitness portion of the bar exam, whether they are past due, in collection, or charged off. When you create debt, you have created a contract, a promise to pay. If you violate that contract, we are going to ask what right you have to be a lawyer if you cannot hold up your end of a contract or promise, if your word is no good. When it comes to debt that has gone to collection or is charged off, too many bar applicants take the position that the obligation is no longer owed, but that is not correct. You still have a debt and an obligation to pay. When you are completing your application for the bar, it is crucial that you disclose everything accurately. If you have debt issues, address them now. Pay your debts—if you cannot afford the full payment, pay a smaller amount or contact the creditor. Don't just ignore the debt—it won't go away.*

Overcoming the hurdle for bar admission is not an invitation to be any less vigilant about your credit. Both private- and public-sector employers are increasingly adding background checks and credit checks to contingencies placed on offers of employment. In the past, only certain jobs, usually government positions requiring security clearance, were contingent on items like back-ground checks and credit checks and many didn't even bother to check references. It is an entirely new ballgame now. It is not at all unusual for offers from a variety of private sector employers, in addition to most job offers in the public sector, to be contingent on

2. National Conference of Bar Examiners and the ABA Section of Legal Education and Admissions to the Bar. *Comprehensive Guide to Bar Admission* *Requirements 2008,* (2008) at viii. Available at: http://www.ncbex.org/fileadmin/ mediafiles/downloads/Comp_Guide/ CompGuide.pdf

favorable background checks, including credit checks. How disappointing and embarrassing would it be to receive an exciting job offer that is later rescinded due to a negative background or credit check?

When you are filling out the paperwork for bar admission and background checks, it is imperative that you are forthright and honest. Do not omit negative items, hoping that they will not be discovered. Willful omissions, misinformation, and falsifications on your applications and bar paperwork are not only unethical and dishonest, they are also cause for concern regarding your employability and fitness to be a legal professional. Although being honest about credit issues won't guarantee you'll be admitted to the bar or get the job you want, it is professional and correct to deal with these issues outright, and it is also your best chance for mitigating any damage. If you have some time before you need to apply for admission to the bar or for employment and you are worried about credit and debt-management issues, seek professional advice immediately. (Some universities provide debt-counseling services.) The sooner you work to correct these issues, the better your chances for a positive outcome.

It is also important to think of the debt load you are carrying in terms of future employment options. Sure, you might be *able* to earn six figures upon graduating from law school, but are the jobs that pay that much the jobs you really want? And even if they are, do you want to be forced to keep that high-paying job for the next ten to twenty years to be able to service your debt and make your payments? It's always good to allow yourself options, including the possibility of moving to a lower-paying job if you find one that is more fulfilling. If you had to borrow heavily to attend law school, though, all is not lost—an experienced public-interest practitioner offers this advice:

> High debt does not mean you cannot choose a public interest career. It does mean that you have to make deliberate choices about lifestyle, goals, what your real passion is, and how you can afford to do what you love and feel called to do. Maybe you will start your career in public interest and find that after a few years you cannot afford it and you need a job in the private sector. Maybe you will decide that your debt load is so high right out of law school that a few years of highly compensated work is what you need before your goal of public

interest is possible. In either situation, maintain your public interest ethic. Stay in touch through pro bono work, be a voice of support for pro bono in your bar association and in your private-sector job, make financial support for pro bono a priority. Your voice from outside the public interest community can be as important and as strong as those within the public-interest community. And when you are ready, there are many pathways back into the public interest community, with new ones being created every day.

Karen J. Sarjeant, Vice President for Programs and Compliance, Legal Services Corporation

Remember, every small amount that you save as a law student and that you do not have to borrow is future money that isn't committed to loan repayment, so do what you can now to manage your debt.

Law students with high student loan debt should also be aware of a recent legislative development. The College Cost Reduction and Access Act of 2007 offers an income-based repayment plan for graduates whose debt is high and income is low. It also provides loan forgiveness after ten years of full-time work in public service, as defined by the law. For students who are committed to a career in public service, this may be an excellent resource. It might be worth investigating this law to see if you qualify for either an income-based repayment plan or loan forgiveness to help you manage your student loan debt.

It's Never Too Early to Think About Your Retirement Plan!

As premature as it sounds, you should already be thinking about your retirement plan! Having enough money to retire when and how you want to is an important consideration for many people, and though your retirement is likely decades away, there are many advantages to saving early, even in small amounts. The key is to save regularly and to make it part of your standard money allocation habits. The compounding effect of even small amounts of money that you invest for retirement at a young age can be phenomenal—and the further you are from retirement, the more you'll gain from the compounding effect. Small amounts invested regularly now can add up to large sums of money for your retirement. Seek professional advice about which retirement investment tools may be best for you at this stage of your life.

Retirement plans and retirement savings options are an often overlooked, but important, aspect to the compensation package you may receive from your employer when you graduate. As such, learning about the retirement plans offered before you accept an offer with an employer is a perfectly acceptable practice that many students do not follow, either because they don't think about retirement as part of their compensation package, or they simply don't know or don't care to ask about it. As with all compensation-related questions you may have for a potential employer, it is best to ask about retirement options once you have an offer in hand. You should learn whether the retirement plan is a defined contribution plan (most common in the private sector), a defined benefit plan (more common in the public sector), or if you can select among these options. If it is a defined contribution plan, you should know what amount, if anything, your employer will contribute to the plan. Many law firms do not contribute to associate retirement accounts, but some do, so be sure to check. Do not assume that a high salary equates to a large 401(k) contribution; often, the reverse is true.

You should also be aware of the vesting provisions for the potential employer's retirement plan—the number of years you will need to be employed by that employer to become fully vested in the plan. Federal and state government plans may credit years of service through other employers, and some states recognize and give credit for service in another state, so be sure to know your plan and ask questions to learn about all aspects of the plan provisions.

Karen's Story

Karen stared in shock at her law school's financial aid advisor. She was at her exit interview, the mandatory meeting that graduating law students with student loans must have before leaving school. She listened numbly while Ms. Strock went over the various loans Karen had taken out over the past three years to finance her tuition, fees, books, and living expenses. Yes, each year she remembered filling out her FAFSA form faithfully, responding to all inquiries, and receiving her award letter that described the loans, grants, and scholarships comprising her student aid package. (The award letter was always light on the grants and scholarships and heavy on student loans.) Yes, she knew she had taken out the maximum amount in loans each year that she was allowed—after all, she wasn't permitted to work her first year, and she was way too busy her second year. By her third year, Karen realized she would be working for the rest of her life, and she decided to take it easy with a lighter class load and no job after her summer employment wrapped up. Yes, she had signed the promissory notes each year for these loans in the maximum amount. Yes, she even knew and understood that she had to start paying them all back six months after she graduated.

What Karen hadn't realized, or hadn't wanted to tally up, was the grand total of all her loans. Added to her undergraduate debt, the amount was staggering. And if that wasn't bad enough, the likely monthly repayment amount that Ms Strock calculated was the equivalent of a mortgage payment. Karen definitely could have survived with a little less loan money during law school, maybe even worked part-time a bit, but getting the loan money had been so easy. "In for a penny, in for a pound," she had always thought. Karen realized she was one of the lucky ones—she had a job with the federal government all lined up, and she had passed all the background checks and contingencies. But even though her job was a good one, Karen acknowledged that it would not provide the six-figure income she'd anticipated before starting law school.

"Stupid, stupid, stupid," she muttered under her breath. As smart as she was, to let herself get this far into debt without realizing what it was going to cost her on the back end made her feel like an idiot. She couldn't believe she had let this happen—denial did not seem like a good course of action now. Even with loan consolidation, she was looking at a sizeable chunk of her income going to loan repayment each month, and that was with an extended repayment option of twenty years. Karen was utterly depressed at a time when she should have been looking forward to an exciting new career. Although she knew others had it worse, she certainly didn't feel like one of the lucky ones.

Chapter Four
Other Gold Mines for Developing Necessary Skills

Developing Leadership and Management Skills

Many practicing lawyers are talented leaders, but unfortunately others are not. Within firms and other organizations, the successful lawyers are usually the ones selected for leadership and management roles. However, the skills that make a lawyer successful are not necessarily the same skills that make him or her a successful leader or manager—in fact, the skill sets are often very different. This is true in other disciplines, as well; although people might excel at the profession itself, they falter when assigned to a leadership role. Within the legal field, this disconnect can result in newer or junior lawyers feeling frustrated about their positions—not having a strong leader or mentor can have a large impact on your job satisfaction. Rest assured, you can seek leadership and mentorship from other sources (a topic that will be discussed in great detail in Chapter Eleven).

You need not fall into that same trap—you can be a successful lawyer AND a great leader. And you can begin to develop your leadership and management skills in law school, as well as in practice—in fact, the sooner, the better. Developing and improving your leadership and management ability is a skills development process that can and should continue throughout your career. The best leaders never assume they are done learning, and they never stop trying to enhance their skills and leadership abilities.

Leadership and management skills encompass a broad spectrum of proficiencies, including teamwork, mentoring, coaching, providing feedback to others, seeking and acting upon feedback you receive, supervising, delegating, listening, motivating and inspiring, influencing, setting a strong example, enhancing diversity, decision-making, and project management. There are many ways you can strengthen your abilities in each of these areas while you are in law school and beyond. Improvement in leadership and management comes through practice (using these skills as often as possible), stretching beyond your current level of expertise, trying new things, learning from mistakes, and obtaining valuable feedback on your efforts from a trusted mentor, supervisor, or colleagues and peers. Because your view of your own performance in these areas is necessarily one-dimensional, it is important to solicit and take note of feedback on your efforts. Only through listening carefully to others' perceptions of your performance can you obtain a complete picture of your current skills and learn which areas need improvement.

In Chapter Two, we discussed the importance of becoming involved in life at law school and beyond, and the many reasons that you are well-served to become immersed in student life and extra-curricular activities during law school. Building your leadership and management skills is another natural outcome of your involvement both in and beyond the classroom in law school. The same is true when you are a practicing lawyer. The more involved you are, the more opportunities you will have to stretch your leadership muscles.

Holding a position in a student group or community service organization is perhaps the most obvious way to practice your leadership skills, but don't overlook other available opportunities. It is not necessary for you to become President of the Student Bar Association, Editor in Chief of the Law Review, or a Director of a board in order to build your leadership skills. It is not even necessary for you to have a formal position of authority to provide leadership and strengthen your skills. Being a "leader" does not mean you have formal power or the ability to tell others what to do— although when you do have formal power or supervisory authority, you have a duty to provide strong leadership!

There are many definitions of leadership, but one of the most concise and useful comes from Angie Morgan and Courtney Lynch, founders of Lead Star LLC, a leadership consulting firm, and authors of the best-selling book, *Leading from the Front*.[3] According to Angie and Courtney, who base their leadership principles on training they received in the United States Marine Corps, leadership is the ability to influence outcomes and inspire others, and it is not dependent on formal authority or position.[4] Angie offers these thoughts:

You don't have to wait for a formal management position for an opportunity to lead. Leadership isn't about a job title or fancy corner office. Your leadership is about your ability to influence outcomes and inspire others. Everyday you're presented with leadership opportunities, like working with a group of peers, taking the time to help a colleague professionally develop, or even volunteering for a specific assignment. If you view yourself as a leader, you will identify opportunities where you can achieve more success and positively impact those you come in contact with. Leadership skills are so critical for success, but many do not spend time developing them. Oftentimes it's up to the individual to make leadership development their top priority. If you make it yours, you'll distinguish yourself as a resource and solutions-provider.

This definition of leadership is useful because, as a law student and lawyer, you will have many opportunities to influence outcomes and inspire others by providing leadership and guidance in everything you undertake. Even if you're not in a leadership position, by joining a student group, for example, you can still provide leadership to your peers in the group.

Tonya's Story

Tonya was a first-year law student, and she was excited to join the student Health Law Association at her law school during the first semester. Having worked as a nurse before law school, she had a strong interest in health law and in

---

3. Angie Morgan and Courtney Lynch, *Leading From the Front* (McGraw–Hill, NY, 2006).

4. *See* http://www.leadstar.us/angie-courtney/about/.

combining her nursing career skills with her legal career. Unfortunately, Tonya quickly discovered that this student group existed almost in name only. It wasn't very active, and the current president was not effective at having regular meetings or at accomplishing much within the infrequent meetings that were held. Tonya saw that many students were interested in health law and that one of the challenges for the students was learning about career opportunities in the health law field. Early in the second semester of law school, so as not to undermine the authority of the current Health Law Association president, Tonya invited her to lunch so they could talk about the group. Tonya asked the president if she would consider having the group sponsor a health law information fair—by combining forces with the career-services office and various alumni in the field—to provide health law career information and networking opportunities to the students. Tonya envisioned an event that would have a panel discussion, a table fair, and a networking reception. She thought students would be very interested in attending such an event, and she offered to help coordinate it. The president, who was overextended and short on time to do much in her leadership role with the group, promptly took her Tonya up on her offer, and she promised to arrange a meeting to discuss it with the membership.

Over the next few weeks, Tonya talked to the more active and vocal students in the group and enlisted their help in organizing the event. She also approached her career advisor and obtained a commitment for help and support from that administrative office. She carefully listed all the tasks that had to be accomplished, developed a timeline, and sought help and feedback from her fellow students, incorporating their ideas and advice. When the information fair took place eight weeks later it was a rousing success, and the current president benefited greatly from her organization sponsoring such a helpful and well-received event. Students who attended learned a lot about career opportunities in the health care field, and they got a chance to speak one-on-one with a variety of practitioners.

In planning the information fair, Tonya forged strong friendships, built relationships with some practicing attorneys, learned about event planning, and gained valuable leadership skills, all of which would serve her well in upcoming interviews and in her career. Tonya was never given a formal title or role when organizing this event, but she was the driving force behind the whole undertaking. She was a leader in every sense of the word—she truly influenced outcomes and inspired those who worked with her. Not surprisingly, Tonya was elected president of the Health Law Association the following year. However, her leadership efforts had begun long before she had any formal authority or title.

Consider how Tonya's efforts may have been received if, instead of enlisting the support of the current president before acting on her idea, she had tried to discredit the current president and complained about the lack of meetings and accomplishments of the group. Although this negative approach to eliciting change may have gotten others to agree with Tonya and complain along with her, it is unlikely that nearly as much would have been accomplished in eight short weeks. Instead of the spirit of teamwork and success that permeated the health law career information fair, a negative approach likely would have led to unproductive venting, divisiveness and bad feelings, and no useful information for the students. Yes, outcomes may have been influenced if Tonya had acted in this manner, but it is doubtful that many people would have been inspired by this approach.

Although your first instinct may be to point out what is wrong with a situation, a leader stops, reflects, and considers how he or she can correct the situation through positive action. If you think of leadership as acting to influence outcomes and inspire others, you can approach all facets of your life from a leadership perspective.

Developing leadership skills is a process. Some people have more natural leadership instincts than others, but anyone can learn and improve their leadership abilities. Student groups, community service, church or other organized groups, and volunteerism are a few of the venues in which you can enrich your leadership potential. You might volunteer to serve as a mentor for a high school student, or a pre-law undergraduate student, for example. You can select opportunities by considering all of the proficiencies that strong leaders master: teamwork, mentoring, coaching, providing feedback to others, seeking and incorporating feedback on yourself, supervising, delegating, listening, motivating and inspiring, influencing, setting a strong example, enhancing diversity, decision-making, and project management. Any task, position, or situation that offers you the occasion to exercise and strengthen any two or more of these proficiencies is likely a terrific leadership opportunity.

In addition to stepping out into positions of leadership (formally or informally, such as Tonya did), there are other ways to bolster your leadership skills. Law schools are increasingly offering leadership courses, recognizing how important the development of leadership skills is to long-term success. If you are fortunate enough to have such an offering within your law school, make every effort to take advantage of it. Regardless of your career goals, enhancing your leadership abilities will be helpful to you throughout your professional life. If your law school does not offer a leadership class, consider exploring whether a related business school has curricular options in which you could enroll and potentially earn credits toward your law degree. If nothing is available in your college or university, or you have already graduated, consider continuing education courses at other local colleges, or weekend or one-day seminars, which are frequently offered through schools, community groups, consultants, and other associations, but are often open to the public. Your employer may also offer some form of leadership education or opportunities to participate in seminars or online training sponsored by training organizations, so do not overlook that possibility.

You can also learn about leadership through books and other material resources, but reading alone will not be enough to enhance your skills—you will need to work to put into practice the information you obtain. However, there are a variety of excellent leadership skills resources that you can read, consult, and use to enhance your knowledge and leadership skills.

You should also explore options within your college or university's career counseling offices, whether you are a current student or an alumna/e. Many undergraduate, business school, and even law school career counselors can either provide you with, or point you in the direction of, leadership assessment tools such as StrengthsFinder 2.0,[5] which is the updated version of the original StrengthsFinder assessment developed by Gallup. Leadership assessments are generally

---

5. Tom Rath, Strengthsfinder 2.0 (Gallup Press, NY, 2007).

short surveys, rankings, or multiple-choice questionnaires that you complete, and the interpretation of your answers can provide insight into your leadership strengths and styles as well as areas that need development. Some assessment tools, such as StrengthFinders 2.0, are available on-line, allowing you to take the assessments in your own home, at your leisure (sometimes free of charge, sometimes for a nominal investment). Leadership theories and theorists abound, as do assessment tools based on various leadership philosophies. It's always a good idea to take more than one assessment and to use the tools and feedback as one of many indicators about your skills and how to improve them, not as the sole indicator.

Finally, leadership consulting is big business, and consultants and career coaches assist clients—even students and new lawyers—who want to improve their leadership and management skills. At this stage in your career (either as a law student or newer lawyer), when your earning capacity is more limited, you probably won't want to spend money on these services; just be aware of this as an option for the future. If you are struggling at any point in your career, or you become particularly worried about your ability to succeed, there are a host of resources available to you. Exhaust your opportunities to improve your leadership and management skills—it's valuable to obtain expert assistance at various points through your career. Your goal is to gain as much knowledge and skill as you can on the leadership front and recognize that there is always room for improvement. There are many paths to enhancing your leadership skills—take as many of them as you can.

For Further Reading

- Ken Blanchard, *Leading at a Higher Level: Blanchard on Leadership and Creating High Performing Organizations* (FT Press, 2006).
- Daniel Goleman, Richard E. Boyatzis, and Annie McKee, *Primal Leadership: Learning to Lead with Emotional Intelligence* (Harvard Business School Press, 2004).
- John Kotter, *Leading Change* (Harvard Business School Press, 1996).

- James M. Kouzes and Barry Z. Posner, *Leadership Challenge,* 4th ed. (Jossey Bass, 2008).
- John C. Maxwell, *The 21 Irrefutable Laws of Leadership: Follow Them and People Will Follow You* (Thomas Nelson, 1998).
- John C. Maxwell, *Developing the Leader Within You* (Thomas Nelson, 2005).
- Angie Morgan and Courtney Lynch, *Leading from the Front: No–Excuse Leadership Tactics for Women* (McGraw–Hill, 2006).

Developing Your Public–Speaking Skills

Let's face it, lawyers get asked to speak in public—a lot. Whether it is in front of juries, small groups, the media, or large audiences, public speaking is a fact of life for most lawyers. Even lawyers who are not litigators will be asked to address groups in a variety of settings. Whether teaching a class or seminar, giving a keynote speech, introducing a luminary, or advising at a city council meeting, lawyers are often the "go-to" people for speaking at events. And for litigators who are in court every day, public speaking is a way of life. So if you are one of those people whose heart starts racing, stomach gets queasy, and palms get sweaty just thinking about speaking to a roomful of people, take heart—public speaking is a skill that can be learned and mastered.

Although you can improve certain aspects of your public-speaking skills through reading books and articles providing public-speaking tips, there is no substitute for actually doing it—and doing it often—as the means to becoming a polished and interesting speaker. Therefore, you should take every opportunity to speak to groups, no matter how large or how small. You might be saying, "Yeah, right, I'm going to volunteer to put myself out in front of a group? No way!" You are not alone in your reaction; in fact, very few people are comfortable with public speaking without some training and effort first.

The first step to becoming a seasoned and skillful speaker is to take a class on public speaking and to sign up for law school classes (such as seminars) that have a presentation component to the grading. If you are already practicing law, you can investigate continuing education classes on public speaking. Courses aimed at teaching you how to improve your public-speaking skills are, hands down, the best way to develop a skill that you will be pressed to use time and time again throughout your career. The comforting fact about most classes in public speaking is that you'll be among people who feel the same way you do about speaking to a group. Most of them will be at least as nervous as you are, if not more, about tackling the speaking beast. Classes in public speaking usually provide you with a foundational set of skills: How to plan your presentation, write speaker notes, capture and keep audience interest, improve your speeches, and re-move nervous habits from your speech patterns and gestures, as well as other basic speaking skills.

At the same time as teaching foundational speaking skills, such classes generally require the participants to give a series of presentations to the class. One day you might be required to introduce someone you know or someone you have re-searched. Another day you might conduct a training session for the benefit of the class. You may be asked to teach a new procedure, give an informational talk on a topic you know well, accept an award, or give any number of other types of talks throughout the course curriculum. These presentations to your fellow public-speaking classmates, with the guidance of your teacher, are valuable because they provide practice in public speaking before a friendly and empathic audience, which will increase your comfort level with speaking in general. Such classes also typically provide a lot of detailed feedback from both the teacher and your fellow classmates, which you are not likely to get in formal speaking situations.

Frequently, the instructor will videotape your presenta-tions and provide a copy for you to review at home. If that is the case, make sure you take the time to watch it. There is nothing like hearing yourself say "umm" for the hundredth time in a speech to cure you of that bad habit! It's also much easier to see if you are talking too fast—a common affliction when nerves are involved—or if you use any annoying and distracting gestures while speaking, like clicking a pen. Being told about these bad speaking habits is one thing, but actual-ly seeing yourself with irritating mannerisms or speaking habits really helps you to consciously avoid them in future presentations. When you watch later recordings of your public-speaking attempts, you will be able to see your progress, which is very heartening. It is actually pretty easy to improve public-speaking skills with some concentrated practice! The natural ease and rapport that excellent speakers have is often the result of many, many presentations. In this arena, practice is essential.

If you don't have any curricular options for taking a public speaking class, either in your law school or a larger university, or as part of a continuing education program, consider becoming a member of or starting a local Toastmasters International Club. Toastmasters is a not-for-profit organization that helps people improve speaking, communication, and leadership skills. Each club meets weekly or biweekly to practice speaking by assigning different meeting roles to members of the group for each session. Some groups meet over a meal; others do not. There are no instructors— it's a peer learning opportunity (and a great leadership-skill-building and networking opportunity). For small fees you can join an existing club or start your own, depending on your preference. For more information and to learn how to join, see the Toastmasters International Web site at www. toastmasters.org.

Public Speaking Quick Tips

1. Know exactly who your audience will be, and prepare your message accordingly. Prepare your key points with your audience in mind.

2. Keep your notes to key words only, and to one page, if possible. Don't write out your entire speech or memorize it. Both will lead to a stilted presentation.

3. Approach your speech or presentation as a conversation—incorporate interesting stories, examples, and humor, if appropriate.

4. Start with a bang—don't begin by introducing yourself, coughing, or saying "Okay, I'm going to get started." Memorize your opening sentence, and say it confidently.

5. Practice your presentation many times to ensure you know it well, and use your key-word outline

to keep it flowing. For best results, practice in front of a mirror several times. Run through the presentation at least twice the day before, and then again on the day of the presentation.

6.   If you plan to use technology, be prepared for glitches and have a back-up plan. Test all your equipment in advance of your talk.

7.   If you use PowerPoint or another electronic presentation software, do not overuse words in the slides, and do not write out your speech. Use PowerPoint only to add graphic illustrations, pictures, and other interesting elements to what you are discussing. Otherwise, if you write out what you are saying, the audience will read your speech instead of listening to you.

8.   If possible, familiarize yourself ahead of time with the room in which you will be speaking—check out the size, layout, microphones, and technology options.

9.   Make eye contact with people all around the room, not just those sitting right in front of you.

10.   If you are allowing questions at the end of your presentation, be sure to repeat the question that is asked before answering it. Most speakers neglect this important step and thus frustrate people in the audience who were not able to hear the question.

11.   At the conclusion of the question period, do not end your talk abruptly. Take a moment to conclude with a compelling statement that sums up your talk and formally brings it to a close.

12.   As a beginning speaker, focus on topics you know a lot about. If you have to address a topic with which you aren't familiar, make sure to research it thoroughly beforehand so you are knowledgeable about and comfortable with the material.

13.   Try to relax and enjoy speaking. Take a deep breath, speak slowly and clearly, and remember— your audience wants you to succeed!

Public-Speaking Resources

You must practice your public-speaking skills in order to perfect them, but books can be a great source of ideas and advice. One of the following books was specifically developed for lawyers; the rest are general public-speaking resources for you to explore:

- Dale Carnegie, *How to Develop Self–Confidence & Influence People by Public Speaking* (Pocket Books, 1991).

- David J. Dempsey, *Legally Speaking: 40 Powerful Presentation Principles Lawyers Need to Know* (Miranda Publishing, 2002).

- Stephen E. Lucas, *The Art of Public Speaking* (McGraw–Hill, 2003).

- J. Lyman MacInnis, *The Elements of Great Public Speaking: How to Be Calm, Confident, and Compelling* (Ten Speed Press, 2006).

- James O'Loghlin, *Umm . . .A Complete Guide to Public Speaking* (Allen & Unwin, 2007).

- The Princeton Language Institute and Lenny Laskowski, *10 Days to More Confident Public Speaking* (Warner Books, 2001).

Developing Your Time–Management and Organizational Skills

Seth's Story

Seth hurriedly combed through his desk, looking for the latest document about the huge deal on which he was working. As a first-year lawyer, he was happy to be involved in an exciting case with such a huge client, and he didn't want to make any mistakes. He was dismayed with how many piles had accumulated on his desk in recent months, but he told himself that such messes came with the territory—he was a busy lawyer and, as such, piles and the inability to find the occasional document were normal and even expected. After searching for ten more minutes, Seth still could not find the document he needed, so he gave up and asked his assistant to get another copy from the assistant to the lawyer in charge of the case.

Seth's assistant rolled her eyes. His request was not unusual—he was always losing documents, frequently late for appointments, and generally a bit unreliable. Although she offered repeatedly to help Seth get organized, he said he didn't need help—and he certainly didn't have time to spend worrying about non-billable pursuits such as organizing his desk. Seth's assistant reluctantly followed his instructions and requested another copy of the document. Unfortunately, the assistant whom she called was overheard by the lawyer in charge of the case, Sandy, who was more than a little troubled that Seth's copy had been misplaced.

Sandy had worked with Seth on a few occasions, and she was impressed with his quick mind and analytical skills. However, he was always slow to respond to e-mails she sent asking for updates on projects, and she had one request to him that was still outstanding—without any acknowledgment. Hearing that he had misplaced a copy of a highly confidential document was concerning at the least, so she decided to stop by and have a chat with Seth.

When Sandy arrived at Seth's office, the sight of his desk took her breath away. Not only was there no available workspace, but documents, files, mail, and other items were piled haphazardly on every available inch of space, seemingly without any order or organization. There were piles on the floor, as well, and Sandy could barely see Seth in his chair.

Sandy approached Seth and asked him how things were going. He said that everything was going well, which prompted Sandy to ask why he had not responded to the e-mail she had sent two days ago. Seth was caught off guard—he didn't remember getting an e-mail from Sandy, and he told her so. He could see that Sandy was unhappy with his answer.

Actually, Sandy was trying very hard to keep her temper in check. Seth was a first year lawyer and already she could tell that Seth had some bad habits that did not bode well for his future. Sandy asked Seth to show her how many e-mails were in his in-box and was not surprised that there were more than 500. Seth acknowledged that his e-mail in-box had gotten a bit out of control lately, and he may have missed her e-mail. Sandy replied that from the looks of things in his office, his entire professional life appeared to be out of control. Sandy gave Seth a week to get his office, his e-mail, and his act straightened up, and suspended his work on the current deal until it was done. She told Seth that he was very lucky it was her and not a client whom he had failed to respond to, because she wanted him to succeed. A client would simply fire him—and the firm—if responses were not forthcoming.

Sandy suggested ways for Seth to get his professional life organized and recommended a few books for him to read. Although she was calm and helpful, there was no mistaking the fact that Seth had disappointed her and other lawyers in the firm on a number of occasions and that his career there was actually in question—all due to his lack of organization. They were frustrated by his inefficiency, how often he couldn't locate important documents (thus potentially breaching client confidentiality), his repeated requests for staff to do tasks on his behalf, delayed (or no) responses to the attorneys with whom he worked, and an unprofessional-looking workspace. Despite his excellent legal skills, Seth's job was in serious jeopardy.

Tackling Time Management

A lack of organizational skills and the inability to manage time effectively can be extremely detrimental to law students, but even more so to new lawyers. Even though as a law student you may feel overwhelmed and behind most of the time, there is even less margin for error and less flexibility in practice. Many new lawyers quickly discover that the survival techniques they employed in law school do not necessarily translate into law practice. In addition to increased time demands, once you're in practice you do not have the same breaks from the pressure—holidays, spring, and summer—to use as catch-up time. Furthermore, law practice lacks the closure to pending matters that you receive at the end of each semester in law school. If you fall behind one semester, you get a clean slate at the start of the next in law school. Clean slates in law practice generally do not exist, and if you fail to

keep up with your responsibilities, the effects become com-
pounded over time. Effective organization and time management are key to your success, and you should work to develop
sound practices as quickly as possible. Although these techniques will be more relevant when you are practicing law
than when you're in school, it is smart to employ these skills
even as a law student.

You should always keep a comprehensive and prioritized
list of tasks you need to complete. This "to do" list is your
guide to spending your time effectively, and some form of it
should be kept with you at all times. That way, you can add
to it as you receive requests, quickly re-prioritize in light of a
new deadline or urgent and unexpected matter, and delegate
as needed. Some people prefer to keep their task list in
hardcopy form of some sort—in a notebook, journal, organizer, or planner system. Others prefer the electronic version—
in a PDA or through calendar and task functions in programs
like Outlook. The form you prefer does not matter; using it to
manage your workload effectively does. You may elect to keep
a similar prioritized task list for your personal life, or make it
a subsection of your workload list.

Some people find it effective to sort their list into three
sections: tasks with a short time frame, those with a longer
time frame, and longer-term projects. Other people prefer to
categorize tasks by the estimated time they will take to
complete, or to organize them in deadline order. If you use a
spreadsheet, you can sort by all three methods. Tasks that
you have delegated to other people should also appear on
your task list so you don't forget about them and can track
their progress.

Your calendaring system should work hand-in-hand with
your prioritized task list. The calendaring system you employ—whether hardcopy or electronic—is your day-to-day appointment guide, your deadline handbook, and a reminder of
all important events, and it should have the capability and
functionality to serve as all three. Your calendar will be a
useful tool for networking and contact management, discussed in detail in Chapter Five. You can record dates you
need to remember such as when to follow up with certain
contacts, birthdays and other important events in the lives of
your contacts, and when it is time to reach out again. Your
calendar and prioritized task list together, if used properly,

will keep you on track each day and make workload management less complicated, whether you are a law student or a practicing lawyer.

To manage your time properly, it can be helpful to have some uninterrupted work time each day. To do this, block out an hour or two (or whatever you will need) on your calendar—that way, you can be sure appointments and meetings will not be scheduled during that time. When you block out your work time, you will want to consider whether you are at your best and most productive in the morning or the afternoon, and schedule time for the most demanding work and projects in those productive time periods. Treat this blocked-off work time as if you were in a meeting—do not stop to pick up the phone, check your e-mail, or otherwise interrupt the work you are doing. Inefficiencies result from repeatedly stopping and restarting work projects. Each time you return to a project, it is necessary to reread the work you had started and figure out where you were in the process. If an interruption is unavoidable, take a moment to jot down where you are in the project and what task you were about to do so you can re-orient yourself to the project as quickly as possible when you return to it.

At the end of each day, study the tasks on your list, make adjustments in the priority and delegation of tasks (if necessary), and select those tasks that either need to be completed or those that you intend to devote work time to the next day. This way, you can flesh out a focused plan of action for how you will spend your time the following day, taking into account meetings and other appointments that are already on your calendar. If you have a plan in place when you arrive the next morning, you will be less likely to waste time and more likely to be efficient throughout the entire day.

Goal-setting transcends your task list and is another process you should employ and review on a regular basis. You should set both short-term and long-term goals, commit them to writing, and review them regularly to assess your progress and make necessary amendments. An example of a short-term goal might be to become involved in a pro bono case in the next two months if you are a lawyer, or to join a student group in the next month if you are a law student. A longer-term goal might be to sit on a board of directors in the next three years or to become a partner in your firm if you are a lawyer, to earn a certificate in an area of law by the time you graduate, or to secure a public-interest fellowship if you are a law student. Specific tasks should flow from each of these types of goals. By setting out the steps you must accomplish to reach your goals, and by completing those tasks in a timely manner, you will stay on the path to achieving your goals. Periodic assessment is necessary—your objectives should not be so rigid that you cannot capitalize upon opportunities that you did not envision when you set your goals. Flexibility should be paired with focus to realize your goals.

Procrastination Is Only a Temporary Reprieve From the Inevitable

One of the deadliest enemies of effective workload management and efficiency is procrastination, and we are all possible victims. Some people procrastinate endlessly until the deadline is so close that they have to shift everything into high gear, pull an all-nighter, or resort to other extreme measures. The final product is never as good under these conditions. Some people justify their behavior by saying they work better under pressure, and that their focus and work product exceeds what they can do in a normal day. You are just as likely to hear them admit, though, that if they'd had just two more hours, the project would have been so much better. Other people are not as extreme, but they procrastinate in smaller ways, putting off those tasks that they are not motivated to tackle until the end of the day, or wasting time throughout the day to avoid having to start a project. Although it is not as extreme as procrastination into the eleventh hour, all procrastination is inefficient. One employer says:

> I am a big believer in Murphy's Law. If it can happen, it will, so don't procrastinate on completing assignments on a timely basis. You don't want to run into scheduling difficulties and perhaps miss out on other events. In particular, summer-long assignments can creep up on you quickly, so it is important to work on these long-term projects a little bit at a time rather than leaving everything to the end.

Gayle P. Englert, Director of Human Resources, Cole, Schotz, Meisel, Forman & Leonard P.A.

Additionally, if you develop a reputation as an attorney who procrastinates, there are other possible consequences:

Procrastination inevitably leads to missing deadlines, sloppy work, or both. The danger of procrastination, particularly for law students and new lawyers, is that people will summarily choose not to work with you again, robbing you of future opportunities. Timeliness, on the other hand, demonstrates that you care, that you respect other people's time, that you are reliable, that you are organized, and that you can follow directions, plan ahead and prioritize.

Kari Anne Tuohy, Principal, KAT Consulting

Unfortunately, procrastination is not always easy to conquer. Even the hardest workers and most productive people face this enemy at times, and some struggle to overcome it every day. If you are a likely victim of procrastination and you have a particular project that you are dreading, try to break the project down into as many manageable tasks as you can. Force yourself to complete the smaller tasks in each work period you have, and as you finish them check them off on your list. That process of visually seeing your progress may help motivate you to keep going. If you are a person who is responsive to rewards, provide a small incentive to yourself at the midway point of the project or at other milestones. Another technique can be to commit yourself to working on a particular project or task for a short period of time—maybe fifteen or thirty minutes—and then go on to a task you really enjoy. Make sure to schedule the work you are dreading most at the time of day when you are most productive. If that time is after your second cup of coffee in the morning, then tackle the most difficult work as soon as you've had that second cup of java. Generally, it is rewarding to get the worst tasks done early so you don't spend the whole day fretting about them or putting them off.

Some tasks, writing projects particularly, are so large and overwhelming that it can be difficult to get started. The best advice here is just to force yourself to start the work and acknowledge that it will not be perfect—perfection is not your goal at the beginning. Your aim is to *start* on the project; you can fix it up later. To overcome writer's block, begin by just getting some thoughts down on paper or on-screen. It can be a complete stream-of-conscious attempt at writing a required memo, for example. Do not pause to insert citations, do not worry about mechanics or grammar—none of that is important at this point; just get words down on paper or on-screen. Because it is always easier to edit a draft, as soon as you get over the hump of getting started you will find that your words start flowing. You can amend, organize, delete, and correct as you go, but by getting some thoughts out, generally some inspiration will come to you.

If you are a law student prone to procrastination, you would be well advised to practice the tips above and work to overcome the tendency to procrastinate while you are still in school. Once you are a practicing lawyer, procrastination can cost you cases, clients, and jobs, and there is a much smaller margin for error as a lawyer than as a law student.

Tackling Files and Piles

Organizational skills and the ability to find what you need when you need it are similarly essential proficiencies—as important as time management skills. You will need a strong organizational system for both paper and electronic files. Your system should give you immediate access to all current projects and provide for occasional access to previous work to which you may need to refer. You will need some long-term storage for those items that must be retained but to which you do not need immediate or frequent access.

Increasingly, files are kept electronically, rather than in hardcopy form, so if you have that option, opt for the e-version. It takes up less space, you will have access to more information more quickly, and you may have a search function that makes locating even obscure files a simple task. If you are saving files on a hard drive that is not periodically backed up on your company's server, you will need to manually back up your data, in order to prevent a computer failure from causing you to lose all your files permanently. Most employers have backup mechanisms as well as storage and retention policies that will guide your organization system and the storage of both electronic and paper files.

With all aspects of time management (keeping a prioritized task list, maintaining a current calendar, and committing to short-term and long-term goals) as well as organization of your paper and electronic files, you should rely on your assistant to help you set up and maintain a filing system that will work for both of you and that is in keeping with your employer's policies. If you are still a student, you can learn about such filing systems during your legal jobs and internships.

E-Mail, Voicemail, and Snail Mail Management

Other traps for unorganized professionals include e-mail, voicemail, and the paper mail that arrives each day. All of these communication forms are necessary, and they help you succeed at your job. However, if not managed correctly, each can detract from your success. With all messages and outreach you receive, whether e-mail, voicemail, or snail mail, you should react promptly and respond appropriately. A same-day response is preferred, regardless of the form of communication.

Sometimes e-mail can be the most intrusive form of communication, even though you can read and respond to e-mail on your own schedule. When someone shows up in your doorway, you generally have to stop what you are doing so you can respond to him or her. Despite the flexibility that e-mail offers, too many people treat it as if it were a person standing in their doorway. As soon as the "new mail" signal beeps or pops up on the screen, many professionals stop whatever they are doing to look at the e-mails coming into their in-box. Just as it is important to schedule work time in your calendar for some interrupted time to focus on pending projects, it is much more productive to check your e-mail at regular intervals throughout the day, rather than stopping a task to check your e-mail each time you hear a new message land in your mailbox. Turn off your e-mail sound indicator, and close or hide the program so you can't see when new messages arrive.

It is important that you respond to the e-mails you receive the same day you receive them. If you are going to be out of the office for a day or more, make sure to put an "out of office" alert on your e-mail letting senders know when they can expect to hear from you. For the e-mails you receive that will require research or other tasks in order for you to respond, you should still reply to the sender—just let him or her know that you are looking into the answer and will get back to them with the requested information. Because e-mail can become overwhelming, it is best to develop a first-rate response and filing system that meets your own preferences. Do this early on so you make a habit of it. It is also good to set aside time to respond to e-mails each day with your task list close at hand. That way, you can add tasks to your list, prioritize them, and delegate as necessary as you receive requests via e-mail.

If you have an excellent e-mail response and filing system, you'll be well equipped to make immediate judgments and decisions when you read e-mails the first time. Otherwise, it is easy for your in-box to become unmanageable and out of control. When reading an e-mail, the first question to ask yourself is if it needs to be retained or not. If not, and you can respond immediately, send your reply and delete the e-mail. If so, and you can respond immediately, send your reply and file the e-mail in the appropriate folder. If you cannot respond immediately, take advantage of flags, timers, color coding, or other labeling techniques available in your e-mail system to ensure that you do not forget to obtain the necessary information and respond to the sender. Some professionals create a "pending project" folder that allows easy storage and retrieval of e-mails that require research before responding. Once you have responded to the e-mail, delete it or file it away, depending on its importance. If you commit to handling your in-box every day, it will stay within a manageable volume, and you will be able to quickly and easily retrieve any stored or archived e-mails.

Voicemail management is not usually as tricky as e-mail management, but it is no less important. There are a number of subjects, issues, or discussions for which e-mail is not well suited. In those cases, a face-to-face meeting is optimal, but a telephone conference is second best. Also, there will be professionals who do not prefer e-mail at all, and for them you will need to engage in phone conversations. The disadvantage to phone calls is that they sometimes take more time, and they often include side conversations or small talk that can run counter to efficiency. However, these conversations can greatly enhance your relationship-building! Therefore, it is often time well-spent.

It is best to return phone calls the same day you receive them. Again, listen to your voicemail messages with your task list close at hand so you can add to it, if necessary. If you cannot provide the requested information immediately, at least call the person back to let them know you are working on it. There will be times when you are at peak workload and simply cannot afford a lengthy phone conversation with a chatty person. If that is the case and it is possible to send the person an e-mail, you can respond the same day without risking a lengthy encounter. An e-mail along these lines can do the trick, and it shows you to be responsive even when you can't reply by phone: "Sherry, I received your voicemail, and I'm attaching the information you requested to this e-mail. Please forgive the e-mail response—I am working on several deadlines this week. Do you want to grab coffee next week after I'm through this time crunch so we can go over the attached information? Let me know if you need anything else in the interim. Sam"

The mail and paper you receive should be handled similarly to e-mails and voicemails. The difference here is that poor management of snail mail will affect your workspace as well as your responsiveness and ability to retrieve needed information quickly. Set aside time to open, manage, and respond to your mail each day (or every other day if your volume is low and you are not likely to receive highly time-sensitive information via mail). Work with your task list close at hand, and employ similar techniques as with your e-mail management. Can you respond immediately? If so, respond and either file the document appropriately, if it needs to be retained, or discard it if it does not require retention. If you cannot respond immediately, let the sender know you have received their letter and that you are gathering information. Then add the task to your list, prioritize it, and have a pending project folder ready for the hardcopy request.

With all of these organizational and time management techniques, if you have an assistant, he or she can be an extremely helpful ally whose efforts can really save you significant time and make you infinitely more productive and efficient. Do not be afraid to ask your assistant for help in managing files, paper, and outreach, and do not shy away from delegating appropriate tasks when possible. Often, your assistant will be more adept at filing and document management than you are, and you can learn a lot from him or her. If you set up a manageable and intuitive system that works for you from day one, you will find that it takes minimal effort to stay organized and on track.

Chapter Five
Making Networking a Part of Your Life

As you gain seniority in your position, there will come a time when business development may become critical to your success. You may have a need to promote your business to a readily available network, or you may need a network for a variety of other professional pursuits. If you feel your network is unimpressive now, take action to bolster it. Join the local Chamber of Commerce or a volunteer organization. Reach out to past alumni networks or even on-line network associations. Bring your business cards everywhere, and make it a priority to follow up with every card you collect. You may not need to leverage each contact after you are introduced to them, but it's important to maintain the relationship. As you continuously expand your network, contact management will become more and more critical. Don't be afraid to invest in a business card scanner and contact management software. Also, don't be afraid to reach out to your immediate circles—you might be surprised by the great contacts your friends and family members have (as well as their willingness to support you in your professional or business development efforts).

Courtney Lynch, leadership expert and consultant, cofounder of Lead Star LLC, and co-author of the best-selling book, *Leading from the Front*

If the word "networking" brings to mind images of making small talk at a stuffy cocktail party, it is time to rework your impression. Networking is key to your long-term success, regardless of your career path, and it need not be difficult, alarming, or extensively time-consuming once you have a system in place. The best way to become a successful networker is to incorporate it into every aspect of your life, such that it becomes a natural extension of all you do. This does not mean that you transform yourself into a cheesy used-car salesperson. It does not mean that your network is used only when you need a job or something else and you want help doing it—although those are both valid uses of a strong and vibrant network. It *does* mean that you consciously seek to make solid contacts, and once you make those contacts you spend time staying in touch. Networking is not about being needy or stalking people. It is about meeting people, being interested and interesting, staying in touch, and developing reciprocal relationships that benefit both you and your contacts on a personal and/or professional level. Although some relationships are more likely to be helpful to you than to your contact initially (i.e. a faculty member), there really is something in it for everyone. As Skip Horne, a former career counselor and now recruiting manager, says:

> *Consider this: When you started law school, you joined the legal profession. True, you're at the very beginning of the timeline, but think about the fact that everyone else in the profession is on the very same timeline—they're just a bit further along than you. And how did they get their jobs? Through networking with practicing attorneys. And how did those attorneys get their jobs? Through the same tried-and-true methods. Think about the entire legal profession as your very own network. Connections you make now, at the beginning of the continuum, will benefit you in numerous ways as you progress through your legal career. Even though getting that summer associate position, judicial clerkship, or entry-level attorney job is paramount, keep in mind that you're in the legal profession for the long haul, and continue to establish and build relationships at every turn.*

Skip Horne, Global Recruiting Manager, Diversity and Law School Outreach, Latham & Watkins LLP

So, how do you begin?

Contact Management Is the First Step

The best networkers start with some kind of contact management tool. You can use anything that works for you. In the past, contacts were managed with a Rolodex, business card holder, or address book. Today, the most versatile contact management tools are e-versions of their original counterparts. You can manage your contacts in the contact application of your e-mail (for example, Outlook Contacts), through a database application like Access, or using any number of software programs. There are a variety of products on the market, but check first to see what might be available for free on the web (Gmail, for example) or within your existing software.

The finest management tools will allow you to keep vital contact information (name, address, and business, cell, home, and fax numbers) along with notes about the contact that can be updated (for example "met at soccer game 9/14/07"; "has three children: Jason, Michael, and Liz"; "sent note about new job in October") and categories that you select (such as family, professional, church, school, public speaking, and litigation). Often more than one category or group will apply to a single contact. Being able to search your contacts based on categories or by creating groups provides a great way to help you stay in touch as certain events happen, or if you have information to share that may be of interest to a specific subset of your network.

Now if you are thinking that you don't need any such tool because you keep all your contacts or "friends" on My Space or Facebook or a similar site, it is important to remember that many of your professional contacts may be from a generation not accustomed to using social networking sites. As such, you should have a mechanism as discussed here for tracking your contacts. Although social networking sites are a great networking tool if used appropriately—and professional networking sites are catching on as well—not everyone in your network will embrace them. Knowing your audience is as important in networking as it is in public speaking. (Social networking sites will be discussed in greater detail in Chapter Seven.)

You DO Have an Existing Network!

Once you've selected your contact management tool, the first step is to organize all the contact information for everyone in your existing network. If this information is currently kept in different places, now is the time to consolidate and organize your network into a central location for easy maintenance and management. You might be thinking that you do not have an existing network, but rest assured that you do.

Rule number one: Family counts! Don't overlook your family as an important part of your network—and be sure to enter family members into your contact management tool. In Chapter Two we discussed the importance of maintaining the relationships you had prior to law school. So that is the second wave of your existing network—all of your pre-law-school contacts: friends from high school; friends from college; fraternity brothers or sorority sisters; people you know from prior jobs (including former supervisors); family friends; prior faculty members or teachers with whom you developed relationships; people you know from sports, clubs, a church or synagogue, etc. Your list of contacts is virtually endless, so be as thorough as you can in committing your network to your contact management tool.

Planting the Seeds: Grow Your Network in Law School

Once your existing network is officially listed, you've accomplished a great deal! After listing all your current contacts, the next step is to expand your network based on where you currently are in your career (first-year law student, second-year law students, new lawyer, etc.). This is the piece of the networking puzzle in which many law students get stalled. But, as mentioned earlier, if you make networking a conscious part of all you do, it will become so automatic and natural that you won't think twice about it.

To build your network, start by adding fellow law students with whom you've developed a friendship, regardless of their year in law school. Upperclassmen might have more leads and advice for you than the direct peers in your class, but all your connections are potentially valuable. Although your peers may seem like unlikely prospects to help you find a job or further your career at the moment, networking is about planting seeds that sometimes take years to grow (and can pay off sooner than you imagined). Fifteen years from now, your current peers will be law firm partners, corporate general counsel, faculty members, judges, politicians, lobbyists, and in any other number of positions of leadership and power. They will be sources of future business, referrals and references, and influence.

Lawyers often lament not staying in touch with their former law classmates and friends, many of whom went on to become successful and who would be excellent additions to any network. If these lawyers had just taken the time to keep in touch with the people who shared the law school experience, their network would be infinitely stronger. As career counselor David Diamond explains, his law classmates were a healthy source of referrals:

> *I attended a large national law school, and most of my classmates were bound for large law firms. I landed a job at a small law firm and because of that, many referrals came to me from my classmates. Cases that the large firms couldn't handle were a great source of business for me. You cannot overlook your own classmates as a source for referrals—if you treat them well and act professionally, they will remember you. On the other hand, I also had a classmate who did not represent himself well or make many friends in law school. Several years after graduation, he was reprimanded by a judge in a ruling for a case he was handling, and the opinion was quickly forwarded by a former classmate to many of us. It was a sure bet that he didn't receive any referrals from any of us. It also was not surprising that his failure to play nice in law school carried over into practice, where he didn't play nice with opposing counsel, as noted by the judge in the case. It definitely pays to get along with and stay in touch with your law school classmates.*

David M. Diamond, J.D., M.A., Director, Center for Career Strategy and Advancement, Northwestern University School of Law

If you have already graduated, revitalize your network by adding in your contacts from law school, and commit to staying in touch.

After adding your law school peers to your network, start adding law faculty members with whom you've developed a relationship. If you haven't yet taken the time to get to know at least two of your faculty members fairly well, you need to make that a priority immediately. Adding two faculty members to your network should be your first official networking assignment. As Assistant Dean Bill Chamberlain says:

> *I have obtained every job I've had since law school in part because of a recommendation from a faculty member for whom I did research and wrote a long paper. Certainly for judicial clerking, either right after school or down the road, relationships with faculty members are key. One of the best things a first-year student can do during the summer is research for a faculty member. Don't be afraid to approach a faculty member in whose class you performed well or whom you like or whose area of research interests you.*

Faculty members can also be excellent resources if you have questions as you're practicing. Faculty members know you and your work—it is always important to maintain good relationships with faculty. If a faculty member does serve as a reference for a job, be sure to follow up to let him or her know whether you got the job. Stay in touch over the years. Let them know what you're doing. Ask them about their research, life at the school, their families and whatever else you know interests them. Faculty members are a key part of your professional network.

William Chamberlain, Assistant Dean, Northwestern University School of Law

Law school faculty are in a unique position to provide references to students who are seeking legal internships or summer jobs, and they are helpful in any number of ways throughout law school and beyond. They can provide career or curricular advice, review writing samples, help you gain experience as a research assistant, assist in improving your writing and drafting skills, support the efforts of student groups, provide interesting, cutting-edge legal articles to read, alert students to job openings that are not yet posted or advertised, and help to clarify course content to improve students' grades. Although you need not become the faculty member's best friend, you do need to begin making these contacts. You can start by selecting the two most approachable faculty members you know, such as the teacher of a law school class you particularly enjoyed or in which you excelled, or by starting with your faculty advisor or small group advisor.

Visiting faculty during their posted office hours is a great way to begin a relationship. If you don't have a specific reason to visit a faculty member, start by asking for advice, or find out how they dealt with a certain issue in law school or their job search. Most people enjoy talking about themselves, so asking questions is a great way to break the ice. Because faculty are busy and have many students with needs, it will be your responsibility to continue to reach out and stay in touch in a way that is respectful of the faculty member's time. It's always a good idea to ask contacts such as a faculty member how he/she would prefer to be contacted. Although e-mail might be easiest for you, your contact may not check e-mail frequently or may find it annoying, so it's always best to ask if you don't already know.

As discussed in Chapter Two, all the people in your law school are natural prospects for your network. So, beyond your classmates and faculty members, don't overlook members of the administrative staff and adjunct faculty. The career services staff, the Dean of Students and his/her staff, clinical staff, and admissions and financial aid staff are all viable contacts for your network. Treat them well, as you would any other faculty member, and watch your network grow.

For those of you who are already practicing law, you should add to your list of contacts everyone you have met or with whom you have worked since you started practicing. Include all your contacts at work as well as contacts you have met externally, through bar association meetings, networking events, community service, and the like.

Using Alumni to Increase Your Network

Alumni of your law school are a potentially rich source of contact development for your network and can be particularly good contacts to cultivate. Many alumni are interested in hearing from and helping current law students and recent graduates as a way to "give back" to their school or community. As practitioners in a variety of career enterprises, they can offer career-related advice, leads, and assistance with items such as cover letters, resumes, and writing samples. Tracking down alumni is usually pretty easy, but before you begin your quest, make sure you are taking advantage of all the opportunities your law school provides for you to meet and develop relationships with alumni. As Dr. Britton of the University of Tennessee College of Law says:

> Many law schools have on-line alumni Web sites or alumni networking programs. Prospective students could use these alumni to test their perceptions about a school's ability to prepare them for career success in this line of work, and the networking "reach" of that school in that area—including alumni support. Enrolled students can contact alumni for advice about job searches and for general career information. You can't expect an alumnus to find a job for you, but reaching out to alumni who have shown a willingness to

provide advice and assistance is a critical element of basic networking.

Dr. Karen Reagan Britton, Director of Admissions, Financial Aid, and Career Services, University of Tennessee College of Law

Career services offices at law schools typically offer a variety of venues in which to interact with alumni throughout the year, including panel discussions, career fairs, mentoring programs, mock interviews, and alumni resumé reviews. Special events related to college sports, alumni awards, and symposia are other means that your school may offer to meet alumni. Furthermore, many schools maintain lists of alumni who have volunteered to serve as a resource for current students—sometimes by location or by the fields in which the alumni practice law. If you haven't taken advantage of these opportunities, you should begin to do so immediately.

The value in these opportunities, however, is in how you approach them and what you make of them. If you attend a panel discussion, for example, and sit in the back of the room, leaving as soon as it concludes, you've only received the benefit of the substance of the panel discussion, and you've lost the opportunity to develop a potential contact. If you sit in the front of the room, however, and make a point to go see the panelists at the conclusion of the discussion to thank them and chat for a few minutes, you've gained new contacts. If you then follow up with an e-mail or invite one of the panelists for coffee, you've really taken the steps to make the most of an opportunity.

If you've exhausted the occasions your law school provides for you to mix and mingle with alumni, there are other ways to identify alumni who may be potential additions to your network. One approach is to search for alumni who practice in the geographic region in which you plan to practice. Particularly if a few alumni are concentrated in a certain geographic area, they are usually more than willing to help students or recent graduates who want to land in their area. Many times, they can also direct you to other alumni in the vicinity. A number of on-line directories exist that can help you locate alumni by law school and place of practice, such as West's Legal Directory.

It is always helpful to contact alumni with whom you have something in common. While attending the same law school is a powerful link, adding another commonality can really impress your potential contact. To that end, be sure to research for alumni of your law school who attended the same undergraduate institution you did. You can also search for common participation in sports, a shared hometown, membership in the same fraternity or sorority, or similar community involvement. Any shared interest provides an opening for you when making a contact and getting the conversation started.

Another Tool: Informational Interviews

Although it is perfectly acceptable to contact alumni or other lawyers simply to ask about their career path, specifically requesting an informational interview can be an easy way to provide structure and purpose to your first meeting with a potential contact. An informational interview is typically requested by a job seeker, but not for the purpose of being considered for a particular position. The informational interview is meant solely for gathering information about a specific career path, practice area, firm or company, geographic region, or type of job. The job seeker is the person who asks the questions throughout the interview, the reverse of a typical job interview.

If you are conducting informational interviews in a different geographic location from where you attend law school, you can either do them in person or over the phone. However, it's a little more difficult to establish rapport over the telephone since you can't read gestures or body language. So, if you would like to conduct them in person at a long distance locale, it's best to set up interviews when you know you will be in town for a few days. Simply let the attorney know that you'll be in town during the week of March 17, for example, during your spring break, and you would love to meet with him or her then. If the location you select is not a place where you have family or friends with whom you can stay, be sure to get the biggest bang for your money and time by meeting with as many people as possible while you are in town. Follow-up with contacts is much easier by phone or e-mail once you have met in person.

When you are requesting an informational interview with a professional, you should make clear that your purpose is to learn, not to be considered for a job. You can do the initial outreach by e-mail, phone, or letter. If you select e-mail or snail mail, be sure to say that you will make a follow-up phone call to the attorney to see if he/she would be willing to schedule an informational interview with you. You can also ask if the attorney would prefer that you work through his or her assistant to schedule the meeting. Set a clear amount of time for the interview, and stick to it—usually no more than thirty minutes. (Although you may have much to learn, lawyers are busy people, and it's much easier for them to commit to thirty minutes than an hour.)

Once you have secured your informational interview, the burden is on you to prepare for it. Learn as much as you can about the lawyer and his or her firm, agency, company, or organization. Next, develop your question list. This should reflect that you've done your research but you want to learn about what the lawyer has to say. Your goal is to find out as much as possible, so develop your questions based on what will be most helpful for you to learn about, and then list the questions in priority order. That way, if you run out of time, you will have asked your most important questions.

After you have arranged your informational interview, and you have researched the lawyer, and you have developed a solid list of questions to structure your time together, are you done? No, not quite. You should treat an informational interview as you would an actual job interview. (See Chapter Nine for a complete guide on professionalism in the interview process.) First, confirm the date and time of your meeting with the lawyer or his/her assistant. Second, make sure you know how to get there and what the parking situation is, and allow plenty of time for unexpected contingencies. Third, dress professionally, and bring along the tools you will need— your questions and some paper upon which to take notes, at a minimum. Finally, arrive a few minutes early, and check in with the receptionist.

Even if the conversation is flowing smoothly and the lawyer appears to be enjoying your time together as much as you are during the informational interview, when the time is up you should say so out loud and offer to end the interview at that point. For example, you might say, "I've so enjoyed talking to you, and I that see our thirty minutes together has flown by. I know you are very busy, so we can conclude here if you need to get to another appointment." If the attorney assures you it's fine to keep talking, feel free to chat a while longer, but don't abuse the privilege. At the conclusion, be sure to thank the attorney for his or her time. You might also consider asking if you can follow up with him or her periodically. This is one way you could approach it: "Thank you so much—I've really enjoyed our time together this afternoon. I have learned so much that will help me with my summer job search. Would it be okay if I update you from time to time on my progress?"

Following the interview, be sure to send the attorney a brief thank-you note sincerely expressing your appreciation for his or her time and efforts. (See Chapter Six for professionalism guidelines in correspondence.) Even if the informational interview did not go as you had planned, or you did not learn what you had hoped to, or the attorney was less than helpful, the attorney should still be thanked after the fact—it is a common courtesy that too many law students overlook. After all, that attorney took time out of what was probably a very busy day to meet with you. Assuming that your informational interview went well, you should add that attorney to your contact list. Then update him or her on your progress, and share other information you think he/she might enjoy receiving.

Informational interviewing is a technique that can be used again and again to assist you in your search, learn more about certain aspects of the legal profession, and expand your network. You should feel free to ask the lawyer you are interviewing for other people he/she would suggest you talk to. If the lawyer is willing to supply you with a few names, ask if it is okay for you to indicate that the lawyer gave you his/her name when you contact the person. For example, if the lawyer you are interviewing suggests that you contact Jane Smith to learn more about a tax practice, you can say, "I'll be sure to follow up with Ms. Smith—would it be okay if I tell her you provided her name when I contact her?" Then it is *imperative* that you follow up with Jane Smith within a few days—you should never ignore or neglect important referrals like this.

Additionally, do not limit your search for informational interviewing prospects to alumni. Although alumni of your law school provide a natural link, you are free to contact anyone in a position that you would like to learn more about. Using other criteria, such as women who are juggling families and a law career, prior accountants who are practicing in estates and trusts, and lawyers who are in alternative careers you find interesting (such as human resources, editing, etc.) are all valid reasons to contact someone for an informational interview. This technique is only as limited as your creativity.

Remember that not all attorneys are created equal, and some will naturally be more helpful than others. As such, if your first experience isn't tremendous, do not let that keep you from trying again. All it takes is one stellar informational interviewing experience to make a network contact for life and potentially be referred to other terrific contacts. Long-term relationships can develop from informational interviews—you never know who might be that next great contact.

Sample Informational Interview Questions

The following questions are provided as samples to assist you in developing your own informational interview questions. As you develop your own questions, think about what is most important to you. Then formulate questions that will assist you in your job search or other networking goals.

CAREER GUIDANCE QUESTIONS

- "As a new law student, I'm pretty undecided about my practice area of interest—how did you settle on employee benefits?"

- "As a first-year student, I'll be starting my search for summer employment soon, and I've heard that opportunities are more limited for first-years—did you work during your first summer and, if so, what did you do?"

- "If you had to start law school all over again with the benefit of your current knowledge, what would you make sure to do or take advantage of while in law school to help your career prospects?"

- "When you are reviewing resumés of second-year law students, what is your focus, beyond grades?"

- "What extracurricular activities did you find most helpful in law school, and why?"

- "I contacted you specifically because you are a partner in a major law firm, as well as a mother, and are very involved in the community. I'm interested in hearing how you are able to balance everything."

- "What is the most challenging part of being a practicing lawyer, and how do you meet that challenge?"

SPECIFIC AREAS OF LAW QUESTIONS

- "Can you describe for me what the typical day of a litigator is like?"

- "How were you able to incorporate aspects of your prior career as a nurse into your current health care practice?"

- "If I am particularly interested in being a transactional lawyer like you, what law school classes should I take, and what extracurricular activities do you recommend?"

- "What professional organizations exist for lawyers in tax and estate planning, and are student memberships available?"

- "If you had to fill a job for a new lawyer in your area, where would that position most likely be posted?"

GEOGRAPHIC QUESTIONS

- "How difficult did you find it to relocate to Texas upon graduation from law school?"

- "Is there a strong law school alumni network in this city?"

- "What professional organizations exist locally that might be good for me to investigate, and can I join them as a law student?"

- "What local publications do you suggest I subscribe to in order to learn more about the local legal market?"
- "Where are legal job openings in this city most likely to be posted?"
- "How would you describe the current legal climate (or market) in this city?"
- "What are the opportunities for new young professionals who move here to meet others?"
- "What do you think is the best way to really learn about this city and the legal network here?"

SPECIFIC ORGANIZATION OR FIRM QUESTIONS

- "When starting as a new lawyer at the State Attorney General's office, what kind of assignments are common?"
- "What advancement opportunities exist for attorneys within this organization, and at what stage of your career is it typical to advance through them?"
- "What do you like best about working here?"
- "What are some of the challenges you face in your job?"
- "If working here upon graduation is my goal, what experience do you suggest I obtain while I'm in law school?"
- "I hear that the internship program here is very competitive—what experiences should I highlight, and how can I set my application apart?"

Everyday Opportunities to Develop Your Network

We have discussed ways to build your network using alumni and informational interviewing techniques. There are a host of other ways to expand your network, whether you are still in law school or you have already graduated and launched your legal career. Local and state bar associations usually provide student memberships at a greatly reduced cost and are "must-join" organizations for new lawyers. By joining the bar association and sections or committees in which you have an interest (for example, the new lawyers committee or the insurance law section) and by attending meetings and events of these committees—in short, by getting involved—you will increase your interactions with possible contacts for your network.

Few law students take advantage of these opportunities, so the lawyer members tend to pay special attention to the one or two students who show an interest in becoming involved in the work of a committee. Particularly if you are located in the geographic region in which you plan to practice, this is a great way to become a member of the legal community prior to practicing. Even if you plan to relocate, it pays to have networking contacts everywhere! New lawyers typically find bar association sections and committees a natural way to meet peers and colleagues across the city and state. Bar contacts can become lifelong friends, supportive colleagues, and long-term professional contacts.

In addition to bar associations, there are professional groups in every city. Often, their meetings and special events are posted in the business section or community calendar sections of the local newspaper to assist potential members in locating them. Some professional groups exist because of a common interest, others are specifically for the purpose of networking and meeting professionals across a variety of disciplines, and still others exist for the purpose of performing good deeds for the community. Whatever your interest, these are all valuable networking opportunities for you to consider, both as a student and as a newer lawyer.

If you have specific career interests, you should also consider attending seminars related to your practice interest or CLE (Continuing Legal Education) courses in your region. Many bar associations and other groups offer discounted attendance fees for law students and will welcome your attendance. If you are a new lawyer, you may not have immediate CLE requirements, but you can still attend. Use these events as an opportunity to meet and connect with professionals who are in the area in which you are planning your own career or that you are trying to master.

In addition to all of these structured and formal opportunities for you to connect with possible contacts, you should approach each day as a networking opportunity. Do you consider a visit to your doctor's office a potential way to make new contacts? What about attending your nephew's soccer game? Going to the grocery store or post office? If not, it's time to rethink your approach to building your network. All of these are *potential* networking opportunities. It does not mean you should count on making a new contact every time you stop for gas or board the subway, but it does mean that you should always be alert for opportunities. It is a small world and an even smaller legal community, and the person you meet at a sporting event could be the cousin of the hiring partner at your top-choice law firm, for example, or the nephew of the chairman of the board of a client your firm is cultivating. You just never know who knows whom. Karen Hough is an improvisational performer who became a businessperson and then found out that the concepts of improv could be revolutionary to the business world. She offers these thoughts:

> As a new professional, it is essential that you develop a variety of tools to advance your career. An "elevator pitch" is a critical tool. The elevator pitch is a one to two sentence pitch that tells your story, provides a hook to the listener, and invites further comment. My elevator story is, "Hi, I'm Karen Hough, founder of ImprovEdge. We create learning experiences using improvisation to teach business skills." For a new attorney, it might be, "Hi, I'm Janice Jones, a lawyer with Charles & Darby. I have a legal practice that helps business owners navigate the challenges of expansion, growth, and market conditions." In addition to creating the elevator story, you have to use it—always.

> An example? I was on the sidelines of a soccer field cheering for my daughter, wearing sweats and not looking so hot. Another parent, also in sweats, asked me what I do. I really did not feel like engaging at that point, and I almost took the lazy way out by responding, "I'm a trainer." But I told myself that I had just added this tool, my elevator pitch, to my professional toolkit, and I needed to use it. So, despite my reluctance, our surroundings, and the way we were dressed, I responded with my elevator pitch. Her response was, "Wow, tell me more." To this day, she is one of my best clients, and she has brought me an enormous amount of business. Not the likely outcome if I had taken the easy way out. Networking is about believing that anyone can be a valuable part of your

network. Conversely, watch out for assumptions or judgment calls about people before you know them.

Karen Hough, Founder and CEO, ImprovEdge

Nourishing and Using Your Network

So you've recorded your network in a great contact management tool, and you are continually adding new contacts to your network. What's next? Well, it doesn't do you any good to just collect names and addresses for your network if you don't stay in touch and develop relationships with your contacts. Without attention, your network will wither, but with a bit of time and effort, your network will thrive. And a thriving network is a useful network. Therefore, it's important that you stay in touch with all of your contacts on a regular basis. By using groups and labels in your contact management tool, you can personalize your messages. You should work your way through your network, and contact every person at least once every three months (preferably every month). It pays to stay in touch when you are not in search of assistance, so your network contacts do not always associate outreach from you with requests for help. A one-sided or needy relationship will not last long.

In that vein, send quick updates on your life or your progress with school, for example, and do small, thoughtful things for your contacts like forwarding a link for an article you think the contact may be interested in reading. Most important, check in to see what is new and exciting in your contact's life, find out if there is anything you can do to assist him or her, and occasionally suggest an in-person meeting over coffee, perhaps, to catch up. If one of your contacts ever needs a favor from you, be as responsive and helpful as you possibly can. And while it's imperative to stay in touch at obvious times like the holiday season, it's also important to select non-obvious times just to check in. Be sure to send birthday greetings to those contacts in your network whom you know well enough to have recorded their birthday. Your contacts will be impressed with your memory, organization, and thoughtfulness.

The notes you make and keep about each of your contacts will help you stay in touch. For example, if an attorney you met mentioned that she was going on a vacation in Spain, note that in your file, and then ask her about the trip when you next reach out to her. When you actually do need assistance of some kind, it's fair to approach some of the members in your network, depending on your level of acquaintance. Contacts can serve all kinds of useful purposes, such as providing feedback on a resumé, cover letter, or writing sample; giving you a head's-up on future job openings; serving as a reference; and helping you locate interesting articles or an obscure citation for a paper. If you are searching for a job, it's perfectly fine to let your network know what kind of work you are seeking, what your preferences are, and to please alert you if they have ideas of other people you should talk to or organizations that might be hiring. Be sure to share your good news, too. If you are elected to a leadership position, for example, or you receive a writing award, let your contacts know. As one consultant, formerly in charge of lawyer recruitment and professional development at a large international law firm, says:

> *Be professional and follow up with those individuals who help you in your professional endeavors, including career coaches, mentors, faculty members, lawyers, family contacts and peers. Inform them about the outcome of your applications and interviews, as well as your career choices. If you do so, people will perceive you as interested, invested, professional and respectful. They will be more willing to go to bat for you and support you in the future. Most importantly, you will begin building relationships that are essential to a long and rewarding career.*

Kari Anne Tuohy, Principal, KAT Consulting

Professionalism in Networking

It is true that your network can be a great tool for helping you along the way at the start of your career and through your progression. It's equally true that a professional network—which is how you should approach yours—deserves the highest standard of professionalism from you. Professionalism in e-mail and written communications should be observed at all times. (This will be discussed in detail in Chapters Six and Seven.) Refrain from forwarding to your contacts chain e-mails, jokes, political statements (unless that is a shared interest between you and your contact), and e-mails filled with quizzes or pictures of cute animals.

Although it is vitally important to stay in touch with your contacts regularly, be mindful of the limited time busy professionals have. Yes, you should stay in touch, but be careful not to cross the line between professional and personal with those contacts in your network who are not in the "family" or "friends" categories (and even with friends, keep in mind how you met them and what you want your future relationship to be). Don't assume too much familiarity with a contact, and don't become too casual with your professional contacts. For instance, do not send communications that have abbreviations and e-shorthand in them (for example, "LOL") to anyone in your professional network.

It is always best to obtain permission to stay in touch with a new contact, but if you were not able to do that, assess your relationship occasionally. If you find that your outreach to a contact has become completely one-sided, you may want to check and see if they would prefer you not continue to reach out to him or her. People do have periods in their lives in which it is difficult to respond to outreach, so it could just be that your contact is exceptionally busy or stressed at the moment and does not actually want to cease all contact. If that's the case, let him or her know you understand and that you don't expect an immediate response.

Finally, recognize that you will gain and lose contacts all the time. If one of your contacts is not interested in maintaining a networking relationship, move on to a new contact who is. Your world is full of potential contacts, so if one relationship has died despite your efforts to stay in touch, focus on people for whom the networking relationship is reciprocal. Not all seemingly valuable contacts will turn out to be so. However, don't drop a contact from your network just because he or she hasn't provided you with a great tip or any help recently—as long as he or she is willing to stay in touch with you, you should nurture that relationship.

It is absolutely critical that you treat everyone you meet with the utmost friendliness and professionalism. . .*everyone*. You will see the phrase "it is a small world and an even smaller legal community" again and again in this book— because it's true! You never want to fall prey to the assumption in any given situation that you will not see someone again or that a person is insignificant and therefore you shouldn't bother treating him or her well. Nothing could be further from the truth.

Many law students and cocky young professionals have learned the hard way not to make assumptions about people (based on appearances, actions, or the place you meet them, for example) because you never know who knows whom, who is related to whom, and who is in a relationship with whom. The person you ignore or treat shabbily could be sitting behind the desk at your next interview. It may sound far-fetched, but you never know when you may find yourself in an uncomfortable situation that could have been avoided. Karen J. Sarjeant, Vice President for Programs and Compliance, Legal Services Corporation, says it best, *"Do not burn bridges. With all of the movement in careers today, you have no way of knowing who you will meet along the path of your career. Therefore, always radiate professionalism when you are in public; this will serve you well and in ways that might not be immediately known."*

Fast forward ten years into your future, and envision your network at that time—a large, flourishing network that has contacts you made before and during law school as well as professionals from various disciplines that you've met throughout your career. By keeping your long term networking goals in sight now, and focusing on building your network today the dividends will be evident in the near future and also at many points throughout your career. If you master the skills of networking—which is possible without ever attending a single cocktail party!—you will have added another valuable professionalism skill to your repertoire. Networking is a talent that will be highly valued by your employers (for example, in private practice, networking is essential to success as a rainmaker). Mastering networking skills now will serve you well throughout your professional life. If it seems difficult, you will become skilled over time. Listen to the advice of Karen Hough:

> *The only time we truly develop as adults is when we move outside of our comfort zone—that's when we learn the most. So, start by engaging people, even if it's not comfortable. I recommend a great book:* How to Win Friends and Influence People *by Dale Carnegie—this is an oldie but a goodie. One of the best ways to impress people is to let them talk—learn to be a strong listener. This is a basic skill in engaging other people:* **Be a person that people want to talk to.**

Karen Hough, Founder and CEO, ImprovEdge

Sarah's Story

Sarah heaved her backpack onto her shoulder, smothered a sigh, and prepared to board the plane for the two-hour flight back to school after visiting with her family for a week. She was dead tired and had a pounding headache. The pain in her throat suggested that she was getting a cold, too. This was the worst possible time for her to get sick; the new semester of law classes started the next day, and she had not yet purchased her textbooks, let alone done any of the reading. Being behind in schoolwork and reading before the semester even started was not fun and made it difficult to catch up. Sarah hoped the flight would depart on time. She needed to get home so she could hit the bookstore before it closed. Until then, all she wanted to do was lay down and go to sleep. Luckily, she was one of the few people who could actually sleep on an airplane.

Sarah boarded the plane and found her seat next to the window. She wasn't sure how full the flight would be, and she was hoping that the aisle seat next to her would be empty. She watched as person after person walked by, and she was beginning to think she'd have the row to herself when a man in a suit dropped into the seat next to her. Sarah inwardly rolled her eyes as she prepared to be cramped instead of comfortable. She just hoped the man wasn't a talker—she needed to get some rest.

Five minutes later, Sarah's hopes were dashed—the man was definitely chatty. Sarah smiled at him and politely answered his questions, even asking a few of her own. She wanted nothing more than to lay her head down and go to sleep, but the man seemed nice, and she didn't want to be rude to him. As they chatted, the man said that he was trying to get home from a week-long business trip. He should have been home by now, but his flight the day before had been cancelled, and today he'd been rerouted. This was the final leg of his connection, and he was anxious to get home. His son's birthday party was that night, and as long as all went well with this flight, he was going to make the party, although he'd be slightly late. Sarah listened politely and wished him good luck.

Sarah's seatmate asked what she did, and she explained that she was in her final year of law school—she would be starting her last semester the next day. The man was a pleasant conversationalist, and he asked a lot of questions. Sarah soon found herself confiding that, although she enjoyed most aspects of law school, she wasn't actually planning to practice law. She explained how she had been pretty sure of this before starting law school, and she had used her time in school to explore her options. Most people did not understand the concept of graduating from law school and not practicing law—her own parents included—so she didn't usually get into these details with someone she had just met. She told him about her goals and even mentioned a few of the companies she had researched. Far from not understanding, the man really seemed to appreciate how the law degree would be helpful to her career goals.

Once they reached cruising altitude and were able to use portable electronic devices, the man pulled out a laptop and settled in to start working. With an apologetic smile at Sarah, he explained that he really needed to get some work done. Sarah smiled genuinely and said that was fine with her—she was hoping to catch a little sleep before arriving home and getting ready for the new semester.

Two hours later, Sarah woke with start as the jet touched down for landing. She gathered her things, turned on her cell phone, and prepared to get off the plane. Her seatmate turned to her and handed her a business card. "Sarah," he said, "we have an opening at my company that may appeal to you. I'd be interested in talking with you about it to see if it might be of interest when you graduate this spring. If you want to discuss the possibility, give me a call next week, and we'll arrange a time to talk."

Sarah was shocked. She didn't even know where the man worked, let alone that he owned a company. She said, "Thanks—I'd be happy to follow up with you. It was really nice meeting you."

"Likewise." He turned to exit the plane, and she followed. Once she was in her car, she pulled out the business card and looked at it carefully. His title and the company caught her eye: president and CEO of one of the smaller local companies that she had been researching. She was ecstatic, but she didn't want to get her hopes up. She was glad she had been polite and responsive to the man, even though she hadn't felt like talking with anyone. To think that she had hoped no one would sit next to her!

Sarah conducted a little more research about the company and Brad Helman, the man from the plane. She called him the next day and left a message since he wasn't available. Later that day, he called her back and arranged to have her come in the following week. He mentioned that there were a couple of other people he wanted her to meet while she was there and that she should plan on spending about two hours at the company.

The following week, Sarah's visit to the company went very well. Brad introduced her to a number of people, including the human resources manager. Even though she hadn't been sure what the visit would entail, Sarah prepared as if it were a formal interview—she did her research, brought copies of her resumé and other application materials, and prepared a number of questions to ask, based on her research about the company. That served her well, because the visit really did take the shape of an interview, and having her materials with her was helpful. She learned a lot about the open position, and she was actually very interested in it. Sarah left the company that day with a good feeling, and sure enough, she was invited back for a final round of interviews. She was offered the position a few days after her second visit to the company. Sarah promptly accepted the job.

A number of years later, Sarah had advanced through a number of positions within the same company. To this day, she remembers how her career began and how a fortuitous meeting on an airplane when she was not in the mood to make small talk with a stranger led to a wonderful job and career path. She also continues to be nice to everyone she meets, regardless of how she feels when she meets them!

Chapter Six
Mind Your Manners: A Primer on Business Etiquette

John's Story

John was nervous and excited about his interview with a small boutique firm in town. As a third-year law student, he had been working on his job search all year, but it had only picked up recently. With graduation approaching soon, John was really hoping that one of the interviews he'd had with his target employers—smaller law firms—would turn into an offer of employment. This was his second interview with this particular firm, which was at the top of his list. He had enjoyed the first interview a lot—he seemed to "click" with the other lawyers in the firm, which he felt was important in the more intimate environment of a smaller firm since he'd be working closely with each of the lawyers. The founding partners of the firm had invited him to lunch today, and John hoped this would be the final hurdle before an offer was made.

At the restaurant, Ned, a partner in the law firm who had met John at his first interview, waited with Tom, the other founding partner of the law firm, for John to arrive. John was right on time, and the three of them were seated immediately. Ned was looking forward to this lunch—he had a good feeling about John and his fit with the firm. They rarely hired new associates, especially ones fresh from law school. It was always a hard decision to add another lawyer, especially one that wasn't bringing a client base along, but they were busy—too busy—and had decided it was time to take the plunge and hire an additional associate. They were looking for a long-term fit—someone who could learn the practice and develop business over time, as he or she established a reputation and expertise. John had appeared to fit that bill, and everyone he met at the first interview really liked him.

The men ordered their food and talked about baseball while they were waiting. Ned was a bit surprised when John tucked his napkin into his shirt collar like a bib, but he was enjoying the conversation—he was a huge Cubs fan, and he couldn't get enough of baseball. Once their appetizers arrived, John ate hungrily, like it had been a while since his last meal. Ned tried to focus on the conversation—he had a lot more he wanted to learn about John—but he was distracted by John's eating habits. Not only did John talk with his mouth full of food, he also chewed and smacked loudly. Finally, the appetizers were gone, and Ned could focus again.

The reprieve was short-lived, however. The main course arrived, and John had ordered a large, juicy hamburger. Throughout the rest of the lunch, watching John manage that hamburger would have been entertaining if Ned hadn't been so dismayed about wanting to hire this guy. He understood now why John had tucked the napkin into his collar— the guy definitely needed a bib. With every other bite of that hamburger, more stains landed on the napkin. Ned certainly hoped they could skip dessert. Although Ned was used to seeing guys "pig out," he'd never actually witnessed it at a business or interview meal, and he was extremely uncomfortable. Finally they finished the lunch, with John seemingly unaware of what a disastrous dining companion he was.

After they had parted ways, Tom turned to Ned and said, "Geez, what were you thinking?" Ned responded, "Going forward, meals are a mandatory part of the interview process. I guess I'm glad we decided to have lunch. What a shame. The guy is smart, and I really liked him at the first interview, but he's not going to make it if he doesn't learn some manners. There's no way I'd trust him to take our clients to lunch. Back to the drawing board, I guess."

An Introduction to Etiquette

Etiquette, it can be argued, is a dated word. It brings to mind columnists like Emily Post and Miss Manners, and it may also stir up memories of parents or teachers telling you to stand up straight, say "please" and "thank you," or to wash your hands before coming to the dinner table. But even if the term "etiquette" seems antiquated, good manners never go out of style—and that's especially true in a business setting. Ensuring that you know the basics for situations requiring protocol and good etiquette, such as correspondence, introductions, meetings, cocktail parties, and meals, is essential at this stage of your career. Later, as your professional and personal interests develop, you can explore more advanced topics that may interest you and that will help you in business entertainment situations such as wine selection and working with a sommelier, mastering various cuisines and restaurant selection, multicultural considerations in business, and hosting large-scale events. The more you know, the more comfortable you will be in a variety of settings.

Do not worry, however, if this all seems unfamiliar to you. You are certainly not alone—many new professionals feel a little discomfited by all the new situations in which they find themselves. Most will not discuss their unease, however, so it may feel like you are the only uncertain one—but you are not. All of the basics are easy to learn and master if you do not already know them, and with a little practice you will soon be handling many common business situations with ease.

Correspondence Basics

A basic review of business etiquette should start with the written word. You will need to know how to draft and when to use various types of business correspondence, including cover letters, business letters, thank-you notes, and business invitations. Although the mechanics and situations for each will vary, one critical item does not—each of these types of correspondence must be absolutely error-free. That means you should not only draft them carefully, you must also run them through spell-check and reread them word by word, line by line, to catch additional errors that spell-check alone won't catch. If possible, have an additional pair of eyes do a complete review. If that is not an option, once the correspondence is drafted, put it away for several hours or overnight, if possible, and then edit it thoroughly one more time. You will be surprised at errors you catch by taking a break from the project before tackling your final review and editing.

Cover Letter Savvy

Cover letters are a crucial part of your application for any position—whether it be a job application, a volunteer opportunity, a leadership position in an organization, or a board of director's opening—if the selection process requires any kind of an application, you should include a cover letter. Many students and newer professionals treat the cover letter as if it were merely a letter of transmittal with the sole purpose of leading the recipient to the enclosed resumé and application materials. This approach is a big mistake—a cover letter is actually the first writing sample of yours that decision-makers will see. In addition to mentioning that your other application materials are enclosed, it should also expand upon and summarize your qualifications for the position in a brief and thoughtful manner. The cover letter is meant to be a persuasive writing exercise and your opportunity to convince the decision-makers to select you for further consideration.

To begin, your cover letter must be addressed correctly, and you should include your full name, address, and other contact information. It is very important that you verify the correct name, spelling, and address of the person to whom you are sending a cover letter; this information should appear at the top of the letter, along with the date. Where possible, avoid the generic "Dear Sir or Madam" or "Dear Hiring Partner." (And *never* say "Dear Sir"!) Take the time to do your research and ascertain to whom the letter should be addressed. Do not use the person's first name; say "Dear Ms. Smith," for example, not "Dear Jackie."

In addition to being one-hundred percent error-free, a well-written cover letter provides additional information about your other application materials. It should not simply regurgitate facts that can be found on your resume but should detail how your specific skills and experiences fit with the qualifications sought for candidates of the position. Highlight at least three areas in which your skills match the position, and illustrate why. Some circumstances, but not all, warrant a cover letter that is longer than one page. Know your audience before sending a longer cover letter.

Do not simply make blanket statements in your cover letter about your skills, such as, "I have excellent writing and communication skills." Anyone can say that. You must illustrate that you have these skills and provide specific examples. "I have worked to develop my legal writing skills throughout my time in law school. Not only did I take an advanced legal writing course, in which I received an A, but I also wrote on to the *Law Review*. Most recently, my journal article was selected for publication. I have also had the opportunity to write during my two summer positions, as a research assistant for Professor Hanson and as a law clerk for Dan Wolf, Esquire. Both Professor Hanson and Esquire Wolf have agreed to serve as references for me and can address the writing I have done for them in different contexts, which includes memoranda, briefs, and articles." This example gives specific, persuasive examples of your strong writing skills.

It is also important, in the interest of submitting a cover letter that serves as a sample of strong writing skills, that you ensure that the verb tense is consistent throughout your cover letter, that your subjects and verbs match (singular or plural), and that you use transitions effectively throughout. A cover letter in which every sentence or paragraph begins with "I did," "I am," and "I was also," does not flow well and is not effective. Other common grammatical errors include split infinitives and dangling prepositions. If these terms don't sound familiar, be sure to invest in a good book about basic grammar to ensure that all of your writing is grammatically correct.

Some Grammar Books to Explore

There are a variety of helpful grammar books on the market, from classics to those just published. It's always good to have one or two on hand that you find easy to use, so you can refer to them as you are writing. Here are a few of the many excellent resources from which to choose:

1. Jane Straus, *The Blue Book of Grammar and Punctuation,* 10th Ed. (Jossey-Bass, 2007).

2. William Strunk, Jr., *The Elements of Style* (Coyote Canyon Press, 2007). Reprint of original edition.

3. Michael Strumpf and Auriel Douglas, *The Grammar Bible: Everything You Always Wanted to Know About Grammar but Didn't Know Whom to Ask* (Holt Paperbacks, 2004).

4. Anne Stilman, *Grammatically Correct: The Writer's Essential Guide to Punctuation, Spelling, Style, Usage and Grammar* (Writer's Digest Books, 1997).

5. Susan Thurman and Larry Shea, *The Only Grammar Book You'll Ever Need: A One–Stop Source for Every Writing Assignment* (Adam's Media Corporation, 2003).

6. Rebecca Elliott, Ph.D., *Painless Grammar* (Barron's Educational Series, 2006).

If you are sending hardcopy applications, cover letters should be printed on good-quality paper that matches your resumé. In the legal profession context, it is best to select white or off-white paper for your cover letter and resumé—other colors are not usually well-received by potential employers. Don't invest in the formal presentations that are available such as folders or fancy envelopes that allow you to mail your materials without folding them. These are unnecessary since, in most cases, your application materials will be opened by a support person who will either copy or scan your resumé and cover letter. The copies or scans will be sent around to internal decision-makers either electronically or by hardcopy, and no one will receive the benefit of your fancy, expensive materials. They are simply not worth the investment in this context.

If you are sending an electronic version of your application materials, it is imperative that you send them in PDF format, rather than in the format of whatever software program you used to create the letter. A PDF file ensures that the formatting of the letter and resumé will be retained through the electronic-transmittal process. Sending letters and resumés in other formats can result in type and font issues, odd spacing, and a letter that does not look professional.

With recent software version upgrades, the "track changes" feature can be tricky to remove from your final document if it has gone through an editing process or if you have received comments in the form of "track changes" from a third party, like a professor or career advisor. Many unsuspecting law students and recent graduates have e-mailed an attachment in Word or another format that has all the changes and edits highlighted. This, needless to say, looks unprofessional and will not help your credibility. If you are in doubt, send a copy to yourself first, before you send it to potential employers. When you send a PDF, what you see on your screen is what the recipient will receive, and that ensures a professional presentation.

Finally, be sure that you retain copies of all of the cover letters you submit, along with a copy of the original job posting, if applicable. If you are applying for numerous jobs or the call for an interview comes at a much later date, you will be able to prepare more effectively for the rest of the application process if you can refer to the original posting and your application materials.

Business Letter Fundamentals

Formal business letters are a common type of business correspondence. Although e-mail is increasingly used for purposes that used to require a formal business letter, you still need to know the basics of crafting effective and professional-looking business letters. Even if business letters are transmitted via e-mail, the same structure and formality rules apply. As with cover letters and resumés, business letters that are sent electronically should be in a PDF format to ensure a professional presentation to the recipient, thus removing the risk of edits or "track changes" appearing unexpectedly.

Examples of business letters that you may be called upon to draft include letters of transmittal, which are brief and to the point; informational letters (conveying the status of a case, for example); demand letters; opinion letters; and confirmation letters. In practice, the recipients of business letters might include your clients, prospective clients, adverse parties, other lawyers, witnesses, and administrative officials, among others. The form and substance of your business letter will vary greatly by the purpose and intended recipient, but a few basic tenets should be followed for all business letters.

As with cover letters, it is important to verify the correct name, spelling, and address of the recipient. Also include the date and your full name and contact information. (Typically, business letters will be sent on firm or company letterhead that already includes some contact information.) It's helpful to add a line regarding what the letter is about, for example: "Re: Smith vs. Jones, Case number 08–34827."

It is likely that your employer will have a standard format for business letters drafted on company or firm letterhead. If this is the case, you should familiarize yourself—and comply at all times—with your employer's rules of style, as well as your employer's filing and record-retention policies for maintaining copies of correspondence.

The body of a business letter should be written clearly with formal tones, but you should avoid unnecessary legalese or verbiage. Do not use any slang, casual language, profanity, or inappropriate language. The purpose of the letter should be stated in the beginning, followed by any explanation or summary, and should include any requested action by the recipient. The closing should be formal but can reflect the preference of the sender; for example, "Sincerely," or "Very Truly Yours," are both acceptable forms of closure. If you are enclosing additional documents or attachments, note that at the end of the letter, and mention if anyone else is being provided a copy of the letter. The earliest business letters you draft in a job will likely be drafts that you prepare for someone else to send. When drafting letters for someone else's signature, it's always a good idea to ask for a sample of their previous work so you can approximate their style and use the correct closing preference of the sender. As you become more skilled and experienced, you will start sending business letters under your own signature. In either case, accuracy counts.

Thank-You Notes and Other Necessary Follow–Up

Another form of business correspondence that is frequently used and important to master is the thank-you note. Students and newer professionals tend to not use thank-you notes enough, even though they are a critical part of the job application process as well as an important facet of network-ing. Thank-you notes should be sent whenever someone takes the time to meet with you, whether for a formal interview, an informational interview, or for certain meetings that happen at your request. Thank-you notes should also be sent when-ever you receive a gift from someone—regardless of the value or how much you like it—and any time someone does some-thing nice on your behalf, assists you, or goes out of their way for you.

Students often assume that it is fine to send an e-mail thank-you note, and it's true that e-mailed thank-yous are becoming more widely used and accepted. However, you should not assume that e-mail is always the best way to thank someone. It is certainly fast, easy, immediate, and free. However, it is also less personal and can appear less thought-ful. In addition, e-mail thank-you notes may actually offend some recipients, so as with any type of writing you do, the first imperative is to know your audience, or in this case your intended recipient. If you're at all concerned about a possible negative reaction to e-mail, send a thank-you by snail mail instead.

If you need to thank someone and have decided that e-mail may not be appropriate, the next decision is whether to send a computer-generated or handwritten thank-you note. The rule of thumb is that a handwritten thank-you note has a more personal touch and is, therefore, the preferred mode. One exception, however, is if your handwriting is not legible. If your writing is impossible to read and would make for an unprofessional-looking end product, compose it on the com-puter. Handwritten thank-you notes are also more prone to grammar and spelling errors, since there is not a computer to alert you to these mistakes, so be very careful to double check and reread all notes before sending them.

In the interview context, whether or not you want the job for which you interviewed, and whether or not you enjoyed the interview, you owe your interviewer a thank-you note. He or she took time away from billable pursuits to meet with you, and that fact alone is worthy of your thanks. You may, from time to time, hear advice to the contrary—that thank-you notes should not be sent after every interview. Oppo-nents of thank-you notes will tell you that such notes will not land you the job, and mistakes in them will only hurt you or possibly cost you the job. They may even say that employers do not appreciate the effort. These arguments miss the point of common courtesy—you are not sending the note to gain favor, but rather to supply thoughtful thanks for a courtesy that has already been extended to you. Therefore, you should always send a note expressing your appreciation.

If you meet with multiple lawyers in an interview, should you send individual notes to everyone with whom you met? At some point, the volume can become overwhelming, so it is acceptable to send a note to your main contact or interviewer, and in that note, ask him or her to extend your thanks to everyone who took the time to meet with you. Of course it is also acceptable to send individual notes to each person, but if you do, be sure to personalize them so you don't send identical notes. It is likely they will all be forwarded to the recruiter for your file, and if the notes are all the same, that will quickly become apparent.

You Are Invited! Invitation Essentials

Another type of correspondence you should be prepared to draft is a business invitation. In the legal field, you may be called upon to extend invitations for seminars and other educational events, cocktail parties, employee- or client-appreciation events, holiday get-togethers, open houses, and a plethora of other business affairs. It is still preferred to send such invitations via hardcopy, although e-mail invitations are becoming more common. For formal events, stick to a high-quality paper invitation and seek professional assistance in selecting them and drafting the language. Generally, the nature of the event to which you are extending invitations will drive what is acceptable language and style on the invitation, but invitations to business events should not stray too far from a formal look and feel. They can be more fun for casual events, but they should never be cutesy or silly.

On business invitations, use font sizes and types that are clear and easy to read, avoid the overuse of capitalization (all caps are very difficult to read), and ensure that all the basic information—who, what, where, and when—is included. Keep the invitation brief, but be sure to personalize it in some way, either by hand-addressing the invitation or by adding a small handwritten note expressing your hope that the recipient will attend. It is good practice to send out all business invitations with ample notice, followed by a reminder closer to the event, if appropriate. If you want your invitees to RSVP, be sure to include that information at the bottom. Finally, it is also smart to ensure (before sending the invitations) that your event does not conflict with any other event to which your invitees will be invited, or with any holidays or religious observances.

Introductions

Introductions are a fact of life in the business world. Learn early on how to make a smooth and polished introduction; it will not only save you from awkward and uncomfortable situations, it will also cement your networking and business-development skills. There will be circumstances in which you need to introduce yourself, and times when you will need to introduce two people that you know to each other. You should be skilled at both situations.

When you are at a meeting, party, or other gathering, and there is someone you do not know, you should introduce yourself to that person, particularly if no one is around to introduce you to each other. Hold out your hand, and say something along the lines of, "Hi, I'm Jane Jones with Abbingdon, Meyer." The other person will likely respond in kind. Be sure to give a firm handshake (few things are more distressing than a limp handshake when you are meeting someone new) but not so hard as to cause physical pain (yes, that actually happens!). Focus on the person's name, and ask some conversational questions.

Every once in a while, you will introduce yourself to someone whom you have met previously but you didn't remember or recognize. Usually, the other person will call your attention to that fact. Simply acknowledge your mistake, and indicate how nice it is to see him or her again. The reverse can also happen—if someone you've met previously introduces himself or herself to you again, it is perfectly acceptable for you to say that you've met before, mention where, and tell them it's a pleasure to see them again. If you can recall the details of your previous conversation, ask follow-up questions about the topic you discussed.

Finally, there will be times when you need to introduce two people whom you know to each other. Peggy and Peter Post advise that is it proper for the person of higher "rank" to "receive" the person of lower rank.[6] Thus, the higher-up person's name is said first, followed by the introduction of the second person, as follows: "Jane Smith, I'd like to introduce you to Sally Sweet, our newest attorney." The guest of honor always ranks highest, as does any official. A client or someone external to the company ranks higher than a colleague or coworker. If a person's rank is not readily apparent, you can start with the oldest person. If the people being introduced are apparent equals, either name can be said first. In all cases, your introduction should be warm and friendly, clearly stated, and include a bit of information about the people you're introducing.

Meeting Etiquette

Meetings are a large part of all professionals' lives at work. They can be extremely productive or the bane of your existence. There are many meeting do's and don'ts, both spoken and unspoken rules of etiquette that you should understand and follow. To some extent, whether meetings are more casual or formal will depend upon who calls the meeting, the purpose of the meeting, and who is in attendance. When you are the person who organizes a meeting, there are additional guidelines to follow.

If you are invited to attend a meeting called by someone else, first and foremost, you must be prepared for the meeting. If you are expected to speak, to have documents prepared, or will be called upon regarding researched or compiled information, prepare in advance, and familiarize yourself with the materials. Even if you are not responsible for the content, review all relevant documents prior to walking in to the meeting. It is important to arrive ahead of or on time and imperative that you turn off (or leave behind) your cell phone, BlackBerry, or other such devices. Avoid being chronically late to meetings—it is annoying to the person who called the meeting, as well as to the other participants, and such behavior does not show respect for the time and responsibilities of others. If, unavoidably, you know you are going to be late, tell the meeting organizer in advance. You should arrive at the meeting with all necessary materials, including some means to take notes (your

6. Peggy Post and Peter Post, *The Etiquette Advantage in Business: Personal Skills for Professional Success* (HarperResource, NY, 1999), 267.

laptop if that is acceptable in your environment, or a pad and pen, if not). Listen carefully to this sound advice from an experienced law firm recruiter:

> *Law students and lawyers are always looking for ways to distinguish themselves. Sometimes, a distinguishing factor can be as simple as always showing that you are interested and engaged, particularly when it comes to meetings. Promptly responding when invited to training programs and meetings, showing up on time, being prepared, being present and paying attention in meetings seems like common sense, but those simple steps can really distinguish someone from his or her peers. Recently, I've heard about increasing instances of bad meeting etiquette by law students working over the summer. In one firm, the managing partner was giving a presentation to the summer associates and one summer did not bother to show up on time. Unbelievably, the summer associate walked in well after the presentation had begun—and the only seat that was still available was up in the front row! When a firm's managing partner takes the time to talk to the summer associates, they should all be there and seated in advance of the start. In another instance of bad etiquette, a summer associate's cell phone went off in a meeting with senior lawyers. While that was bad enough, she proceeded to answer the call and talk while the meeting was going on around her! If you must be late to a meeting or are expecting an important call, it is always wise to notify the speaker or presenters in advance. That way they know that you respect the time that it took for them to prepare for and present their program, or that your personal phone call is not more important than the meeting with your colleagues.*

Irena McGrath, Chief Associate Recruitment Officer, Hogan & Hartson LLP

During a meeting, be careful not to dominate the speaking time, and guard against interrupting. Listen carefully to what others are saying instead of thinking about what you will say next. If a course of action is agreed upon, take careful notes, and follow through with any assignments you agree to take on. It is critical that you pay attention and appear to be engaged throughout the meeting. Few things annoy a supervising lawyer more than a junior lawyer who sighs heavily, looks bored, fidgets, and otherwise acts like he or she has better things to do. Meetings can get long and dull, and they are grueling at times, but you should work hard to pay attention and appear interested, regardless. Meetings can be your opportunity to show that you are willing to learn, interested, and engaged.

If you are the meeting organizer, you have an extra set of responsibilities. Careful preparation should ensure a professional, well-run meeting that will accomplish your objectives. Provide adequate notice of a meeting, and obtain availability responses so that all critical parties are free of previous commitments and can attend. The location and time of the meeting should be clear. Send out the agenda ahead of time, and if others will be responsible for leading the discussion or presenting materials, coordinate with them in advance. The agenda should clearly list the topics of discussion and the approximate time to be spent on each. Start the meeting on time, regardless if everyone is present, and conclude the meeting on time, even if you have not been able to get through the entire agenda. If all of the topics on the agenda were not covered in the allotted time, set up a follow-up meeting to address the remaining issues. In today's busy professional world, it is extremely important that you respect the time demands everyone is facing.

During the meeting itself, follow the agenda, and be sure that everyone has an opportunity to talk. If you find that someone is dominating the conversation, speak up and ask for another person's thoughts. If you know in advance that one person tends to talk a lot, set some ground rules at the start of the meeting, such as speaking in turns around the table, to ensure that everyone has the opportunity to be heard. As the meeting organizer, it is your responsibility to ensure that the meeting stays on point. If digressions occur, politely steer the conversation back to the agenda at hand, and stick to the times you set for a discussion of each topic. At the conclusion of the meeting, summarize what was accomplished, and repeat any follow-up assignments and the responsible parties. Set a deadline to complete tasks, and schedule a follow-up meeting, if necessary, or devise another way to ensure that everyone stays on deadline and completes their tasks, as agreed.

By following these simple professional steps for attending or holding a meeting, you'll ensure that your meetings are goal-oriented and useful, and you will impress those with whom you work with your professionalism at meetings.

Travel Basics

The first time you travel for your career could be to attend an interview with a prospective employer who is not located in your city or state. It is exciting to be invited for a long-distance interview and very important that you act professionally, even in matters of arranging travel and incurring expenses. In many, but not all, cases, if you are invited for an interview, the employer intends to pay your reasonable travel expenses. Or the prospective employer may say that he or she would like to meet you whenever you're in town, in which case you are responsible for the costs of traveling. If you have any doubt about who's paying, be sure to ask—it is better to verify the prospective employer's intentions before you incur any expenses. If it's clear that the prospective employer intends to cover your costs, you should ask how he or she would prefer for you to make your travel arrangements and if they have any guidelines with which they can provide you.

When you are traveling to an interview, you are generally expected to obtain reasonable transportation (coach airfare or mileage for your personal car, for example); transportation to and from the airport, if needed; hotel accommodations, if you're staying overnight; and reasonable meal expenses. You should refrain from using room service, ordering movies, making long-distance calls, or otherwise adding charges to any bill that a prospective employer is paying. If you must incur additional charges, pay for them with a personal credit card, and do not seek reimbursement for them. Being invited for an interview does not give you permission to live high on the hog on someone else's dime. You should spend your prospective employer's money while you are traveling with as much care as if it were your own money.

Government employers may have maximum amounts for which you will be reimbursed for interviews; private sector employers will likely pay all reasonable expenses. Public interest organizations may need to rely on you to foot your own travel bills. Here's some advice for law students pursuing public interest opportunities:

> Students desiring public interest positions for summer and post-graduation should brace themselves and plan to foot the bill for travel to interviews with non-profits and direct legal service providers. Unlike large law firms, which often sched-

ule and pay for student travel and lodging for interviews, public interest employers typically provide little or no travel subsidy for candidates. One way to make the most of your travel budget is to attend large public interest career fairs such as the Equal Justice Works Career Fair and Conference in Washington, D.C. Each fall this fair provides the opportunity for students to meet with a huge variety of employers from throughout the United States in one large venue. Many employers conduct first-round interviews on site. Students often share transportation and housing costs to further save money. Regional career fairs, such as the Midwest Public Interest Law Career Conference, provide students the ability to submit materials in advance of the career fair and give candidates enough notice to purchase tickets well in advance of travel or to share ground transportation costs within the region. Another way to save funds is to see if your law school or local community offers video-conference technology for students. If the employer agrees, this is a fabulous way to save money and time by interviewing close to home and saving money for interviews later in the process.

Cybele Smith, Director of Public Service and Public Interest Programs, The Ohio State University Moritz College of Law

Julie's Story

Julie shifted around on the plane as it prepared to land; she was anxious to get to her destination. She was accompanying Robert, a senior lawyer from her firm, on her first deposition, and she was very excited. She had gotten up early that morning, carefully packed her bags, and arrived at the airport way ahead of Robert. She was through security and sipping a cup of coffee by the time he arrived. Robert was now seated several rows back on the plane, and when she caught his eye he gave her a thumbs-down. Their flight had been delayed an hour, and Julie knew Robert didn't want to be late to the deposition. Julie looked at her watch again and sighed. It looked like they might be a little late, depending on how quickly they could get out of the airplane and into a taxi.

The plane landed and immediately taxied to a waiting gate. Julie grabbed her belongings and exited the aircraft, waiting just outside for Robert to work his way off the plane.

He walked toward her with purposeful strides and said, "We made it! We should be able to get there with a few minutes to spare—let's go grab a taxi."

Julie said, "Right—I just need to get my bags. Don't you have any?"

Robert stared at her. "I have my bag right here. We'll only be gone overnight. You said you checked bags? As in, more than one?"

Julie could tell that Robert was annoyed, but she had no idea that she shouldn't have checked bags—that's what she always did when she traveled. She confessed that she had two checked bags. With a heavy sigh, Robert led the way to baggage claim. Fifteen minutes later, when the luggage still hadn't been unloaded, Robert began making calls to let everyone know they were going to be late. Julie was mortified—despite careful planning, packing to ensure she wouldn't forget any necessities, and her early arrival to the airport this morning, she had inadvertently caused a lot of grief for Robert and the other parties to the deposition. This wasn't the way she had envisioned her first deposition getting underway.

Traveling is often a necessary part of life as a lawyer. Junior lawyers are usually excited about the opportunity to travel on business, while senior attorneys are more blasé or even dislike it. If you are new to business travel, there are some guidelines you should know that will save you from annoying more senior and experienced travelers who might be accompanying you on a business trip. Learn your employer's policies in advance of making any travel arrangements. From in-house travel agencies, to preferred providers, to encouraging the on-line purchase of tickets, every employer has its own policies—make sure you follow yours when making travel arrangements, spending money while on travel status, and documenting money spent.

You should know what receipts you will need to save and present for reimbursement, or if you will receive *per diem* amounts for meals. Some employers may require you to submit airline and train boarding passes for reimbursement; others may not. You should also understand what is reimbursable by your employer and what isn't. Some employers cannot reimburse for alcoholic beverages, meals above a specified amount, and certain kinds of tips. Be sure to review and be familiar with all written travel guidelines and policies. If in doubt, ask before you leave.

The main rule of business travel is to expect the unexpected. Frequent travelers know that there are often delays because of weather, overbooked trains or planes, heavy traffic, accidents, or any other number of factors beyond your control. If it is critical that you arrive to your destination by a certain time, you may want to travel there the night before, assuming that is acceptable from a cost standpoint. Build in as much time as you can to anticipate delays. And be sure to have the contact numbers of all relevant people you will be meeting at your destination with you and easily accessible in case you need to notify them of unexpected delays. You should also bring a complete travel itinerary, with all of the places you will need to be, the times you are expected, and the addresses and phone numbers of all destinations. If you are relying on taxis, you will need to give specific addresses to the driver.

If you are traveling by plane with other professionals on an overnight trip or longer, plan ahead regarding your luggage. If you'd prefer not to carry all of your items on with you, be sure to ask if others will also be checking bags. As a junior lawyer, you do not want to cause busy senior professionals to have to wait on you or delay their arrival to a meeting by forcing them to wait at the baggage claim for your luggage. Most senior lawyers are seasoned travelers who pack light and carry everything onboard with them—for good reason. Unless you are going on a long trip, best practices are to pack everything in a bag that you can carry with you. If you will only be bringing carry-on luggage, ensure that you are following all FTA rules, including size requirements and the types of items that are allowed in the cabin. You don't want to be forced to check your bag unexpectedly and cause additional delays for your party.

Travel often involves using many services offered by providers who are compensated partially through the tips they receive. You should learn tipping guidelines (as well as what will be reimbursed by your employer) and ensure that you are a respectful, professional traveler who rewards good service. It is smart to carry some cash when you travel—not so much that you could become a robbery victim, but enough that you can comfortably pay cash for expenses that may arise during your trip. Ensure that you have enough small bills to tip as appropriate while you are traveling.

There are some general tipping guidelines you should learn and follow, when possible. Taxi and limo drivers should generally be tipped fifteen percent or more of the total bill. (Some employers will not reimburse tips in excess of fifteen percent; others will.) Drivers should receive a little more than fifteen percent if they help you with your bags. Doorman should generally receive a dollar or two if they hail a cab for you; more if they assist you with your bags. Valet parking services should be provided one to two dollars or so each time your vehicle is retrieved. The concierge should be tipped for any in-depth services provided, which may range from a couple of dollars to ten dollars if a lot of time was spent helping you. The bellhops/porters at a hotel or airport are generally tipped one to two dollars per bag. (It is fine to decline extra service if you can easily handle your own luggage.) Hotel-room maids should generally be tipped two to five dollars per night for the services they provide.

When you eat at a restaurant or order room service, the tip should be between fifteen and twenty percent of the bill—generally the tip amount should be figured on the pre-tax portion of your bill. If you are in a group of six or more at a restaurant, the tip will often be added in—check to see if the gratuity has already been included before you add in a tip. You do not want to double tip, but you also do not want to leave your server without a tip. If the gratuity has already been added, you can still leave an additional tip. Generally fifteen to eighteen percent is added to the total for large groups, so you may want to add another two to five percent or more if the service was good. For coat-checking services at restaurants or events, tip a dollar per coat unless the service already has a charge—in that case, the tip is optional.

When you are traveling on business, it is more important than ever to be prepared regarding rules and regulations that may govern your travel. It is your responsibility to ensure that you have your driver's license, your company credit card, and your passport, if necessary. The heaviest restrictions are generally in place when traveling by plane, so you should know the rules in advance and be prepared to go through the security checks as quickly as possible. If you are visiting large buildings in certain cities or any government buildings, allow extra time for the security checks that may be required there. Always have the necessary documents with you and easily accessible, and take the time to ensure that you return them to their proper place so you do not inadvertently lose them.

By planning ahead, traveling only with necessities, having all contact information and phone numbers with you, and being prepared for unexpected delays, you will handle business travel with ease. It does not take too many business trips to become efficient at preparations, packing, and expecting the unexpected. Before long, you'll have earned the status of "road warrior."

Giving and Receiving Business Gifts

Often in professional settings you will find that you are the sender or recipient of a business gift. As with any other aspect of professionalism, you should investigate and understand your employer's policies regarding both giving and receiving gifts before you are faced with the situation. Gifts, including food baskets, wine, exotic coffees, and chocolates, can be a thoughtful way to express thanks and appreciation for a business or networking relationship. In some cases, business-related gifts are imprinted with a firm or organization logo, so the gift-giver also receives some branding and marketing benefits. Gifts can also include services, meals, and entertainment—anything from concert tickets to sporting events. Your employer may encourage such gift-giving and may have a budget set aside or credit cards at your disposal for just that purpose. If your employer has a more limited budget, you may have to spend your own money on a small gift card or book, for example, to thank a contact who has been helpful to you. Whatever the circumstances, you must ensure that you are not violating any employer policies or budget constraints in your gift-giving.

Many government employees are prohibited from accepting gifts above a certain value, so do not be surprised if they either ask you how much it cost (sometimes there are exceptions for gifts of nominal value, under a certain dollar amount) or refuse the gift if it exceeds that guideline. If that is the case, acknowledge your understanding of the restriction, and do not attempt to press him or her into accepting the gift anyway. Attempt to ascertain such restrictions in advance, if possible.

If you are given a gift, be sure that your acceptance of it is within the guidelines provided by your firm or organization. Many newer lawyers do not think twice about accepting business gifts, only to bear the consequences later. If you are entitled to accept the gift within the guidelines of your employer, be sure to thank the gift-giver warmly for the kind gesture. Your verbal thanks should always be followed with a handwritten thank-you note expressing your appreciation, even if you do not like or intend to use the gift.

When all policies are followed, the frequency and expense is not excessive, and the items given are professional and appropriate, business gift-giving can be a memorable and friendly way to show appreciation for a business relationship. Small tokens of appreciation can also be a nice way for you to personally thank those contacts in your network who have been kind and helpful to you. Items like a nominal coffee-shop gift card or movie tickets are an appropriate way to show your gratitude without breaking the bank. In all cases for business and networking purposes, be professional and tasteful in your gift selection and presentation.

Cocktail Parties Can Be Fun!

Earlier you were promised that you did not need to attend cocktail parties in order to network. That is true, but the fact remains that cocktail parties or similar events can be a necessary evil in the life of most lawyers. At this point, with a solid understanding of networking, skill in making introductions, and an understanding of the basics of business relationships, professional attendance at a cocktail party should seem almost easy to master. There actually are not a lot of etiquette rules you need to learn before venturing out to your first business cocktail party, but do commit those few mentioned here to memory and try not to violate them.

Chief among the rules is to keep your drinking to a minimum at all business events where alcohol is served. This is true whether you are a summer associate and the cocktail party is specifically for the summer associates, or it's an employee-only party, or if external clients and vendors are invited. Almost all large and noticeable professional gaffes that are committed at events like these happen because someone broke this basic, foundational rule and had too much to drink. Whether it's a summer associate falling into the water due to over-indulging on a boat outing, or an inebriated junior lawyer telling a sexist joke to a client or senior lawyer because of the effects of alcohol, there is too much at stake to risk becoming even slightly impaired in a business situation. Save your heavy partying for personal events, preferably in the privacy of your own home. The business arena is no place for you to let your common sense, judgment, and worse, your confidentiality imperative become weakened by alcohol. Never was the saying "loose lips sink ships" more applicable than when alcohol interferes with your professional obligations to your clients, your employer, and your colleagues. Even if your behavior is simply embarrassing, rather than violating ethical obligations, it is not something your employer will take kindly to. And if you are an intern, summer associate, or interviewee, the consequences are usually immediately negative—no continued employment for you upon graduation.

If you find that you are in a professional environment in which heavy drinking is the norm, you should still keep your drinking to a minimum at business functions. Even one night of overindulgence at a professional event can cause long-lasting harm to your reputation. Switch to club soda with lime or have the bartender make you a "virgin" drink if need be. By keeping your alcohol intake low, you'll be better at networking and will be more likely to impress—rather than embarrass—your clients and supervisors.

The second rule at cocktail parties is to introduce yourself to as many people as possible. Although it feels safer and more comfortable to head to the corner where your best-known co-workers and colleagues have gathered, professional events are about mixing, mingling, and forming new relationships. Even if this makes you uneasy at first, you'll be surprised at how naturally you are able to reach out and introduce yourself after only a few tries. Many people are uncomfortable in a venue like this, and they will appreciate your overture of friendliness. If you have the opportunity to see the guest list in advance, do a little research on the invitees. Identify whom you would like to be sure to meet at the event.

Finally, there are a few procedural issues to remember regarding nametags, food, and drink. When circulating at a party, wear your nametag, if available, on your right lapel or right upper chest so people can easily see it, and keep your right hand free for shaking hands. All food and drink should be in your left hand—with a little practice, you can hold both a small cocktail plate and a drink in one hand. If tables are provided, it is fine to sit briefly to eat, but only after you have circulated around the room once and as long as you circulate again when you've finished eating. If food is passed on trays, you should select your serving with the small napkin provided, and either eat it immediately or place it on your cocktail plate. No matter how delicious the food and drink offerings are, they are not the main purpose for your attendance at the event, so they should not be your primary focus. It is always a good idea to eat something *before* you attend a cocktail party—that way you will not be sipping a drink on an empty stomach, and you will not need to make eating your top priority. You are there in a professional capacity to focus on networking and making the most of the opportunities inherent at business-related events.

Tracy LaLonde, a partner with Akina, a national sales coaching and consulting firm, offers this wonderful advice for making the most of cocktail parties and similar events:

> *Two keys to maximizing any networking event, cocktail party or otherwise, are 1) to have an objective for the event, and 2) to secure a Definitive Next Step. Many times we attend cocktail parties because we think it's a good idea or we feel like we "should." To give meaning to the event, create an objective that you want to accomplish at the cocktail party. An objective could be to meet three interesting people, to reconnect with an old friend, to meet people in a particular industry, or to seek opinions on a particularly hot topic. By having an objective, you will make sure your time is better spent.*

> *The other key to making the most of a networking event is to secure a Definitive Next Step. Rather than ending a conversation with "we should get together for coffee sometime" and never seeing that person again, a Definitive Next Step seeks the next conversation in the moment. For example you could say, "I've really enjoyed talking with you and would love to pick your brain more on this topic. When I return to the office, could I send you an e-mail to get coffee sometime in the next two weeks so we can continue the conversation?" Ending a conversation like this ensures that you will see the person again and helps you to develop or maintain the relationship.*

Hungry, Anyone?

A business meal can be the most intimidating of functions, especially if you have not attended many. Dining events seem to have more decisions, rules, accessories, and things to remember than other such business situations. They are also rife with opportunity for mishap, such as selecting a disappointing restaurant, spilling food or drink, eating messily or with the wrong utensils, and ordering incorrectly or out of turn; the list of possible snafus may seem endless. If you are having an interview lunch or dinner with a prospective employer, the pressures you feel may intensify. Really, an interview lunch or dinner represents the opportunity for you to get to know a potential employer in different surroundings, and it gives them a chance to see how you handle yourself outside the office (but since it remains part of the interview, we'll give this situation more attention in Chapter Nine). Regardless of whether your business meal is an interview dinner, a client lunch, or brunch with your supervising attorney, sharing food is meant to be an enjoyable and somewhat more relaxing means to trade ideas, discuss business, and learn more about each other than you would at the office. But as Bill Chamberlain, Assistant Dean at Northwestern University School of Law cautions, *"We tend to think the world revolves around us (or should). It's not about us—it's about the client. And at a business or interview lunch, it's not about the food—it's about getting the job or the client. And speaking of business lunches, always remember: solids on the left and liquids on the right!"*

Who pays the check? The general rule is that the person who invited the other will pay the bill. (During an interview, the prospective employer will pay.) If you have a standing "dutch treat" arrangement with a colleague, it is perfectly fine to ask for separate checks at the beginning of the meal. But if you extended the invitation to dine, you should expect a single check, which you will settle.

To start off your business meal correctly, immediately place your napkin (which might be found in the center of the plate or under your eating utensils) in your lap when you are seated, and leave it there throughout the meal. If you have to get up from the table for any reason, place your napkin on your chair, and put it back on your lap when you return.

Beyond the placement of your napkin, you will notice many other utensils and dinnerware at the table. There are a variety of arrangements and combinations of silverware that you may find at a place setting, but some general rules prevail, so using the right utensils at a business meal need not be confusing. Beginning in the top right corner of a place setting, the water or beverage to the rear right of the serving or dinner plate is yours—all beverages should be placed to the right, including water and any other drinks you order. Moving to the left, the bread-and-butter plate to the left rear of the setting is yours. Which plate belongs to whom can be a source of confusion for many at the dinner table, especially when the one to the right appears closer to your plate than the one that is really yours. Sometimes in a group, one person will use the wrong plate, which causes a snowball effect of everyone else having to do the same. When rolls are placed on the table in front of you, pass them to your right without taking any—you should select last, after the basket or plate goes around the table. Once you have selected your roll, place it on your bread-and-butter plate (remember, yours is to the left). Any butter or spread should be transferred to your bread-and-butter plate before using it. The roll should be eaten by breaking off small pieces and buttering each piece before eating.

Utensils should be used from the outside in—if you remember that, you'll be fine, even if you are faced with items you do not recognize! Your salad fork, for example, will usually be the outermost fork on your left, and your dinner fork will be the next one in. The dessert fork will either be closest to the plate or at the top of the plate. If you are not having a salad, begin your meal with the dinner fork, even if the salad fork has not been removed from your place setting. Once you have used an item of silverware, do not place it back on the table—it should be positioned on the plate, and soup spoons should be set on the saucer, not in the cup or bowl.

Some restaurants will have a service plate on the table when you arrive—this plate will either be used as a base for other plates or bowls during the soup or appetizer course only, or it will be removed before any food is served. When accessible (i.e. you're not seated in a booth), food should be served from the left, and dishes should be removed from the right. It is important to remember that when any course is served, you should not begin eating your food until everyone at the table has their food. If someone's meal is delayed (or yours is) it is proper for the person whose meal has not arrived to ask the others to begin eating while their food is warm, rather than waiting for the delayed meal to arrive. If the person whose meal is delayed does not invite you to begin eating, however, you should wait.

As a matter of seasoning, etiquette demands that you taste your food before adding salt or pepper to it, no matter how much of a saltaholic you are. And if someone asks you to pass the salt, the pepper should always be passed with it—just remember that you should not split up the salt and the pepper. As you are eating, food that needs to be cut should be tackled in small quantities; only cut a bit or two at a time. It is not proper to cut an entire steak at once into bite-sized pieces, for example.

As far as table manners go, never talk with food in your mouth, and always chew with your mouth closed. Do not interrupt when someone is speaking. All personal grooming—using toothpicks, applying lipstick, or anything along those lines—should not be conducted at the table, and you should not lay your personal items on the table. Your cell phone and other e-devices should be left behind, turned off, or turned to vibration mode. Under no circumstances should you answer your phone or check your BlackBerry at the table. Finally, although your forearms can rest on the table, your elbows cannot.

Concerning alcohol, the same rules apply to a business meal as to cocktail parties. Keep your drinking to a minimum, and if you are not the host, take your cues as to whether to drink alcohol at all from the person who invited you or from the more senior lawyers. Generally, alcohol should not be consumed at a business lunch or at any part of an interview meal, whether it is lunch or dinner.

Finally, remember to be polite to everyone in the restaurant throughout your time there. You should say thank you to the host or hostess who seats you and to your servers and bus people when they bring food or drinks or remove used items from the table. Much of their income is dependent upon tips, so if they provide exceptional service, remember that in your gratuity.

Sometimes, despite your best planning and good intentions, mishaps occur. Do not panic if a beverage is spilled or your food is undercooked or the person next to you inadvertently uses your bread-and-butter plate. Your calm and collected response to a tiny disaster will put your dining companions at ease and illustrate your professionalism. All people make mistakes and have accidents. If one occurs, help to make it right. If you cause a spillage that results in stained clothing, you must pay to clean or replace it. But remember, it's not the end of the world.

You can gain a level of comfort by knowing good manners and sound etiquette, and that foundation of knowledge will allow you to conduct business meals with ease. If your school or employer offers an etiquette class or seminar, take advantage of the opportunity—it is a rare chance to practice while learning, and one with very little pressure. Once you are out on that interview or business meal, relax, project confidence, and handle mishaps with ease.

The Golden Rule Rules

Although there are some particular details to master in various business situations, you'll rarely go wrong if you simply remember the Golden Rule: "Treat others as you would want to be treated." Proper etiquette and protocol is not always quite that simple, but the Golden Rule is a great fallback if you aren't sure how to handle a particular situation. If things were reversed, think about how you would want to be treated, and chances are you will do the right thing, have the proper response, and handle the situation appropriately.

In keeping with the Golden Rule, it is also important, as you become more seasoned and comfortable in various business situations, that you work to give others that same level of comfort. When you are the interviewer rather than the interviewee, do not forget the nerves, pressure, and tension that the interviewee is likely feeling. Do everything you can to put him or her at ease. As you become more senior, take junior lawyers out to meals so they can develop their business meal skills in relative comfort, before they have to entertain a client. Work to introduce newer members of your firm or organization around, help them build a network, and mentor them in all aspects of business etiquette. After all, being a professional is not just about mastering the skills you need to succeed, it is also about helping others develop that same mastery.

Chapter Seven
Traps for the Uninitiated: Technology Pitfalls

Is a Lawyer's Life Private in the World of Electronic Communications?

Years ago, one's professional life and personal life could be easily compartmentalized. When lawyers left the office at the end of the day, it would be rare for them to communicate with work until the next morning. If there was contact with the office, it would be in the form of a phone call on a landline, and then—in the days before answering machines and voicemail—only if the lawyer happened to be at home. But in today's world of rapid and constant electronic communication, it is more difficult to decide where work ends and home life begins. Most lawyers are wired everywhere they go, with laptops and the Internet, e-mail, instant messaging, podcasts, Webcams, BlackBerries, cell phones, camera phones, voicemail, and text messaging all providing endless means to stay in work mode anywhere, anytime. People conduct business in airports, on trains, from the waiting rooms at doctors' offices, in their living room, at their kids' soccer games, and even from distant vacation destinations.

There are many consequences—both positive and negative—to this constant communication, but one thing is certain: The line that used to be clear between the professional and personal spheres of one's life has become a lot more fuzzy. This can be particularly challenging for newer lawyers who are seeking balance in their lives (which will be discussed in greater detail in Chapter Thirteen) and for whom it is more common and effortless to run afoul of professionalism.

Increasingly, new lawyers are surprised to learn that there are professional ramifications for events that happen in what they believe are their personal lives. Even though one is entitled to a personal life, it is important to remember that many of the forms of communication we use today enable us to make personal communications very public. Becoming a lawyer means becoming a professional—one that can easily find himself or herself in the public eye. Therefore, it is essential to take precautions early on to ensure that no communications pitfalls trip you up.

E-Mail: Friend and Foe

No doubt about it, e-mail has made staying in touch much easier. Chances are, you hardly remember life before e-mail; the newest professionals—like you—grew up using e-mail to communicate. To you, it is a given. But remember, there are three other generations in the workplace right now, and they *can* remember how life was before e-mail. Some members of older generations do not appreciate the changes (or havoc) technology has brought to their practices. Many professionals of all generations have embraced technology and its positive impact, but not everyone views its prominence with the same appreciation, so it is important to use e-mail smartly and to know your audience.

When it comes to using e-mail for professional purposes, such as a job search, make sure you have an e-mail address that is professional in nature. Partyanimal@yahoo.com or buggy501@hotmail.com would not be the best choices for e-mail addresses to use for your professional network. Your school-assigned address is fine, as is a personal account that has your name or initials or some combination thereof. If you have a personal e-mail address with a less-than-professional-sounding name, open a new one for professional purposes only. If you have more than one e-mail address, it is important that you check all your in-boxes regularly. When using e-mail to communicate, you need to be as responsive via this method as any other. Just as you should return phone calls the same day you receive them, you should also respond to e-mails within twenty-four hours (unless you have an appropriate "out of office, unable to respond" message that alerts senders when you will receive and be able to respond to e-mail).

It is fun and trendy to add signature lines, pictures, and even quotations that automatically appear at the bottom of e-mails you send. Be very cautious about doing so in business-related e-mails. You can include a professional signature line that lists your full name, law school and class year, and basic contact information. Refrain from making it fancy or colorful, or sprucing it up with pictures. In general, quotations are not a good idea for professional e-mail. If you have a quotation that you love, frame it and hang it above your computer, but do not include it in your signature line! Also avoid using any elaborate backgrounds or colors in your e-mails for regular communications (e-mail invitations are the exception). In addition to keeping your e-mails neat and professional, remember that attorneys often read their messages on Black-Berries or similar instruments, and the downloading capabilities may be limited. Certain items won't load, will take too much time to load, and/or will not appear as they were sent. This is frustrating to recipients. The KISS rule should apply here—Keep It Simple, (Very) Simple.

One seasoned career counselor, who oversees career services, externships, and pro bono and public service initiatives at his law school, adds this:

> When using e-mail to apply for a job, be sure that your e-mail address is formal and professional, not humorous or inappropriate. I recommend that students and new lawyers create a signature block, which includes name, law school and year of graduation, postal address, phone number, and e-mail address. Quotes should be deleted. If the e-mail provider includes advertising at the bottom of the message, either delete the advertising or select an e-mail provider that does not include such advertising "taglines." Also craft a short, descriptive subject line so the recipient will know that the e-mail is important and not spam.

Robert Kaplan, Associate Dean and Director of Externships, William & Mary School of Law

E-mail is an incredible tool for networking and job-searching purposes. It is free and fast and saves busy law students and new lawyers two things that are usually at a premium for them: time and money. However, e-mail is a common cause of mistakes that professionals make, in one form or another. So when you use e-mail, assume that everything in your message has the potential to become public, and that a permanent record will be kept of the e-mails you send. One commonly heard e-mail rule is: If you wouldn't want to see your e-mail as a headline on the front page of the newspaper, do not send it! Refrain from making unflattering comments about others, sending snarky or gossipy e-mails, and generally putting in writing anything that could come back to haunt you or be embarrassing to others.

This exercise in restraint can be difficult for students and new lawyers to master. You might be used to dashing off quick e-mails to your friends, but when it comes to professional e-mails, or any e-mails sent to networking contacts, it pays to take a little more time and care. As Morgan L. Smith, Assistant Director of Attorney Development and Recruitment at Mayer Brown LLP, advises, *"E-mail is a critical tool in today's world, and it is important to develop good habits. Hopefully it goes without saying that abbreviations used when texting friends and emoticons generally don't belong in business e-mail messages."*

As lawyers or soon-to-be lawyers, you are well informed about the downsides of having negative information in writing. So be very careful about what you put in e-mails, even to your friends. Inadvertent and purposeful forwarding of e-mail messages happens all the time, and once you push "send" you've surrendered all control over the final destination of that e-mail and its contents. As Nancy B. Rapoport, Gordon & Silver, Ltd. Professor of Law at the William S. Boyd School of Law, UNLV says, *"Assume that everything—everything— you write in an e-mail will be read by your worst enemy. Often, that's exactly what happens."*

It pays to exercise restraint, and think before you send!

Forward E-Mails With Care

Another important aspect of professionalism in e-mailing is to avoid forwarding messages indiscriminately. Junk e-mail should never be forwarded to professional colleagues or contacts, and care should be taken not to forward messages or trails excessively to anyone. We all have contacts in our lives who forward anything and everything, so we know what it's like to be that recipient. For most people it's an additional e-mail to delete; for busy professionals it's a real annoyance, especially if the content is unprofessional, annoying, and/or possibly offensive. In most cases the recipient will not actually tell you if he or she is annoyed, and their annoyance will build with every e-mail you forward.

Beyond junk e-mail, forwarding a message to a third party should also be done with great care. In most cases, if someone else needs to be brought into the e-mail conversation, it is a good idea to copy the original author as you forward it on, so he/she is aware that the message has been forwarded. Do not forward e-mails to make fun of the sender's message or for other ill purposes. Messages should only be forwarded under a legitimate "need-to-know" basis so, again, exercise restraint in your e-mailing practices.

It is important to remember that once you forward a message (either junk messages or real content), your name and e-mail address become part of that message—few people take the time to remove all of those annoying and lengthy headers from forwarded e-mails. If it's a junk e-mail with questionable content, your name will be associated with it, and if you used a school or work e-mail account, you are implicating other institutions. If someone authored a message that was meant for you, forwarding it without the sender's knowledge or permission is not a good practice. It will have your name attached to it, so there could be ramifications for you. Use your "forward" button with great care.

Other E–Mail Actions to Handle With Care

In addition to the "forward" button, the "reply" and "reply all" options should also be used sparingly and with caution. Many busy professionals have been embarrassed by replying to all when they meant to reply only to the sender. For e-mails that are sent to the entire organization, such as a request for a benefit election you need to make, replying to all might mean you just shared your personal information with all of your colleagues and bosses.

A list serve (a mailing service that broadcasts e-mail to everyone who is on the list) is an excellent source of professional information in various disciplines. However, you must be particularly careful not to "reply to all" when you receive a message through this medium. Often, peers and colleagues from many firms, companies, and cities will send items of interest to a list serve. Many inappropriate responses have been sent to an entire list serve when it was clear that the sender only meant to send the message to the author of the first e-mail. These are usually uncomfortable and professionally embarrassing gaffes. If the sender had simply adhered to the e-mailing rules discussed here (not putting in writing anything they would not want to see in a headline, refraining from negative e-mail comments about people, double-checking the recipient line before hitting "send"), he or she would have avoided this awkward and possibly damaging mistake.

It is also common to hit "reply" instead of "forward" when you meant to forward the e-mail to another recipient. As mentioned previously, it is best to avoid forwarding e-mails without permission, and this is another reason to handle that situation with care. Always review who is listed in your "to" line before you hit "send" on all e-mails you draft. If you do this as a matter of course, you will be surprised at how many times you catch yourself before sending an e-mail to the wrong recipient. You don't want this to happen to you:

> *In twenty years in the business, I have a lot of embarrassing stories to tell! E-mail has been a great invention, but it can also get you in hot water, particularly if you don't pay attention and are multi-tasking when you are sending e-mails. So, keep that in mind before you hit "send." We are all guilty of misdirecting an e-mail, usually without much impact, but what about the summer associate who sent an e-mail criticizing a partner? The summer associate thought she sent the e-mail to a friend, but she actually sent it to the partner she was criticizing.*

> **Gayle P. Englert, Director of Human Resources, Cole, Schotz, Meisel, Forman & Leonard P.A.**

Communication Issues in E-Mail

There is no question that e-mail saves a lot of time—it is a quick and easy way to communicate, even with friends, family, or colleagues who are halfway around the world. But e-mail is not a cure-all for your communication woes, and it can actually hinder communication in a way that face-to-face conversations do not. There are a number of problems with e-mail as a communication tool. You cannot infuse your e-mail with tone, for example, so something may sound sincere in your head when you draft your message but may be read in a sarcastic tone by the recipient. Emoticons (such as smiley faces) have become a popular way to try to infuse e-mails with tone. However, they should not be used in business e-mail communications. Because it is possible for the tone and, therefore, the meaning and intent of your message to be misconstrued, e-mail should not be used to relay information that is controversial, unsettling, or difficult to explain, or when you are joking or being sarcastic. These types of communication call for some tonal quality, facial expressions, or gestures in order to be delivered effectively, and they also require the opportunity for give-and-take, not the static exchange of messages on e-mail. A seemingly innocuous message exchange can easily spiral into a trail of hard to forgive-and-forget, confusing, upsetting, and even infuriating e-mails. It is important to realize that, although e-mail allows you to share your thoughts with someone immediately, the recipient has needs, too. It may take longer to track someone down on the phone or in person, but the results for certain kinds of communication make it time well spent.

Constructive Feedback Via E-Mail? Not a Chance!

Since e-mail is definitely not the best way to deliver certain kinds of news, it is important to identify the situations, happenings, and events that call for and deserve the courtesy of a phone call or, better yet, an in-person conversation. The most striking example of this is when you need to provide some kind of critical feedback to someone, particularly constructive feedback or counseling information to help someone improve his or her performance. Although this often happens in a supervisory relationship, as a new professional working to master leadership skills you now know that being a leader is not dependent on a formal title, and you may find yourself needing to take on this role long before you step foot into a law firm or other professional job. Once you are in a law firm, you become an immediate supervisor of sorts—even during most summer jobs—in that you will be assigned some kind of support person or professional assistant. You will need to provide feedback sooner than you think. (More information will be provided on handling that quasi-supervisory situation in Chapter Eleven, along with detailed information about getting and providing feedback.)

Providing constructive feedback to get someone on track or help them improve is difficult, and—frankly—most people are terrible at doing at it. If you have someone in your life who is skillful and provides great feedback, take careful notes and learn from his or her talents. For the purposes of this discussion, e-mail is *never* an appropriate communication channel for constructive feedback. It is tempting to shoot off a brief e-mail along the lines of, "Susan, I did not appreciate that you were late for the 8:30 meeting this morning—it's the third time this month. Don't let it happen again." Or perhaps, "Bob, the research you provided me was disastrous. Make sure you do a better job next time."

There are all kinds of drawbacks with these types of messages being sent under the guise of feedback. Consider if you were on the receiving end of either of these e-mails. If you are Susan and you're supposed to have a start time of 9:00 a.m. on your job (and you have class until 8:30 and can't be there before 9:00, which you've mentioned repeatedly), how would you feel about receiving an e-mail like that? If you are Bob and you asked for clarification several times about this research assignment, but your supervisor was too busy to meet with you, what effect would an e-mail like this have on you? Feedback needs to be part of an in-person conversation, and it must be handled with care. Too many supervisors rely on e-mail as the easy way out. They become bolder and more direct than they are able to be in person, and they hide behind the protection of e-mail to avoid having a difficult conversation. Taking this approach does not do the situation justice or show your employees the respect they deserve. Nor does it usually result in performance improvement. E-mails like the ones to Susan and Bob usually foster resentment and anger, and most people would take offense at receiving them. If you are on the receiving end of such an e-mail, take steps to have a face-to-face conversation as soon as possible. Talk through the issues in a non-threatening way designed to open the lines of communication. Chances are, if you handle a negative e-mail professionally and appropriately, you will not receive a similar one from that sender again. Once someone realizes they cannot avoid an in-person conversation by sending an e-mail, they are significantly less likely to repeat that tactic.

If You Wouldn't Say It, Don't Send It!

Providing feedback is not the only e-mail situation in which people become more bold or direct than in person. E-mail provides a protective shield that allows people to say things they would never say out loud, and you should realize that we are all possible victims of the false bravado that e-mail appears to provide to us. Don't fall prey to the temptation. If you wouldn't say it, you absolutely should not commit it to writing and send it. E-mail should not be a shield you hide behind to fire off messages you would not be comfortable saying directly to someone in person.

Anger can prompt us to say things we normally wouldn't. E-mailing when angry is an especially bad idea because it provides a permanent record of a momentary lapse in good judgment. If you are tempted to fire off a quick and not-so-nice e-mail, you should start enforcing a simple rule with yourself: Never send an e-mail to someone when you are angry or are reacting to an angry e-mail you received. If you are on the receiving end of such an e-mail, do not respond immediately, if at all. Although it is tempting to fight fire with fire, you should either wait overnight and draft a calm, professional e-mail, or respond via another method. It can be very effective to pick up the phone or drop in on the person and say, "John, I could tell from your e-mail that you were upset, so I wanted to talk this over with you." This will go a long way toward diffusing the situation, rather than dousing the fire with gas, and there is a strong chance that the other person already regrets his or her impulsive message.

It is also tempting to draft e-mails that you never intend to send. These "therapeutic" e-mails allow you to vent, process your anger, and calm down, all without the other person knowing your reaction. No harm, no foul if you don't press send, right? Not necessarily. As great as therapeutic e-mails might sound, avoid drafting them like the plague. It is too easy to accidentally push the wrong button and launch your diatribe into cyberspace. And if you are on a computer network (as at most places of employment), if you save a draft overnight, chances are it will be saved on a server, and multiple back-up copies will exist *even if you never sent the e-mail to anyone!* The draft that was never meant for any eyes but your own could end up in the wrong hands.

E-Mails Gone Public

Many of us have heard stories about the unfortunate mishaps facing newer professionals when they have sent an unprofessional e-mail to one source that ended up in the in-boxes of millions. A number of these of e-mails have been forwarded so much they even made the news. From the unprofessional reneging of a job-offer acceptance that devolved into an e-mail trail culminating with a young lawyer's reply of "Bla, bla, bla," to the unflattering and ungrateful-sounding e-mail a summer associate meant to share with one friend about his summer clerkship at a prominent firm but accidentally sent to forty attorneys inside his firm instead, examples abound of e-mails that really do literally make headlines.[7] How do you make yourself "headline proof"? By following the guidelines discussed throughout this chapter. First and foremost, starting today, do not put in writing anything unprofessional, juvenile, immature, or malicious. Recognize that e-mail is most definitely not a confidential communication tool.

I Can't Keep Up: Volume Issues

As helpful as e-mail is for staying in touch, in the professional workplace, and particularly in the legal field, staying on top of your e-mail can consume you. It is not at all unusual for a busy lawyer to receive more than 300 e-mails a day. Given that, it will be very important for you not to overuse e-mail as a new professional. Your supervisors and colleagues will appreciate your efforts to keep e-mail to a minimum.

There are a few quick tips to follow that will help you in this endeavor. As a rule, only copy those people on an e-mail who really need to know its contents. In addition to limiting your distribution list as much as possible, ensure that your e-mails are correct and complete the first time you send them. Having to resend something because you did not add the attachment or you left out a vital piece of information only serves to increase the volume of e-mails flying about. Make it a practice to reread carefully, from beginning to end, an entire e-mail before you send it, and double check your "to" line one additional time. Do not use work e-mail for personal announcements or to sell items like tickets or Girl Scout cookies. And do not hit "reply all" if only the sender needs a response. Following these simple tips will go a long way

7. Jake Tapper, "The 'Bla Bla Bla' Heard 'Round the World," ABC News Nightline, February 18, 2006. Available at: http://abcnews.go.com/Nightline/story?id=1635472.

Ben McGrath, "Oops," *The New Yorker,* June 30, 2003. Available at: http://www.newyorker.com/archive/2003/06/30/030630ta_talk_mcgrath.

toward ensuring that you do not contribute to your coworkers' e-mail volume issues.

Drafting E-Mails Like a Pro

When drafting e-mails, you want to ensure that those you send will be well-received. First of all, brevity is key. You are not writing a book; you're sharing information. Lengthy e-mails do not get read in their entirety, period. Accept that fact, and work with it. Put the key information or the point of the e-mail first. Think of it in terms of writing the short-answer section of a legal memo at the beginning. The reader should get the gist in a sentence or two, and if they want elaboration they will read further. If you need the recipient to take some action, particularly by a specific deadline, it is helpful to put that information in boldface. Here's an example of an e-mail written in a way that will frustrate a busy attorney and then rewritten in a way she will appreciate:

Mary:

Per your request, I have combed the files on the Hudson matter, but I can't find any documentation about the issue we discussed yesterday. You also asked me to review the Lambert file if I couldn't find anything in the Hudson file. I did that also, and there wasn't anything in the Lambert file, either. I double checked both files, and when I still couldn't find anything, I had Susan pull the Dozer and Dunn files to see if I could find anything in those. I did locate a memo in the Dunn file that may interest you. I have scanned it, and it is attached to this e-mail. Based on this memo, I think the course of action we discussed yesterday is probably the correct one. I'd like to know your thoughts on that. I also assumed you would want me to do a quick update on the research in the attached memo to ensure that nothing has changed since it was drafted. I did double check, and it is still solid. Can you let me know what you would like me to do next?

Thanks,

XXX

Mary:

As we discussed yesterday, I've located this memo from the Dunn file (electronic version attached) that confirms our planned course of action. I've updated the research in the memo, and it is solid. I'll swing by this morning to confirm next steps.

Thanks,

XXXX

As you can see, although the message is the same in both e-mails (once you can actually locate the message in the first one), unnecessary information bogs down what you are trying to convey in the first one and may confuse and frustrate a busy reader. Keep the extraneous details out of your professional e-mails. Consider these next two examples:

Dear Jan:

I hope you had a wonderful weekend. I sure did, although I didn't get nearly enough sleep. I guess that's what happens when I spend my weekend working on client matters! The weather left a lot to be desired, too, so I figured I might as well bill some hours. I know you want to get together today to discuss the Hart issues. I forgot that I have a doctor's appointment this morning. I am hoping to be in the office by 10:00, although the last time I went to the doctor, I had to wait for over two hours! I really hope that doesn't happen this time, but I just wanted to make you were aware of the possibility. I spoke with your assistant this morning, and she said you had an opening at 1:00, so I took that opening. I will see you at 1:00 for sure, but I will probably be in much sooner than that. Wish me luck at the doctor. E-mail me if you need anything before 1:00. Talk to you soon,

Emily

Dear Jan:

I'm on your calendar for 1:00 p.m. today to discuss the Hart issue. I have a doctor's appointment this morning, so I'll be in the office right after that, hopefully by 10:00. I'll be checking e-mail, if you need anything before that.

I hope you had a great weekend,

Emily

As you can see, there are easy and quick ways to improve the messages you send by making them leaner, more effective, and easy for busy professionals to read and process. Work to make your e-mails succinct and accurate.

Other Common E-Mail Communication Mishaps

There are other e-mail challenges that you will need to manage in the professional workplace. Back-and-forth e-mail trails, like conversations after hours over alcohol, can easily become too casual and informal. As banter is exchanged (either via e-mail or over drinks), colleagues sometime forget time and place (or e-space), lose sense of proper boundaries and devolve into a casual communication mode. Although this might be fine with your friends, it is never a good idea with your supervising attorney or boss. Keep all conversations professional (whether they're in person or on-line) and avoid the casual. It is tempting to try to be funny, or easy to simply forget with whom you are really communicating, but you should guard against this behavior.

Another common mistake when using e-mail is to assume that every message you've sent has been blessed with the three R's: received, read, and remembered. In most cases you are lucky if you hit two of the three—rarely will you get all three. Your e-mail might be received and read but not remembered. Or it might be received and remembered but never read. (Don't believe this? Mark these words—many attorneys will see that they have received an e-mail from you, will read the subject line, and will never open the e-mail, assuming they know what the contents are!) For extremely important information, the tried-and-true "belt and suspenders" method is best: e-mail plus either a phone call, a personal visit, or a note.

For e-mails that require some action by the recipient, it is always helpful if you start the subject line with that information. For example "Review needed: draft of Hart memo" or "Approval sought on letter draft" or "Survey response required—benefits election." Much of the work you do as a new lawyer will seem very important to you—and it is. But do not fall prey to always marking your e-mails with the "high priority" notation—it is not a smart way to get your e-mails to stand out, unless you are truly dealing with a rare and urgent situation. One professional who made a habit of marking most of his e-mails as high priority quickly became the laughing stock of the office. Not only is it annoying to the recipient, it also appears egotistical, as if your e-mails are more important than everyone else's. There is a time and place to mark messages "high priority"—and that time and place is rare.

Finally, remember that the attorneys to whom you are sending e-mail will be accessing them in various ways—through their computer at the office, remote connectivity on their laptop, and/or on BlackBerries. Keep your messages short, without pictures and signatures that take a long time to load, and avoid sending large attachments unless it is absolutely necessary. If you must send a large attachment for a work-related purpose, give the recipient advance notice. One professional who regularly travels to a developing country on business is leery of opening any attachments for fear it will be so large as to shut down Internet access for a few days! Although that is an extreme example, it pays to be mindful of issues and challenges recipients may face in receiving your communication via e-mail.

Social Networking Sites: Too Much of a Good Thing?

Facebook (www.facebook.com), MySpace (www.myspace.com), LinkedIn (www.linkedin.com) and others: Are they your social lifelines? Many students and new professionals spend hours each day on one or more of these and other social networking sites, and for good reason. These sites are a great way to reconnect and stay in touch with friends and colleagues, update your friends on what's happening in your life, find out what people are up to, plan social events, and even build your professional network. To tell young professionals to avoid these sites is a fool's game. These sites are helpful, incredibly powerful, and fun. So what's the issue?

It is really the same issue with which this chapter began: the increased blurring of the personal and professional spheres of one's life, given the technology now available. Some events, decisions, or announcements in your life that are intended to be personal can have unintended implications on your professional life when you use technology to communicate about them. Social networking sites are a public forum, and as such, a fair way to learn more about people. This means, unless you are careful, there could be consequences in your professional life if you do not manage your use of social networking sites carefully.

If you intend to keep a professional-only profile on the social networking site of your choice, you probably do not need to worry much about protecting your profile. Be sure to watch for inappropriate posts, however, on your bulletin board or wall. To be completely safe, secure your profile and pages, thus restricting access to a limited group of people to whom you choose to allow access. Most issues with inappropriate profiles on social networking sites arise from information that is available on public profiles, where anyone can access the information. Although the legalities of using social networking sites as a form of reference or background checking is still a topic of discussion, some employers and individual decision-makers are definitely running profile searches to learn more about the candidates to whom they are considering offering jobs. An experienced recruiter provides this critical information about e-due diligence:

In preparation for a recent presentation at the National Association for Law Placement (NALP) Conference, I conducted a survey of law firms around the country to learn how common it was for a firm to conduct e-due diligence as part of the hiring process. 46% of the 81 respondents noted that they conduct some form of e-due diligence on the Internet before hiring a candidate. There was tremendous interest in this topic at the conference. We had over 150 attendees at the presentation and standing room only which tells me that while this subject is relatively new, law firms and other employers are extremely interested in it. Hiring a lawyer— whether at the entry-level or lateral level—is very costly to a firm and even more so if the hire doesn't work out. Therefore, employers need to learn as much about a candidate as they reasonably can to ensure that individual will be a successful hire. Legal employers implemented background checks years ago for this same reason and conducting e-due diligence is just a further extension of the due diligence process.

Nancy Berry, Director of Firmwide Recruiting, McDermott, Will & Emery LLP

You should keep this in mind as you craft both the content of your profile and the security levels you place on the content. But beware: Pictures and content you post on your private profile could be copied and placed elsewhere. As Robert Kaplan, Associate Dean and Director of Externships at William & Mary School of Law, advises,

It's a good idea to "Google" yourself at regular intervals. Because some employers will use this technique to learn more about you, it is important to know what prospective employers will find about you. Compromising or inappropriate photos, videos, or text—placed on the Internet by you or by others— may adversely impact your job search. You may be able to take steps to have the information removed, but the ability to do so varies greatly among Web sites. Even when a Web site agrees to remove the information, that can be a lengthy process. The Web also may contain compromising information about a different person with your same name. That can be challenging to resolve. You may be able to use a different version of your name (e.g., your full name, including your middle name) on application materials so that Internet searchers can distinguish you from others. If that's not a reasonable option, be prepared to explain at the appropriate time in the hiring process that there are other individuals with your name whom the employer may have discovered.

In the legal profession, a good question to ask for particular content and security is, "Would I want a client or potential client to find this information?" An even better question to ask is, "Would *my employer* want a client or potential client to find this information?" If the answer is no, take failsafe steps to ensure that can't happen.

Blogs and Web Sites: Selling Point or Liability?

The issues with maintaining blogs or personal Web sites are not all that different from those that surround social networking profiles, with a few extra items to be wary about. Generally, blogs and Web sites can be more easily found— they are usually more public and do not require a profile membership to access them, as many social networking sites do. Additionally, some students and lawyers intentionally use a blog or Web site as a professional tool, either to showcase research, present their credentials or writing samples, or converse with colleagues across the country and beyond who have similar research interests.

If you include on your resumé the address of a blog you author or a Web site you have developed, it's fair to assume that potential employers will go there to review the content. If, for example, you play in a band after hours and your band has a Web site, you might include that Web address in the interest section of your resumé. If that's the case, ensure that all content on the site is appropriate and professional. Do not lead potential employers to sites that contain profanity, vulgarity, or other inappropriate content. You must also ensure that the content on your site is updated. You do not want to refer potential employers to a Web site you developed in 2004 that has not been updated since. That will neither create a positive impression, nor highlight your skills or attention to detail.

An equally concerning development in cyberspace, and one over which you may have little control, is what others say or post about you on their blogs, Web sites, or profiles. The best thing you can do here to prevent malicious or inadvertently unprofessional postings about you is to avoid giving anyone cause to talk negatively about you. It may also help to avoid some on-line discussions or posts in which your name would be included in the post. But there is always a chance that someone will portray you in an unflattering or unprofessional manner on some form of e-technology, whether or not their information is accurate or well founded.[8] Pictures that others take of you in less-than-professional situations are another way that your personal life could become public and potentially harm your professional life. The advantages of technology are many, but you must always be aware of the possible consequences.

Other Possible Technology Perils

Your computer and laptop are not the only technology advances that have made life much more connected for you

---

8. Ellen Nakashima, "Harsh Words Die Hard on the Web: Law Students Feel Lasting Effects of Anonymous Attacks," *The Washington Post,* March 7, 2007, p. A01. Available at: http://www.washingtonpost.com/wp-dyn/content/article/2007/03/06/AR2007030602705.html

and all people on a personal and professional level. Voicemail, BlackBerries, and cell phones have all evolved significantly in recent years, and they offer a variety of options for busy professionals to work remotely, stay connected, and manage the barrage of information coming their way each day. They also offer many hazards for the uninitiated professional to traverse.

No one will argue with you that, as a new lawyer (regardless of your job), it pays to stay in touch as much as possible. BlackBerries, cell phones, and voicemail offer you the ability to get information and respond in a timely manner. If you have said that you will be monitoring your e-mail when you are away from the office, then you definitely need to monitor it. But beware that you don't rely so much on remote accessibility that you forgo in-person relationships and professionalism. In other words, don't communicate with one client or lawyer via BlackBerry while giving short shrift to the lawyer or client with whom you are currently sitting in-person.

How is that possible? Consider a scenario in which you are visiting a corporate client, and the meeting you are attending is critical but running very long. If you start checking your BlackBerry, you're not paying attention to the client whose meeting you are attending. What sense does that make? Absolutely none, but guess how many times a day a busy lawyer does that very thing to a client! You may have witnessed it yourself in an interview situation. Did one of your interviewers ever sneak a glance at his or her BlackBerry during the interview? If so, how did it make you feel? How did it affect your impression of that lawyer, that lawyer's firm, and whether or not you were still interested in working there? Imagine if you were a client paying big money by the hour.

In a situation like the one in which a meeting is running long, there is a way to handle it professionally, without appearing insensitive to those with whom you are meeting. Simply say something along the lines of, "We are accomplishing a lot here today, and I don't want to lose this momentum. However, my office was expecting me back an hour ago. Why don't we take a quick five-minute break to check for urgent messages so we can finish this meeting with our complete focus?" As a law clerk or junior lawyer, it is rare that you will be the critical link in a meeting, but you should still give each and every meeting your full attention, without distractions like BlackBerries and cell phones. Don't even bring your cell phone or BlackBerry to meetings within your law firm. If meetings occur elsewhere and you must bring your cell phone or BlackBerry, make absolutely certain that the ringer is off or set to vibrate on all of your technological accessories. Many senior lawyers complain about newer lawyers not only allowing their cell phones to ring during meetings but, worse yet, answering them! It's not only discourteous, it also illustrates publicly a complete lack of good judgment and common sense.

BlackBerries also have the reputation of becoming "addictive" in that many lawyers cannot go for more than a few minutes without checking their e-mail. BlackBerry-checking becomes particularly annoying to family members when it is done incessantly during what should be family or personal time. Newer professionals appear to be self-important when they are constantly checking their BlackBerries, and that can be irritating, too. Accessibility is good—to a point. You will need to guard against overdoing it and alienating your colleagues, friends, and family. Outside of urgent situations in which you are truly on call, make a point to select a few intervals each weekend day, for example, to check your e-mail and respond, if necessary, rather then doing it constantly throughout the day. Managing your habits in this regard will go a long way toward enhancing your professionalism, as well as your relationship with and enjoyment of those around you.

Voicemail Issues

Your voicemail messages, both at home and at work, should be professional, succinct, and clear. Your outgoing voicemail message at work should include your name and firm or organization, as well as notification if you are out of the office or unavailable. When you are away from the office, your voicemail message should direct callers to someone else who can help them in your absence, particularly if you are not able to check your messages. If you are in the office but inaccessible for much of the day, it is a good idea to change your greeting so that callers will understand your limited availability.

When you are in the office, all calls and messages should be responded to the same day you receive them, before you leave the office. If the caller has requested information that is not yet available or that you have to obtain from another source, you should return the call to indicate that the message was received and you are working on obtaining the information, along with a likely timeframe in which you will be able to supply the information. Your failure to respond to voicemail messages in a timely manner will not be appreciated by those with whom you work, and even less by clients who are paying for your services. You should not leave for the day without responding in some manner to everyone who reached out to you that day. Those same rules apply to your home and cell voicemail, particularly if you are in a job search. You should return all calls and outreach from a prospective employer the same day. If you do not receive the message until after business hours, you should return the call early the next day. Callers to your home, cell, and office phones should be treated with the same level of quick responsiveness as people from whom you receive e-mails.

Chapter Eight
Putting It All Together: Professionalism in the Job Search

Although people go to law school for many different reasons, almost without exception students view law school as a means to an end—to become employed in a career position they desire. Your job search, then, is one of the most important aspects of your law school career, and it deserves your energy, enthusiasm, attention, and an unwavering focus on professionalism throughout, whether you are seeking your first legal internship, your career position upon graduation, or something in between. Assistant Dean William Chamberlain at Northwestern University School of Law notes that many of us do not devote enough attention to our career plan. He says, *"We tend to think too short-term: I'll go to this large firm for a couple of years and then decide what I want to do. This job pays the most, so it must be the best. I've got a job for after law school; why do I need a career plan?"* You are the only one who knows your career aspirations and can make them a reality, so take charge of your long-term career plan, and begin working toward your goals.

Law school, internships, summer jobs, classes, and clinics are all designed to acquaint you with various aspects of the law. You may have started law school with a specific career goal in mind, or you might decide on a career path only after trying out different legal fields. If you simply do not know what type of law you want to practice, you are not alone. An experienced career counselor offers this advice:

Often students will tell me that they don't know what kind of law they want to practice or what legal career they want to pursue, yet it seems like everyone else around them in law school knows exactly what they want to do. I analogize that to being a college freshman, when everyone else seemed to have declared a major. Maybe they knew exactly what they wanted to do, but it also may have been that they just felt like they needed to sound confident. There is nothing wrong with taking the time to figure out what you want to do. In fact, you are better off taking a step back, exploring the various options, and ruling out some opportunities while continuing to re-search others. Many classmates that seem committed to one thing early on will have experiences that will open their mind to other possibilities. Reserve the right to change your mind in law school—if you have an experience in a certain practice area and end up not liking it, you can at least cross that off your list.

David M. Diamond, J.D., M.A., Director, Center for Career Strategy and Advancement, Northwestern University School of Law

A Note About the Office of Career Services

Most career service administrators, from the assistant dean to the receptionist, work very hard to help law students and lawyers with all aspects of their job search. They provide counseling and other services, career information, events, programs, and resources to help you learn about various career options. When it comes right down to it, though, they are not responsible for finding you a job—only you can do that for yourself, and it usually does not happen without a fair amount of research, elbow grease, legwork, and a good attitude on your part. Consider these words from a recruiting manager:

While in law school, students have a tremendous support system already in place to help them through the legal job search, including career services professionals, student affairs administrators, faculty members, classmates, family, and friends. These individuals are all here to help you put best practices into place that will benefit you throughout your professional career, whether that involves working in the legal profession or elsewhere. Even with all of this assistance, everyone's job search is ultimately self-directed. Only you can (and will) take responsibility for your own career direction. So use the support systems that you have in law school—ask for help, meet with a career advisor, go to workshops, find a mentor, learn as much as you can—and you'll be preparing yourself for a lifetime of career success once you graduate.

Skip Horne, Global Recruiting Manager, Diversity and Law School Outreach, Latham & Watkins LLP

The office of career services cannot control the fact that large law firms are generally the only legal employers that can predictably hire students far in advance of graduation. Likewise, they cannot control the fact that large law firms can and do pay big sums of money to students and new graduates, or that those large firms have extremely stringent hiring criteria that is focused on students with the highest grades in their class. The harsh reality of the legal market is that smaller to mid-size law firms, public interest agencies, not-for profits, and state and federal government agencies tend to hire on an as-needed basis, not on a predictable annual basis, and as such, they generally do not find it worthwhile to participate in on-campus interviewing. At most schools, the career services administrators spend a lot of time reaching out to these employers, but they simply do not find on-campus interviewing an effective recruitment tool in most cases. That means in order to find these jobs—and there are many great jobs out there to be found—you need to understand the legal market, be aware of the hiring processes and timelines of different kinds of employers, and accept the realities inherent in the market. The career services office cannot control these aspects of legal hiring, but they should educate you about the realities so you can gain solid legal experience and ultimately find a fulfilling job.

Yes, it is much easier for the guy who got grades in the top five percent of his class to land his dream job at a large firm—he can likely go through the on-campus interview process, get wined and dined by employers at call-back interviews, and have several job offers from which to choose. It may seem unfair if you want to work at a large firm, too, but your grades aren't quite high enough for you to be considered. Or it might seem unfair that if you are interested in a career with the government, you have to research, make phone calls, attend numerous counseling appointments, draft version after version of a cover letter for different agencies, pay for your own interviews in some cases, and possibly face many rejections before finally landing a job, sometimes months later. It seems unfair because it *is* unfair, but it is hardly the fault of the professionals in your career services office—they cannot control the system, the hiring criteria, your grades and other credentials, and which employers are willing to come to campus to interview students. Frankly, most of them dislike the system as much as you do.

Almost without exception, the refrain heard on most law school campuses is that "our career services office is useless—they only focus on helping the people in the top ten percent of the class." This statement is typically far from the truth, and those who say it are usually the people who have not mastered professionalism skills, starting with the most important: taking responsibility for the success of your own job search. Your career services office and the administrators therein can be a valuable ally in your job search, and you should take advantage of the many services they offer. If you don't click with a particular counselor, make an appointment with someone else—everyone has different styles and areas of expertise, and a method of counseling that you enjoy may frustrate your classmate. It is good to have options—just be sure to exercise them. You pay for the services offered with your tuition dollars, so it is foolish and shortsighted not to use them, particularly if you are basing your non-use on the faulty rumors that circulate throughout most law school campuses.

Elbow Grease, Leg Work, and Research

Looking for a job is an exercise in rejection. Most of us are repeatedly told "no" over and over and over again, until we hear the magic "yes" and we're offered a job. And who likes to be continuously rejected? The job search is naturally frustrating, especially when you're balancing the demands of a rigorous academic program and myriad extracurricular activities with your personal life. Thus it is absolutely critical that law students keep a positive attitude throughout their law school experience—and this extends to the job search as well. If you consider the "system" to be unfair, just remember that the "system" probably only works for a small number of students. Look on the bright side. This frees you up to create your own "system" of working, networking, volunteering, and gaining valuable experience that will land you the job you're looking for regardless of whether you're at the top of the class or your family has connections or a faculty member has referred you to an employer.

Skip Horne, Global Recruiting Manager, Diversity and Law School Outreach, Latham & Watkins LLP

In order to take responsibility for your job search, the first step is to identify what you would like to do or try in your internships and summer jobs, and conversely, which areas of law you can eliminate because you have no interest in them. An effective, successful job search will require research. Even if you plan to land your position through on-campus interviewing, you must research the employers—first to make your selections about submitting resumés, and second, in preparation for interviews. For all other positions, research is even more essential. Your first task is to understand the legal market and the hiring needs and timelines for each of the types of employers you're interested in. Researching past hiring practices, recently hired alumni, and recent job postings are all solid ways to gain information. Web research, directories, informational interviews, and phone calls can help you discern appropriate timeframes to apply, likely hiring needs, and the qualities certain employers are seeking in candidates. Your career counselor may know this information for some employers and can help you find it for others.

As you research and select employers to whom you intend to apply, save a copy of all your research and advance outreach, either in electronic or hardcopy format. If you do land an interview, your prior research efforts will be easily accessible for interview preparation purposes.

Take Care With Your Application Materials

Once you have identified potential employers and verified the application timeframes for each, you will need to prepare your application materials for submission. These materials are your opportunity to convince a potential employer to invite you for an interview, and they should reflect your integrity and professionalism throughout.

Ready Your Resumé

Your resumé is a summary of your professional qualifications; it must be one hundred percent accurate—no exceptions. There should be no discrepancies, truth-stretching, or incorrect information included on your resumé. Do not estimate, round up, or embellish. The information you put on your resumé about your academics, for example, should match the transcript your registrar will provide you to give to potential employers for them to verify your grades and class rank. Students are sometimes tempted to round up when it comes to a GPA—resist the temptation. Inaccuracies will eventually be discovered, and they will call your overall credibility into question.

There are debates about whether your resumé should be limited to one page or if two-page resumés are acceptable. Rather than following a hard-and-fast rule, this is an area in which your research should drive your decision. Although some legal employers will view a resumé with more than one page as presumptuous or reflective of an inability to be pithy, other employers will appreciate the additional information about your skills and experiences in an effort to distinguish one candidate from another. You should discern in which camp your potential employers are likely to fall, and then ensure that your resumé complies. Here's some advice for those seeking public interest positions:

> *Public interest employers are interested in all relevant experience related to their client population. If your target organizations serve children, give details on how and when you have worked with children on your resume. Go back as far as volunteer experience in high school if your experience warrants it. If you have language skills, be sure to tell the employer your proficiency level. If you have traveled and volunteered abroad, explain your experiences. Volunteer service and non-law-related work with underserved populations show your commitment to public service, so feel free to list it and to submit a two-page resumé for public interest positions. Resumés for this type of employer often have very different headings than a private sector firm resumé. Use headings such as: Community or Volunteer Service, Direct Legal Service Experience, Non–Profit Work, Child or Elder Law Work. Clinical experience gained in law school can be very impressive, so make space to explain your work in all clinics. Lastly, let your excitement about your work shine through on your cover letter and in your interview. All employers hope to find the most qualified and most motivated candidates for their organizations, so let them know that public interest is your top choice.*

Cybele Smith, Director of Public Service and Public Interest Programs, The Ohio State University Moritz College of Law

When preparing your resumé, you may need to make some decisions about whether to include certain information that employers may not be permitted to inquire about. For example, strategically, you may want to include information about the many positions you hold at your church or mention the fact that you balance law school with parenting responsibilities. You can just as easily elect to omit this information—employers cannot use your religious affiliation or status as a mother in the employment decision-making process, and as such, they should refrain from inquiring about it. You are under no obligation to disclose information that cannot legally be used as a basis for an employment decision.

However, your leadership positions at your church may add significantly to your qualifications for a particular position. Or your ability to excel in law school while balancing parenting responsibilities might speak volumes to certain employers about your capability to multitask and prioritize. If you have plenty of other examples, it may not be as critical to include items like these. Only you can decide to include or omit items of this nature, and your decision may change depending on the position you're applying for. It is your resumé—you must be comfortable with the information you choose to include.

Although an interest section is not strictly necessary to include on your resume, many employers do value knowing a little about your interests beyond law school and work. They view those items as an opportunity to see if you are well rounded. If you do elect to include interests, be brief—list no more than three or four. Be specific rather than general. Instead of saying "sports," say "playing tennis and basketball." If you like to watch movies or read books from a particular genre, list that rather than just saying "avid reader" or "movie buff."

You have a choice about the length of your resumé, whether to include certain items, and what, if any, interests to list. But there is no leeway in the need to be absolutely accurate and to ensure that there are *no* typos or grammatical errors on your resumé. In addition to using the spell-check function, have another person review your resumé to ensure that it flows well from beginning to end, that the dates are sequential without gaps, and that the explanations and descriptions make sense. A human resources director gives this resumé-preparation advice:

> *First impressions are important. While everyone makes mistakes, if there are typos in your resumé or cover letter, it raises questions about not only your proofreading skills but you as a person and your abilities, etc. Make sure your resumé and cover letter do not contain any typos and are in good form. On average, resumés receive about eight to ten seconds of a reader's time, so they should be clear and concise. Reverse chronological order is the standard resumé form and the most appropriate for students. Review your resumé for content and grammar, and ask that someone else review your resumé as well. Be sure to use spell check!*

Gayle P. Englert, Director of Human Resources, Cole, Schotz, Meisel, Forman & Leonard P.A.

Some employers will do the first sorting of resumés into two piles—those with any typos or mistakes (the instant cuts) and those that are error-free (worthy of additional consideration).

Cover Letter Reprise

Your application package is not complete without a cover letter. As discussed previously, your cover letter is the first writing sample an employer will see. Although the basics of cover letter–writing were covered in Chapter Six, the need for an accurate and error-free finished product bears repeating. Although it may be tempting to use the same cover letter for every employer to which you apply, you need to be a little cautious with that approach. You'll certainly save time if you use the same cover letter repeatedly, and that might be fine if all the employers are offering similar positions. But if you are applying to different kinds of positions, develop a cover letter tailored specifically for each one.

If you can legitimately use the same cover letter with multiple employers who are offering similar positions, then guard against careless errors when changing the information in the name and address lines, as well as in the salutation and body of the letter. Many careless law students have sent cover letters addressed to "Jane Doe" at "Jones & Smith" law firm that begin "Dear Mr. Pauls." Or the letter might begin correctly, "Dear Ms. Doe," but then continue on in the body to say, "I am writing to apply for a position with 'Knepper & Lyon.'" You can easily forget to update a form letter in all the necessary places when using it for multiple employers—and neglecting to change pertinent information is sure to land your application in the cut pile.

If you elect to transmit your application materials electronically, rather than via hardcopy, remember to convert them into a PDF file first to ensure that they arrive in the recipient's in-box exactly as you intended, with all formatting, fonts, and spacing intact.

References

As you embark upon your first job search, you will need to consider whom you will use for references. You should have three professional references available to submit with every application. If you are in your first year of law school, use one to two law school faculty members in addition to a prior employer and/or an undergraduate professor. As you progress through law school, you will want to add an additional law school faculty member as well as legal employers.

For an internship or career position, personal references are irrelevant so you should not include them. Your references need to be professionals who are familiar with your academic and legal skills, your writing ability, or your performance in a work environment. Although your only legal references at the beginning of your law school career will be law faculty, as you progress you should add more legal employers. If you have room on your resumé, list two to three references there; if not, create an additional application page solely for your references. At the top of the page, include your name and a heading such as "Professional References."

Professionalism dictates that you secure permission before using anyone as a reference. Speak with your proposed references in advance of your job search to obtain their approval to list them as a reference. Additionally, if any amount of time has passed since you last secured such permission, you should update that permission. Once a reference has agreed to be included, you should provide him or her with an updated resumé. If there is a particular position for which you are in the running and your references are likely to be called, it is always helpful to supply your references with information about the specific position and the qualities and experience the employer is seeking, along with your application materials, so they can speak directly to your abilities in that regard if they are contacted. Arm your references with relevant information, and make it easy for them to provide strong and pertinent information on your behalf.

As Robert Kaplan, Associate Dean and Director of Externships at William & Mary School of Law, says:

> *Using references appropriately requires due diligence throughout the job search process. Before using references, contact them—not only to secure their permission, but also to assure that they have current information about you. It always surprises me that applicants use references whom they haven't contacted ahead of time and/or with whom they haven't been in touch for several years. Inform your references that they may be contacted on your behalf. Choose references with whom you have had reasonably recent contact or to whom you have provided updated information about your accomplishments and experience. After you have secured employment, you should, as a matter of professional courtesy, follow up with your references to thank them and to let them know that your job search has been successful.*

Writing Sample

Your writing sample becomes an increasingly important aspect of your application materials as you progress through law school. As a first-year law student, your writing sample is likely to be a basic research memorandum of five pages or less. If your school does not teach legal writing in the first semester, you may need to provide a non-legal writing sample to employers who require a writing sample. This is not preferred, but at some schools you may not have a choice. If you must submit a non-legal writing sample, be sure to indicate on the cover page why a legal writing sample is not available.

As you advance in law school and have a wider variety of writing samples from which to choose, it is smart to have a faculty member or practitioner give you advice about which sample may be the most appropriate one to use, and that could vary depending upon the position for which you are applying. If your best writing is a longer piece of work, it is fine to use a section that can stand on its own as your writing sample. If you do use an excerpt, include a statement on the cover page that indicates the sample is extracted from a longer document and mention that the full sample is available upon request.

Many students and prospective employers wonder whether writing samples are, or should be, edited by others. There are different schools of thought on this. As a candidate, your goal is to present your best work to prospective employers. As such, it is definitely to your advantage to have another pair of eyes review your writing sample to ensure that you have caught all typos and other errors. Light editing to catch mistakes and awkward sentences is fine, but heavy editing that rewrites sections, reorganizes the document, or otherwise changes your work significantly calls into question whether the sample is actually your work or that of someone else. If a friend or colleague gives you feedback and you use it to modify your work, where does that fall in the spectrum between your own work and someone else's? If you write a paper for class, and your professor gives you detailed feedback that you then use to make a stronger memorandum, is that acceptable?

The editing question plagues candidates and employers alike. The baseline consideration is that the work should be *your* work, no exceptions. You should conduct the research and write the sample, and if someone provides feedback to you, the rewriting should also be your work. Lawyers learn from each other, and feedback from others is often used to make their writing stronger, so this process does mirror what happens in practice. The best approach, beyond ensuring that the work is yours, is to be honest about the circumstances surrounding the writing sample you are submitting by providing a bit of detail on the cover page you include with the sample.

A cover page to your writing sample is always advised. The cover page should include your name, as should the header or footer of each subsequent page of your writing sample. To address the editing question, the cover page should describe the circumstances under which you drafted the writing sample. If it was a class assignment with feedback received, you should note that. If you wrote it during your internship with a small law firm, provide a brief bit of background. If the sample is completely unedited by others, note that as well, and that will tell the prospective employers that no one else has provided feedback on your work.

In most cases, in addition to writing assignments that you do for law school courses, you can consider "real work" that you draft for an employer as possible writing samples. The most important aspect of your writing sample is not the context in which it was written or the type of sample it is (memo, brief, opinion letter, etc.) but that it is one of your best samples of writing. Whether it is a memorandum, a brief, an opinion letter, a motion, or something else is not as important as whether it illustrates your ability to synthesize large amounts of legal information into a cogent and concise document. When you elect to use a sample from an internship, externship, clerkship, or other circumstances outside of the classroom, professionalism and ethics dictate that you obtain permission from your employer and/or supervisor before using the sample. In many cases, you will be asked to redact the clients' or parties' names from the document, which you can do easily. Your cover page should note that you are using the sample with permission and that all confidential information has been redacted.

Transcript

In most cases, the final component of your application package will be your transcript. If a transcript is required, you must submit one even if you are not happy with the information on it. Hiding the ball as to grades from employers who rely on them to make interview selections will not gain you an interview. If you have not done as well in law school as you'd hoped, all is not lost. There are plenty of legal employers out there for whom grades are a secondary consideration and who prefer to look at a variety of other skills and characteristics first. Large law firms often elect to rely on grades more heavily than other types of legal employers, so select your potential employers with that in mind. There is more than one way to land a position in a large firm, and you can certainly set yourself up to move laterally into a large firm down the road if that is still your ultimate goal.

Study your transcript as an employer might, to see what information you can or should highlight or address in your cover letter. If you had a slow start the first semester of law school and your grades have steadily improved, highlight your rapid progress. Although you should never make excuses for poor grades, you can certainly let a potential employer know if you experienced a trauma, such as the death of an immediate family member, in a semester in which your grades were particularly low. If you have several courses in which you excelled, especially if they are relevant to the position for which you are applying, you can certainly point that out. If you excel in courses with a strong writing component, that is certainly worth mentioning. Whatever the patterns on your transcript, take the time to read and understand how an employer might view your legal academic record.

When you submit a transcript with your application package, most employers will accept a copy of a certified transcript, and a PDF version of a scanned transcript is almost always acceptable for an electronic application submission. Unless an employer specifically requests a certified transcript to be submitted, you can safely assume that a copy is fine at the early stages of the application process. Some employers will ask for a certified copy later in the process or at the time of employment to complete their records; others will use the copy to contact your school and verify your grades. In all cases, be absolutely certain that you are submitting the most recent version of your transcript, that the GPA and class rank information that appears on your transcript matches the information on your resumé, and that the copy is legible and clear. Sending a dark transcript that no one can read will only frustrate potential employers.

First You Have to Land the Interview

The importance of spending quality time on the application materials for your job search cannot be overstated. Despite the many demands you face in law school and in practice, your application materials are of primary importance, and they deserve your best effort. You cannot proceed in the application process if you do not land an interview, and that decision is made primarily on the basis of your application materials. Of course, there are always circumstances in which your networking efforts will pay off, and you will move to the front of the consideration pile based on relationships you have formed, references who advocate on your behalf, and any other number of other situations in which a contact has stepped out for you.

If you do obtain extra consideration and land an interview through networking or other means, submitting sloppy application materials that you threw together at the last minute, or providing information that is inaccurate or questionable, will cause you to lose any traction you had gained. You will not only hurt your chances in the process, but you will not live up to what your contacts have said about you, and it could very well prevent them from wanting to help you in the future. No one wants to support a candidate who turns out to be a disappointment or even an embarrassment.

Your application materials are the first opportunity for you to demonstrate your professionalism and ethics, and that will continue throughout the application process. If your materials are sloppy and inaccurate, your professionalism and ethics will be questioned, and you will not fare well in the application process. You have to land an interview before you can move toward an offer of employment, and the vehicle to do so is your application. Give your materials the time and attention they deserve.

Persistence, Yes! Stalking, No.

Once you have submitted your application materials to a prospective employer, in most cases it is fine to follow up to ensure that the materials were received. You can also inquire about when you might expect to hear something or what the hiring timeframes are for the position. With smaller firms, public interest agencies, and even government positions, it can be effective to close your cover letter by indicating you will contact the employer in the next week or so to see if they would be interested in arranging an interview. This way, you have the ball in your court for following up, rather than waiting for the phone to ring, and this can be helpful to busy attorneys who are acting as recruiters in their spare time. Here's some advice about being proactive in your job search:

> *I graduated without a job because a cut in government funding caused my offer to dry up during my last semester of law school. I moved to Chicago and put my job search on hold while I studied for and took the bar exam. At some point, I did a mass mailing to every government agency, public interest group and small, mid-size and large firm I could find in a major directory and then sat back and waited for the calls to come. Somehow I thought that constituted a job search. I did receive a few interview opportunities from the mailing, including one from a firm that was not even on my mailing list. The attorney who called told me a friend of his had forwarded my resumé to him. I went on the interview and got the job—therefore, it seemed to me that my strategy was sound.*

Months later I found out that the person who forwarded my resumé actually forwarded the WRONG resumé—he meant to forward someone else's, not mine. The takeaway? If you get your name out there and do it the right way, you can create many opportunities for yourself. If you do it like I did and rely on a single mailing and nothing else, you are merely relying on pure dumb luck.

David M. Diamond, J.D., M.A., Director, Center for Career Strategy and Advancement, Northwestern University School of Law

If you do contact employers by phone, be respectful of their time—lawyers who are handling recruitment matters are extremely busy with the practice of law; recruitment is just an additional non-billable task, albeit an important one. If the contact is a professional recruiter, he or she receives a multitude of applications and inquiries, and such applications are often handled through a full team of staff members. As such, do not be surprised if a recruiter does not have instant recall of who you are and why you are contacting him or her.

If you reach out to a prospective employer and are told they have not made any decisions yet, you should reiterate your interest in the position and indicate that you would definitely accept an interview, if offered. If you leave several messages and get no response, in most instances you should take that as a sign of non-interest and let it go. Persistence is a good trait, but sometimes you simply do not have the right set of skills for a particular position. No amount of follow-up will convince an employer otherwise, so it is better to redirect your energies toward other opportunities. Although in a perfect world you would receive a response to your outreach, if you have not been selected to proceed in the process, many employers would prefer to send you a letter to that effect, rather than telling you personally or over the phone.

For out-of-town employers, it can be effective to offer to meet with them while you are in town and supply specific dates that you will be there. That way, the interview does not cost the employer anything but time, and he or she may be more likely to meet with you.

Generally, follow-up is positive, and it demonstrates your interest in a position. You should track your applications and check in as appropriate with potential employers. Such follow-up can be especially effective if you reach out to alumni of your law school or to others with whom you have a common link. The exceptions to these general rules about follow-up would be for employers that have set recruiting cycles and processes, such as large law firms, and government honors programs that have a defined selection process. In those cases, you should follow the application guidelines exactly, and/or work through your law school's on-campus recruiting program. Always follow the policies at your school that pertain to these employers. If you do directly mail or e-mail an application to an employer that does not recruit on campus, you should follow up if you do not hear anything. But contacting prospective employers more frequently, unless it is in response to outreach from the potential employer or you are concerned that your materials were not received, is usually superfluous and just adds to the workload of those handling the recruiting processes. Employers are usually equipped to handle large numbers of applications at certain times of the year, so your continued outreach is unnecessary and may not be appreciated given their volume of work.

Employers remember two types of candidates in the application process. The first candidates are those who stand out in the process due to their credentials, interview skills, and professionalism. Maturity and good judgment permeate their actions, and employers are so impressed by these "superstars" that they remember and talk about them eagerly and often. The second type of candidates are those who stand out for negative reasons; they are remembered and discussed just as intensely, but not in a good way. These are the applicants whom employers give as examples of what *not* to do in the application process, such as making daily phone calls to prospective employers, sending cover letters that contain bizarre statements in an attempt to stand out, using gimmicks, and not accepting "no" for an answer. Your goal is to be one of the candidates who are remembered, but for the former, positive reasons, not the latter negative ones.

Chapter Nine
Putting It All Together: Legal Interview Savvy

If you have done your homework and selected potential employers, submitted a strong application package to a variety of firms and organizations during the appropriate recruitment timeframes for each, and practiced networking and building your contacts, it is only a matter of time before you begin landing legal interviews. Preparation for the interview stage of your job search is as deserving of your research, time, attention, and effort as the application stage. You may have heard the expression "getting a job is a full-time job," and you'll understand that firsthand. All aspects of the job search require time and effort, and as a busy law student or new lawyer, time is one of the resources that you are most lacking. Pace yourself—you do not need to spend a solid week on your job search to the detriment of everything else. If you devote twenty minutes or so a day to your job search, it will not be so overwhelming. Your efforts will eventually pay off in the form of interviews and, ultimately, job offers will come before you know it.

Reprise: Research Is a Must

We have already talked about how crucial it is to conduct research to learn about and select potential employers. Once you have landed the interview, your research tasks are not done. Research is equally important at the interview-preparation stage. You need to be extremely prepared for all interviews, and that includes being familiar with the employer and the people you will meet during your interview before you ever step foot in the door. Hopefully, you have saved the research you conducted about the employer at the application stage. It is definitely to your benefit and a real time-saver to keep organized records about each employer to whom you apply, as well as a copy of your application materials and the job posting, if applicable. If these items are organized and filed, you will be a step ahead when the call comes inviting you for an interview.

Learn and understand basic information about the potential employer. After you have checked the most obvious sources, such as the company Web site, run a news search online to see if there are any recent press hits of which you should be aware. If you have trouble finding information about a small law firm or other business, it is never a bad idea to double-check with the reference librarian at your law library. He or she may be able to provide you with a rich source of information that you didn't know about or were unable to locate during your research efforts.

Prepare Materials to Have on Hand

When you attend an interview, bring along as little as possible. However, there are a few necessities you should have on hand. If you do not already have one, invest in a decent portfolio that has a pocket or holder for documents and a place for a notebook and pen. It need not be expensive, but it should be clean, unmarked, and professional-looking. Avoid bringing backpacks, book bags, and other large and cumbersome items to interviews. If you have to move from one office to another during the interview, it can be distracting to gather up multiple belongings, and it is difficult to shake hands with others when your hands are full. You are also more likely to leave something behind inadvertently if you carry multiple items with you. If you must arrive at an interview with your luggage due to travel arrangements, get there early enough to find out if you can store your baggage someplace until the conclusion of the interview. It is preferable, though, to leave travel bags at your hotel and check it with the staff there.

Your portfolio needs to be stocked with several updated and good-quality copies of your resumé, transcript, references, and writing sample, all printed on high-quality paper.

If the prospective employer indicates during the interview that additional application items, such as a transcript, are needed, you look organized and efficient if you can pull it out and provide it immediately. Your portfolio should also contain copies of your research about the prospective employer in case you need to refer to it between interviews; the schedule for the interview, if one has been provided; and blank paper and a pen. We will be discussing below what notes you should make and the appropriate time to make such notes. If you have done your research and prepared your portfolio with these items, you will be ready to interview with confidence. Be sure to carry your portfolio—and purse, if applicable—in your left hand so that your right hand is free for shaking hands as you are introduced to people.

Other Necessary Preparations

In addition to having a close familiarity with and understanding of the research you conducted about your prospective employer, you also have an obligation to know your resume and other application materials from top to bottom. Be familiar with every item on your resumé so you can converse about it with ease. It is completely ineffective in an interview to say something like, "Well, it's been a while since I researched that issue for that paper, so I really don't remember the details," in response to a question about a writing award mentioned on your resumé. If you are asked about a prior internship, you should be able to discuss your duties, what you learned, and the challenges of the position. If you are asked about a leadership or volunteer position on your resumé, you should know the particulars and be able to describe your responsibilities and accomplishments without difficulty. In short, if it is important enough to include on your resumé, it is important enough for you to review the item, recall details about it, and know how to answer any questions you are asked about it.

To ensure that you know your resumé entries well enough to answer questions about them, read your resumé item by item. After each one, ask yourself some sample questions, like, "What did you enjoy most about working there?" or "Give me an example of a time you had to talk with an employee about his or her performance and how you handled it." or "What did you find challenging about that position?" or "What accomplishment are you most proud of and why during your time at Langley Builders?" This way, you will become comfortable talking about your experiences in detail, even if you are not asked those exact questions.

You should also review the rest of your application materials, in addition to your resumé. Although it is less common to be asked about your writing sample, it is not unheard of, and you should prepare for that possibility. Reread your writing sample and the underlying documents and research, if necessary, to ensure that you recall the facts, your analysis, and the conclusions you drew. Also, examine your transcript for anomalies or grades that might spark questions, and be prepared to address those, as well. The overall preparation necessary to review your application materials will get shorter with each interview, particularly if you are interviewing frequently. If it has been a while since you had an interview, though, allot time to prepare yourself in this manner again.

Finally, you should ensure that you know exactly how to get to the employer's place of business, and that, if you are driving a car, you know what the parking situation will be once you arrive. If this is your first time traveling to the area and you are finding your own way to the interview, allow yourself extra time and make certain that you have sound directions and an accurate map. If you are driving during rush hour, allocate a larger cushion of travel time. Sometimes parking can be difficult to find, so inquire ahead of time about the best place to park. Ensure that you have adequate money (both cash and change) to pay for parking in case the prospective employer does not validate, the parking lot or garage the employer indicated you should use is full, or you have to park at a metered spot. Plan ahead for any possible contingencies, and plan to arrive early. That way, even if you experience small delays, you will still make it to the interview with time to spare.

Dress to Land the Job

For an interview, dress like you want the job; you should take care with your appearance. Natural beauty is not what we are talking about here. You don't have to be a model or spend thousands of dollars on your interview suit. Taking care with your appearance means that your hair is shaped and tidy, your hands and nails are clean and neat, you do not have offensive body odor or bad breath, and you are wearing appropriate interview attire. If all of these seem like "no brainers" to you, be mindful that there are interviewees every day who violate one of the above grooming rules. You do not want a matter of personal grooming or dress to detract from your primary purpose: to land a job.

Selecting appropriate interview clothes can be the most difficult part of the "well-groomed" equation. Many career counselors recommend that women and men wear navy blue suits, preferably with a skirt for the women, to legal interviews. Certainly, there are different viewpoints about what is okay to wear, but err on the side of caution lest you have an interviewer with a more conservative viewpoint on the spectrum of "acceptable attire." A suit is necessary, but it doesn't have to be in navy blue. Of course it should not be a distracting color, like bright purple or pink. Sticking to neutral or dark suit colors may seem boring and safe, but there is an added bonus: Neutrals match each other and a wider array of colors and apparel, so you can mix and match to build your professional wardrobe more quickly. If you choose suit basics in neutral colors, you can add more personality through blouses or scarves for women and shirts and ties for men.

Although some interviewers and employers would prefer (inappropriately) that women wear skirts, it is up to the female interviewee whether to wear a suit with pants or a skirt. It is important to ensure, however, that that if you do wear a skirt, you don't wear one that is inappropriately short. Skirts should fall at or below the knees. There are regional differences (and practical weather considerations) about wearing pantyhose with a skirt. Use your best judgment, based on how you see the majority of professional women, specifically lawyers, dressed in your geographic region. Be mindful, too, of wearing a blouse or shirt that is too low-cut or unbuttoned by one too many buttons. It is distracting and inappropriate to wear an unsuitably revealing neckline in an interview or professional work situation. You want to be remembered for your skill and ability to do the job, not your inappropriate attire or the exposing view you offered of your cleavage.

Men should wear a tie to interviews. Double-breasted suits are best for occasions other than work and interviews, and sport coats are too casual for most legal interviews.

Select a basic single-breasted suit for interviewing. Both men and women should pay attention to fit and comfort of the suit they are selecting as interview attire. If you must shop for and purchase an interview suit, ask for advice from the experts in the stores, and spend the money necessary to get your suit properly tailored.

Shoes for both men and women should look clean and polished and should match your suit. Women should avoid overly high heels and extravagant shoe designs. Wear jewelry and accessories that are simple, tasteful, and minimal—again, the rule of thumb is that if it is distracting in any way, it is not good for an interview.

If you feel strongly that your dress should reflect your personality, be mindful that if your personality is flashy, your interviewer may not agree with the wisdom of your apparel choices. Only you can decide if it is worth the risk to wear attire that may keep you from getting a job offer. In the employer's mind, if your clothing choices reflect bad judgment, a lack of common sense, and/or immaturity, they may view these as a reflection of your job-related skills and abilities and move on to the next candidate.

With all the decisions you make about grooming and attire—how to wear your hair, and whether to shave your beard, for example—the bottom line is that you should look and feel your best. You want your appearance to make you feel confident and strong, not inadequate, uncomfortable, or unable to breath because of ill-fitting clothes. If you are uncomfortable and ill at ease, you will probably appear awkward and self-conscious to the interviewer. If you feel great, however, you will appear more confident, even if you are nervous about the interview.

There are always exceptions to the general rules about interview attire. Although you cannot go wrong wearing a suit, and it is usually better to "overdress" than "underdress" for an interview, there may be times when a suit is not necessary. Some public interest positions, for example, may not require a suit, and a number of law firms have year-round business casual dress codes; they may indicate that it is fine for you to dress in business casual for the interview. In most legal environments that are deemed business casual, there will still be lawyers in suits due to client meetings, court appearances, etc. It is truly your call whether or not to wear a suit in those situations where business casual has been suggested by the interviewer.

Karen Hough, a former improvisational entertainer, actress, and model, asks you to consider the following as you dress for interviews and on the job:

> *Your professional presentation counts. Always be sure to dress in a flattering but professional manner. Whether we like it or not, we are judged by how we look and, unfortunately, this is particularly true for women. Everyone needs to be very mindful of their professional image, including dress and accessories, body language, and the total body picture we present. Be cognizant of how you are being perceived, and err on the side of professional at all times. You want to be the one who is dressed more sharply than your peers and colleagues. Your presentation should stand out for the right reasons.*

Karen Hough, Founder and CEO, ImprovEdge

Ensure that your grooming and attire do not distract from the purpose of your interview. Although suitable interview attire and good grooming will not necessarily net you a job offer, lack of appropriate attire and good grooming can definitely cost you a job.

The Day of the Interview Has Arrived!

On the day of the interview, plan ahead, and leave early enough that any unexpected delays can be handled without being late. Bring along the name and telephone number of your contact at the interview. Although it is your responsibility to be on time, if an absolutely unavoidable delay occurs, you need to be able to get in touch with the prospective employer immediately. One law student witnessed an automobile accident on the way to her interview, and because the other witnesses left the scene, she felt obligated to stop and provide a statement to police, thus causing her to miss her interview. Because she called and explained the situation, she was able to reschedule for another day without any negative reflection on her.

If you arrive to the employer's location more than ten minutes early, do not check in or ask for your contact until you are within ten minutes of your appointment, unless the employer has requested that you arrive a bit earlier to complete paperwork and forms. If need be, spend a few minutes reviewing your research and application materials.

Arriving too early can be stressful for the employer, who likely won't be ready for you and may, in fact, be finishing up another interview.

It is extremely important that you adhere to the Golden Rule and treat everyone with professionalism and respect while on an interview. It is possible that anyone and everyone you meet will have the opportunity to comment about you to the decision-makers. Also, you might unknowingly meet or be observed by a decision-maker. Assistants and other support personnel often have a lot of power—more than you might think. If you receive and accept a job offer, you do not want to be on bad terms with any staff members because of how you treated them at the interview. Support staff can make or break you (as we will discuss in greater detail in Chapter Eleven), and you simply cannot afford to alienate anyone. From judges to lawyers to government officials, and everyone in between, lawyers rely heavily on their assistants and will not take kindly to you treating them poorly. There is nothing to gain by thinking or acting like you are more important than someone else, and everything to gain by networking and making contacts with everyone you meet.

Fielding Interview Questions Effortlessly

If you have done your research, reviewed your application materials, and dressed sharply, answering the interview questions should be relatively easy. For some people, though, it is very nerve-wracking to be interviewed, particularly if you do not have a lot of practice. If your law school offers a mock interview program, take advantage of it. At some schools, you will have a mock interview with a career counselor at your school, and you will learn a lot from the experience. At other schools, the mock interview program involves matching students with practicing attorneys, who will conduct the mock interview. Either way, it is great practice and will likely give you greater confidence for the first real legal interview. If you don't have such a program, you will be well-served to conduct some informational interviews. See Chapter 5 for information about informational interviewing. Although the format and purposes are different, it is still good practice and will make you feel more comfortable.

Bear in mind that the attorneys who interview you are not, for the most part, accomplished interviewers. For many, the only interview experience they have is when there is an opening they need to fill at their organization or firm. As such, they may do most of the talking, rather than asking you questions, or they may unknowingly or inadvertently ask questions about items they are not legally allowed to consider in the employment process. They're usually friendly, but occasionally you may encounter someone who wants to treat the interview like a cross-examination. Often, busy attorneys have not had time to review your resumé or application materials in advance of the interview. They may even fail to give you their full attention during your time together. From checking e-mail to taking calls during the interview, or looking at the clock, it is sometimes obvious that he or she is multi-tasking during the interview. Although none of these situations, and others you may encounter in an interview, are ideal or preferred, your deft handling of an interview faux pas can turn it into a positive for you.

As you are developing responses for interview questions, it helps to have a framework for approaching the interview. One strategy is to come up with three or four "talking points" that serve as the structure for organizing your answers. These talking points—what is crucial for the interviewer to know about you when deciding whom to hire—should be based on your research about that particular employer and how you best match the requirements of the position. For example, your talking points might be that 1) you are a strong legal writer, 2) you have exceptional multitasking ability, 3) you are good at working with different people and teams, and 4) you handle high-pressure situations well. Again, these talking points should be based on the requirements of the position, so they may change from interview to interview.

After you develop your talking points, come up with one or two ways to illustrate each of them. For example, to show that you are good at working with different people and teams, you could discuss a situation in which you got people with opposing viewpoints to work together on a project. Or you could talk about your solo international travels in which you stayed with strangers who spoke another language, and explain how well you adapted. To illustrate your ability to handle high-pressure situations, you might describe a job in which last-minute deadlines were the norm, and detail how you worked to meet them. Similarly, you could discuss your personal accomplishments in learning a difficult task (flying a plane, investing in the stock market, playing competitive sports, body building, etc.) or caring for a medically dependent family member. The examples that illustrate your skills need not be limited to school or work experience, as long as the items you are discussing demonstrate your proficiency.

If an interviewer asks you about an internship listed on your resumé, think about which talking point you can offer to answer the question. If they ask you a more open-ended or general question, your talking points will help you organize your answer quickly and efficiently. Every question provides an opportunity for you to illustrate your skills and abilities to the employer; do not waste a single opportunity to present your talking points. Even in half hour interview, you have precious little time to speak, so make the most of every opening.

Prepare for Your Interview

What MUST an Interviewer Learn About You in Twenty to Thirty Minutes?

Step One: Develop Three to Four Talking Points

(Base them on the requirements of the position and your experiences, skills, and abilities.)

My four talking points for the intern position at X, Y, & Z Law Firm:

1. I have strong legal writing skills.

2. I have exceptional multi-tasking abilities.

3. I work very well with different people and teams.

4. I handle high-pressure situations calmly and professionally.

Step Two: Develop Two Ways to Illustrate Each Talking Point:

(Develop them by expanding the information on your resumé.)

1. **Strong legal writing skills:**

    A. The writing award for which I've been nominated.

    B. The brief I wrote for my prior employer that was submitted to the Court with minimal changes.

2. **Multi-tasking ability:**

    A. Currently balancing high performance in law school with a part-time job and significant involvement in student activities, including serving as vice president of the Environmental Law Group.

    B. My work experience at the university during my undergraduate years that required balancing various projects, deadlines, and assignments from multiple people.

3. **Proficiency working with people and teams:**

    A. My facilitation of two people with opposing viewpoints working together on a project for the Student Bar Association and how I succeeded in moving the project along.

    B. My experiences with solo international travels to several countries—I stayed with strangers (now close friends) who spoke another language, and I adapted well.

4. **Ability to handle high-pressure environments**:

    A. My employment at Jones Corporation—unexpected, last-minute deadlines were the norm, and I met them.

    B. Obtaining my pilot's license (or learning to play a competitive sport, etc.).

Step Three: Draw from Your Talking Points to Answer Interview Questions

(Frame your answer in terms of the vital information you want the interviewer to learn.)

Question: What do you like best about law school?

Answer: I enjoy many things about law school—I love meeting people, and I'm learning a lot. It's been really exciting to be involved in so many projects and groups. I've always thought that my strong writing skills would be an asset in law school, and I'm finding that to be true—that is probably my favorite aspect of law school. Legal writing is different from other writing I've done, and I've enjoyed honing my skills in that regard. I received a high grade in my legal writing class, and I just learned that I've been nominated for the J. Thomas Peterson Writing Award for a paper I wrote for a seminar last semester.

[Contrast the effectiveness of this answer, which left the interviewer with a strong understanding of your writing skills, with an answer that focuses on a less-relevant aspect of law school. Do not fabricate information to make your answer focus on a talking point, however. Use a talking point only if it legitimately and truthfully answers the question.]

Question: Tell me a little about the job you held at Jones Corporation.

Answer: My job at Jones Corporation taught me a lot about my ability to handle a high workload and unexpected deadlines. It was a fast-paced, high-performance environment, and we were often expected to pull a project together from scratch in forty-eight hours. I actually enjoyed working under the time constraints. Although it sounds like it would be stressful, I liked the challenge and being part of a team that worked to pull it off. I never missed a deadline. In fact, just before I left this position to start law school, I received an award for my work on a project.

[Contrast the effectiveness of this answer, which left the interviewer with an understanding of your ability to handle deadlines and pressure, with an answer that simply repeats the job duties and responsibilities listed on your resumé.]

As you answer interview questions, avoid rambling and talking in circles. If you are asked why you elected to go to law school, for example, do not give a long-winded response about how you wanted to be a doctor, but then you changed your mind, so then you were set on being an engineer, but you didn't like a couple of classes you took, so you finally changed your undergraduate major to English, and you settled on law school because it seemed interesting and you weren't sure what else you could do with an English degree. Instead, give a concise and organized answer that illustrates a talking point.

Let's say you would like to draw from your talking point about strong writing skills. Your answer to the "Why law school?" question might indicate that you explored a variety of career options and, given your undergraduate major in English and your enjoyment of writing, you found law to be a good match for your skills. Instead of wasting valuable interview time rambling about irrelevant information, say that you are pleased with your choice—the writing foundation you received as an English major has served you well, and you have excelled in all your writing courses. You are looking forward to your membership on law review to further refine your legal writing skills. In this way, you have answered the question concisely and provided the interviewer with one of the talking points you really wanted him or her to know about, while illustrating that talking point by discussing your excellent writing grades and your law review membership. Obviously, talking points and illustrations need to be tailored to the position for which you are applying, as well as to your individual strengths and experiences, but this provides a solid example of how to approach questions using the talking point strategy.

Occasionally, you will be asked a difficult question that absolutely stumps you. Don't panic, and do not feel compelled to jump in and start talking right away. It is completely fine to pause and think for a minute to gather your thoughts. It can also be effective to admit that it is a challenging or difficult question, or say that you hadn't considered that question previously, and buy yourself a little time to organize your answer. Generally, you will not be stumped by questions, and the more interviewing you do, the more adept you will be at answering questions in a cogent and complete manner.

Most interviewers will approach a legal interview by spending the first few minutes breaking the ice and making "small talk." The interviewer may ask you about an interest that you've included on your resumé or talk about something inconsequential like the weather. After a rapport has been established, the interviewer will likely begin asking questions based on your resumé. He or she may have made notes on or highlighted your resumé if they had time to prepare in advance. If not, don't be surprised if you're asked a question that is addressed or answered on your resumé. Don't be dismayed—use the repetitive question to expand and develop the information the interviewer is seeking. Try not to be distracted or worry about notes the interviewer is taking during the interview. It's usually a waste of energy to try to figure out if the interviewer likes you or did not agree with something you said.

Keep in mind that interviews vary from employer to employer. Interviews for public interest positions, for example, will likely be very different from interviews for private sector employers like law firms. During public interest interviews, in addition to finding out more about you as a candidate, the employer will assess your interest in and commitment to public interest. Be prepared to discuss your public interest experiences. Karen Sarjeant, a lawyer who has devoted her career to public interest work, offers this sound advice:

> *Being able to talk about your opportunities in law school in which you accumulated client contact experience is an important part of public interest interviewing. It is not the breadth of what you did that is important; it is what you learned from those experiences that the interviewer is most interested in as a way of learning about you.*

Karen J. Sarjeant, Vice President for Programs and Compliance, Legal Services Corporation

Preparing for a public interest interview can be a bit different from preparing for a private sector interview. Cybele Smith, Director of Public Service and Public Interest Programs at The Ohio State University Moritz College of Law, offers this preparation advice for public interest interviews:

Every employer wants to hire the best and brightest candidates for their organization. Students interviewing for public interest positions should be aware that even though some of these employers do not focus only on grades, public interest positions can be very competitive and highly sought after by the top graduates from many law schools. Employers interviewing for direct legal service positions tend to look for evidence of commitment to helping the community and the underserved. Candidates should be able to give examples of volunteer or work experience with the population that the agency serves. If students volunteered at a soup kitchen in college or coordinated a canned food drive in law school, this should be brought to light with employers whose mission is to help the homeless or feed the hungry. Your commitment to community service can be illustrated through enrollment in a law school legal clinic representing abused children or helping families fight eviction.

Your interview is also the time to highlight any activities you have done in your public interest law group or raising money for student-funded fellowships. Employers are aware that most law schools provide opportunities to do pro bono research or raise funds for fellowships. Be prepared to share your leadership experience and that you did take advantage of many opportunities to serve while in law school.

When applying for post-graduation fellowships, your materials and interview should highlight knowledge of your clients' legal issues as well as evidence that you have worked directly with such clients. A fellowship candidate for positions representing kids with disabilities who has, for instance, worked with children with autism is likely to interview more convincingly than a candidate who has merely taken a class on the topic. It cannot be overstated that organizations are looking to hire people who are passionate about helping their clients. Candidates should also focus on advocacy more than policy issues for legal positions.

At some point before the conclusion of the interview, the interviewer will probably ask if you have any questions for him/her. This portion of the interview can be very important. Most interviewers want to hear what kind of questions you ask and may judge the quality of your questions as part of their assessment of you as a candidate. As such, developing questions in advance is an important part of the preparation for each interview. Take the time to write out your questions ahead of time. It is fine to carry them with you for quick reference between interviews, but you should not refer to your notes during the interview itself. The questions you ask should reflect why you are interested in the employer and what you need to know about the employer to make an informed decision, should you be offered the job. You should not ask any questions that could have been answered by your research. For example, it would be a very poor question to ask a firm how many attorneys work at the firm or what practice areas they offer. That only serves to illustrate that you have not prepared or done your homework, and your question will be seen as a negative, showing a lack of interest in the employer on your part. If you're having a series of interviews with different lawyers at the same firm or organization, it's fine to ask some of the same questions to different people to get several interpretations. You can preface a repetitive question with, "Bob mentioned the pro bono opportunities he's had since joining the firm; can you tell me about yours?"

A Word About "Scripted Interviews"

Infrequently, you may be interviewed through a scripted interview format, in which employers provide their interviewers with a set of questions to ask. By giving the interviewer a script and instructing him or her not to deviate from it, the employer is attempting to minimize interviewer mistakes. This is most common in government interviews, but it could certainly happen with any employer. If you are in a scripted interview, it may not feel like the interview is going smoothly or favorably no matter how well you are doing. This is because in a regular interview, the interviewer will likely respond in some way when you answer a question. But in a scripted interview, there probably won't be any follow-up to what you have just said. The interviewer will simply read the next question on his or her script, and it will be unrelated to the previous question or your answer to it. As such, it has the potential to feel awkward and even uncomfortable at times.

If you understand the constraints the interviewer has in a scripted interview situation, you should be able to overcome the awkwardness. Simply answer the questions you are asked, using the same strategies you would in a non-scripted interview. Do not let the swift change of topic or questions throw you, and don't hold it against the interviewer if he or she appears less than friendly. Many law students have left a scripted interview feeling like they failed miserably, only to be pleasantly surprised with a job offer.

The Interview With a Meal

As if there wasn't enough to remember and juggle in an interview, sometimes you will be asked to interview over a meal, or a meal may be part of a longer interview schedule. With large firms, you may go to dinner the night before, have lunch with more junior associates on the day of your interview, or both. With other types of employers, you may be asked to meet over breakfast or lunch, to allow busy practicing attorneys to more easily fit the task of interviewing into their hectic days. Whatever the situation, eating while interviewing does not need to paralyze you with fear. But no matter how casual the meal setting feels, remember that it is still an interview. Ensure that your meal etiquette is up to snuff, and use excellent manners throughout the meal.

As the meal interview proceeds, follow all the same strategies when answering questions as in a regular interview. There may be more small talk over a meal, so take the opportunity to discuss your interest in the employer and your talking points as the meal proceeds.

Be mindful of the food you order—avoid difficult and messy food such as spaghetti, or food that requires you to eat with both of your hands, like a juicy cheeseburger. Nancy B. Rapoport, Gordon & Silver, Ltd. Professor of Law at the William S. Boyd School of Law, UNLV, recalls a particularly challenging mealtime moment in her job search:

> One firm (thankfully, one that had already offered me a job!) took me out to dinner at a Chinese restaurant, along with a few other law students in whom the firm was interested. Well, I managed to swallow a whole hot pepper during our dinnertime conversation, and I couldn't figure out a polite way to say, "Help! I've swallowed a hot pepper, and I think I'm going to die, right here, right now, if you don't rescue me!" I ended up draining glass after glass of water (which didn't really help), sweating profusely, and hoping that no one noticed. Lesson: Be engaged in the conversation, but watch what you eat.

When it comes to meals with potential employers, simple food is best—it allows you to concentrate on how to illustrate your skills rather than on how to get the next bite into your mouth without wearing it. Do not order an alcoholic drink during an interview meal, even if your host does. You have enough to concentrate on without adding alcohol to the mix. With a little practice, interview meals will become more comfortable and less daunting; and they are terrific practice for the business meals that will probably become a regular part of your professional life.

Interview Challenges and How to Overcome Them

As mentioned before, lawyers are generally not professional interviewers and, as such, may be lacking some skills in that area. You don't have to be the victim of a poor interviewer, however. If you come up against one, it is up to you to take charge and turn the situation into one that can benefit you. The lawyer who talks nonstop is a frequent interview challenge. He or she is so busy telling you about the firm or organization, or his or her practice, that you are asked few questions and can hardly get a word in edgewise. Usually, the lawyer is not doing this out of ego (although that is sometimes the case). More likely, he or she has been instructed to "sell" the firm or organization, or the interviewer hasn't been trained to ask insightful questions, so they will fall back on old standbys like, "Why did you go to law school?"

If you get an overly talkative interviewer, don't interrupt—that will only annoy him or her. Everyone has to pause for a breath now and again, and when that happens there are several strategies you can employ to get at least a few of your talking points across, albeit in an abbreviated fashion. The reality is, if a lawyer likes to talk that much, he or she will likely enjoy a good listener. But that doesn't mean being merely a passive receptacle—you can and should take a small role in the conversation.

For instance, if your interviewer is rambling on about his practice and how busy he is and why he hasn't had a chance to review your resumé before now, say something like, "Your practice sounds very busy—it must be exciting. My job at a law firm last summer helped me realize that I really thrive under pressure. What do you like best about your practice?" In this way, you have made two points—you obtained legal experience last summer, and you aren't afraid to work hard—and you've asked a question that allows the interviewer to continue talking, but now they might actually talk about something that will help you learn more about this potential employer. Another example would be if your interviewer, an alumna of your law school, is talking about her experiences in law school more than a decade ago. When she pauses for a breath, you might say, "I didn't like law school at first, but I've made a lot of friends through my involvement in the Business Law Student Group. I'm currently serving as the head of the subcommittee working on a corporate lawyers panel presentation. I'm really interested in your firm because of its strong corporate practice. What is a typical day like for you in your practice?"

Another challenge can be the interviewer who is not engaged in the interview. He or she might be checking the clock, looking at a BlackBerry, or making any number of gestures or body language movements that speaks more than the words he or she is saying. You may not be able to connect with such an interviewer, but it doesn't hurt to try. A good technique is to end your answer to a question by asking one about the interviewer. Most lawyers like to talk about themselves, so asking about their preferences, the biggest challenge in their practice, even what advice they have for you as a first-year/second-year law student or new lawyer has a chance of interesting the interviewer. If the interviewer seems abnormally distracted, you could ask if there is something wrong or if it would be better to reschedule the interview.

Finally, you may encounter an interviewer who asks one or more inappropriate questions, either inadvertently or with the intent of obtaining information that he or she is not legally allowed to consider in the employment process. You do not have to answer the question, though the rest of the interview might be uncomfortable if you abruptly refuse. Quickly decide how to handle the question. If you really don't want to answer it, consider trying to move to more appropriate material for the interview. If, for example, the interviewer asks if you intend to have children, you could answer the question, or you could elect to redirect the conversation. One answer might be, "Yes, I hope to have kids one day, but right now I'm really focused on completing law school and launching my legal career." Another equally appropriate answer would be, "That's not something I'm focused on right now— I'm really interested in launching my legal career, and I see that your agency offers the opportunity to appear in court almost immediately. Can you tell me a little about the training I can expect?" Finally, you would be well within your rights to answer very differently, although it may affect your rapport with the interviewer: "Whether or not I intend to have children doesn't have an impact on my ability to do this job. I have spent my time in law school honing my legal writing skills and learning litigation skills through moot court, trial practice, and the clinic I took last semester. What additional skills do you seek in a junior litigator?"

Questions about having children are not the only area about which you might get some inappropriate questions. In any number of innocuous or offensive ways you could be asked about your marital status, ethnicity, religious preference, disability status, political views, sexual orientation, or any other non-job-related qualities. The strategies for fielding such questions, regardless of the subject, remain the same. Please note: If you are interviewing on campus, most schools require employers who use their interviewing services to abide by the school's nondiscrimination policy. As such, any violations of your school's policy should be reported.

Although the balance of power in an interview is usually tipped in the interviewer's favor, you do need to realize that interviewing is a two-way street. You are there to sell yourself, first, and to find out of this is an employer for whom you could work, a close second. If the interviewer is adversarial, inappropriate, or seems unusually interested in non-job-related characteristics about you, it is perfectly fair to decide that this is not an employer worth pursuing. You are free to withdraw from consideration at any time, and in some cases, even though you do not yet have a job offer, it is definitely the right thing to do. If an employer cannot behave in the interview context, you have to wonder how you will be treated if you chose to work for him or her.

Professionalism Permeates the Interview Process

As you work to maintain your professionalism and maturity and keep up your efforts throughout the interview process, it is normal to become discouraged at points. Interviews can be hard work, and if you pour your heart and soul into the preparation, only to receive a cut letter, it is natural to feel disheartened. Usually, however, if you do not land a specific job, it probably wasn't the best match for you, and you just need to keep trying. Staying poised and positive in the face of adversity can be more challenging than showing maturity in the face of good fortune, but it is imperative that you remain professional throughout the interview process. If you let your discouragement, bitterness, or bad judgment interfere, it will likely cost you a job opportunity.

Avoid saying anything negative about anyone or anything during an interview. It cannot be overstated how small the legal community is, even in large cities. Too many law students make disparaging remarks about a former employer when asked why the left that job, or talk unkindly about a professor when asked about a low grade. Even if the interviewer does not know your former employer or professor, it reflects poorly on you to talk negatively about anyone. Often, the potential employer will put himself or herself in the shoes of the former employer and wonder if you would talk about him or her like that some day. If they do know your former employer or professor and like the person, your comments are even more detrimental. You cannot win by making negative statements about others, even if you believe them to be true. Sarah Staup, Director of Professional Personnel at Dykema Gossett PLLC, offers this important advice:

> Do not say the first thing you think of when asked your opinion. Use a filter when communicating during an interview and in the workplace. If asked what you think about the offices, do not comment upon how worn you found the carpeting on a particular floor. If asked where you see your career in five years, make sure the prospective employer fits into that vision in some way.

It is also important to be honest and accurate when you answer interview questions; it's no different from when you prepare your application materials. Do not overstate your experience, inflate your credentials, or otherwise exaggerate your skills and abilities during an interview. If you make a mistake or misstate something, correct it immediately. If you don't know the answer to a question, don't make it up or lie—that will only come back to haunt you. Here's what one legal recruiting manager has to say on this subject:

> One of my personal professionalism pet peeves involves recruits who lie—or perhaps more accurately, stretch the truth—for their own gain. They may try to "pull a fast one" on a recruiting manager by claiming they didn't know about a particular firm policy that is clearly spelled out in recruit-

ing materials or on a Web site. Or they may concoct a story for their supervising attorney about why they can't meet a particular deadline. Being professional means, among other things, being honest with yourself and your (potential) employer. Believe it or not, recruiting managers and attorneys have long memories. If you come across at all "slippery" during the recruiting or on-boarding process, they will remember that for years to come. One of the worst things you can do in your job search is earn a bad reputation even before you set foot inside your employer's door!

Skip Horne, Global Recruiting Manager, Diversity and Law School Outreach, Latham & Watkins LLP

Answering the Tough Questions

With a little practice, interviewing will become second nature, and you will feel that an interview is what it is meant to be: a two-way conversation for both the interviewer and the interviewee to explore fit for a position. You will do well to remember, particularly during challenging interviews, that an interview serves both you and your potential employer. You are not under any obligation to accept a job offer if you receive one—you should check out the potential employer as much as they are examining you. Although the balance of power is not even—as a law student or new lawyer, you probably need and want a job much more than the employer needs to hire you—you will benefit greatly from trying to make the best match possible in your job search. That's not to say that you should approach interviews with a bulging ego or act like a hot commodity. It is to say, however, that you will benefit from being confident, asking questions that are important to you, and working to achieve a power balance in the interview.

There are times when job options are limited or the job market is tight, and you may have to accept an offer that is far from your first choice. If this is the case, remember that the job you accept for the summer or post-graduation need not be the job you will keep for the rest of your life. You can make the most of the opportunity for a summer or year or two, and then laterally work your way into a different position. Your success in making strong lateral moves, though, will depend upon making the most of every opportunity, as well as building your network and feeding your contacts.

As you explore potential employers, you will get asked some tough interview questions from time to time. If you know a particular part of your resumé will be a focal point, don't be surprised if you're asked the same tough questions about it by multiple interviewers. Areas that typically draw scrutiny and exploration are law school grades, a class in which you received a particularly low grade, gaps in the dates on your resumé, unfinished degree programs, short lengths of employ (less than a year, not counting summer positions), and anything else that stands out as unusual on your resume. You should learn from each interview what provokes interest on your application, and develop strong answers to questions you expect to receive.

If your grades are not stellar or you face a similar challenge, work on an explanation that is not apologetic but acknowledges that you have not achieved your full potential, and mention what goal you are working toward. Talk about what you have learned from the challenging experience and what you are doing to change the situation. If you can point out steady improvement or a circumstance in your life that impacted your performance, be sure to do so, but briefly and not to the extent that you sound like you're making excuses. Accepting responsibility and showing that you have formulated a plan to overcome the difficulty is typically an approach that works well. The bottom line is, however, if an employer is focused on high grades and is going to disqualify you on the basis of your grades, there is nothing you can do about it. Employers for whom grades are important but aren't the determinative factor are more likely to appreciate your well-thought-out answer addressing the grade issue. Focus your efforts on employers whose hiring preferences are a fairly close match with your credentials, but don't be afraid to stretch and take chances with difficult-to-land jobs.

Although you won't be able to anticipate every interview question, expect to be asked common questions about why you went to law school, why you are interested in working with that employer, where you see yourself in five years, what is your greatest strength or weakness, and other questions that typically appear in interview books or guides. Additionally, look at your resumé with a critical eye to determine what items might draw attention and questions from employers. The more you have prepared and the more interviews you've been through, the more seasoned you will become at answering repeat questions, as well as unique ones, with complete confidence.

A longtime career counselor and former practicing lawyer offers this idea for one interview question you may receive:

"Where do you see yourself in five to ten years?" can be a challenging interview question. You may think that the obvious answer is, "as a shareholder/partner/section chief/supervising lawyer at [insert firm or organization name]." But that response may strike interviewers as fawning and disingenuous because they will assume that you'll simply change the firm's or organization's name depending on who is interviewing you. I recommend that you answer this question in terms of your broader professional and personal goals. Rather than reply in a specific employment context, talk in more expansive terms about professional achievements (e.g., "I want to be recognized as an expert in the legal community in which I'm working" or "I want to become a leader in bar and professional associations, a first-rate problem solver, and a respected advocate"). You also may want to refer to a neutral and interesting personal pursuit (e.g., "I will work hard at my legal career, but I also want to continue my involvement in community theatre/hone my tennis game/etc."). That shows that you are a whole person with both professional and personal dimensions.

Robert Kaplan, Associate Dean and Director of Externships, William & Mary School of Law

Another longtime career counselor addresses a different interview challenge:

One challenging interview question is:

"I see from your resumé that you are from (example, the South) and chose to go to college and law school there as well. Tell me what you know about life in (our city, not in the South) and the basis for your decision to establish your life and career here."

Anticipate this question, and provide information in your cover letter to increase the odds that you will be selected and allowed the opportunity to explain further in an interview! Mention family ties or friends there and past travel to the area. Show a working knowledge of the city's economic base and quality and cost of life there. Discuss why you selected

that employer, as well as that city, based on research about
their practice.

Dr. Karen Reagan Britton, Director of Admissions,
Financial Aid, and Career Services, University of Ten-
nessee College of Law

Approach your interviews with a sense of confidence and
purpose. If you tense up, become sweaty and flushed, and
start talking quickly whenever you get a challenging question, not only will you appear nervous and uncertain, your
body language and appearance will detract from even the
most proficient answers. When you are asked a challenging
question, remind yourself to take a deep breath, collect your
thoughts, and speak slowly and confidently as you respond.
Remember, there is nothing wrong with a bit of silence while
you collect your thoughts. Throughout the interview, sit up
straight, speak clearly and at a reasonable pace, and look the
interviewer(s) in the eye. Eye contact, gestures in response to
what the interviewer is saying, and genuine smiles will give
you an aura of confidence and pave the way for an interview
that both you and the interviewer will enjoy.

When Is It Okay to Cancel an Interview?

If you accept an interview, you have a duty to attend it.
The only circumstances in which it is acceptable to cancel an
interview are if you have received a job offer that you intend
to accept—in which case you must cancel the interview—or if
an emergency situation arises (such a death in your family)
that will prevent you from attending the interview. In almost
all other cases, you have an obligation to interview with a
potential employer with whom you have accepted an interview. Sometimes when students begin their job search, they
target multiple cities and then settle in on a particular
geographic area. If you have accepted an interview with a
potential employer in a region that you are no longer target-
ing, you may call to explain the situation, and let the employer decide whether or not to cancel the interview. Let them
know you will be happy to honor your commitment to interview if they want you to, but you are more focused on
another city now. Because different employers have different
views about situations like this, it is best to let the employer
make the call. The employer can then decide if they want to
try to convince you of the merits of their city and place of
employment, or if they would rather focus their efforts on
someone who is more interested in that region. An experi-

enced recruiter confirms that she wants to know if you are no longer interested:

> If a candidate decides to join another firm or go to a different city, it is best that additional callbacks with other firms be cancelled so no one's time is wasted—including the candidate's, the attorneys' who would be interviewing the candidate, the recruiting staff who would be preparing the interview schedule and subsequent evaluations of the candidate, and the recruiting committee who would be discussing whether or not to extend an offer to the candidate. This applies even if a plane ticket has already been purchased for a call-back interview with another firm(s). The cost of a plane ticket is less expensive then the value of the time of all those involved in a candidate's interview with a firm. Also, in any of these situations, the firm will then have an opportunity to extend an additional callback to another student who might not otherwise have had that callback opportunity.

Nancy Berry, Director of Firmwide Recruiting, McDermott, Will & Emery LLP

Do not accept interviews lightly—if you accept an interview, you are making a commitment to a potential employer. Your intention should be to honor that commitment. If a prospective employer has incurred expense on your behalf for an interview that you cancel, professionalism dictates that you offer to reimburse those expenses. If you have doubts, do not accept the interview, so the employer can focus on candidates who are sure.

After the Interview

As the interview draws to a close, it is fine to ask when you can expect to hear from the potential employer. As you prepare to leave, thank the interviewer for his or her time (and ask that your thanks and appreciation be extended to anyone else who was involved in arranging the interview). Even if you do not intend to pursue employment with that particular employer, or you did not enjoy the interview, you should still thank your interviewer for taking the time to meet with you, and appear gracious and confident to the end.

Immediately after you leave the interview, jot down a few notes that will assist you in writing a personalized thank you note. If you have multiple interviews in one day, spend some "downtime" between interviews jotting down such notes—otherwise the people and interviews may begin to blend in your memory, and you will have a more difficult time recalling specifics.

If the interviewer asked for any information or materials that you did not have with you at the interview, follow up promptly to provide it—either the same day or the next day is preferred. Thank you notes should be sent following the guidelines provided in Chapter Six, and they should be sent within twenty-four hours, if possible. Again, it is important to thank an interviewer for his or her time with a note, even if you do not intend to pursue the opportunity or you did not enjoy the interview. This is a common courtesy that should be followed—even if it has no bearing on whether you will receive a job offer. However, ensure that your thank you notes are well written and error-free, so they will not eliminate you from consideration.

After the Job Offer

If all your hard work and preparation pays off, and a potential employer in whom you are interested contacts you with a job offer, you may get so excited that you forget to ask critical questions. No matter how interested you are in the position, you should respond enthusiastically to an offer of employment when it is tendered. Typically, a job offer will first be made in a phone call, then followed by a written offer of employment; increasingly, the written offers are transmitted via e-mail in place of, or in addition to, snail mail. The offer letter usually spells out all the terms, as well as any contingencies, of the offer. One common contingency is the successful completion of a background check, and if you are a practicing lawyer, another contingency will be the clearing of any potential client conflicts.

When the exciting phone call arrives and the offer is tendered, thank the potential employer for the job offer, and express your pleasure at receiving it. If he or she does not indicate the terms or mention that an offer letter will be forthcoming, ask if you can expect a written offer of employment that outlines the terms. Before you complete the offer conversation, confirm the date by which you must answer the offer. Some offers are governed by the NALP Guidelines' General Standards for the Timing of Offers and Decisions ("NALP Guidelines"). NALP was founded as the National Association for Law Placement and is now simply known by its acronym. See Part V, available under the "Principles & Standards" tab at www.NALP.org. James G. Leipold, Executive Director of NALP, explains the rationale underlying the NALP Guidelines:

> *NALP's timing guidelines form the foundation for the legal hiring process for law students. They provide clear guidelines and expectations for all of the parties involved...employers, law school job candidates, and law schools themselves. The guidelines strike a balance between student candidates' interest in having ample time in which to make informed decisions and employers' interest in managing their hiring programs. This balance is achieved by allowing students 45 days during which to accept an offer of employment.*

If the offer is governed by the NALP Guidelines, it is fine for you to confirm that the offer will remain open in accordance with the Guidelines. The exact date the offer expires will be determined by the date of your offer letter.

The NALP Guidelines typically apply to larger employers who are NALP members, but the Guidelines can be a useful resource for most offer-and-decision situations. If an employer is not a NALP member and does not abide by the NALP guidelines, you will need to respond within the timeframe provided by the employer. If the employer is a NALP member and you foresee a possible violation of the Guidelines, consult with your career services office immediately for instruction and guidance.

Sometimes smaller employers will need an answer quickly and may pressure you for a response almost contemporaneously with the offer. Because smaller employers hire on an as-needed basis, they cannot afford to keep offers open for long periods of time. If you are not going to accept the offer, they need to be able to make an offer to their second-choice candidate in a short time frame. Rather than getting frustrated with these time-sensitive situations, try to understand the position that the employer is in—he or she does not have multiple openings and, thus, can only make an offer to one candidate at a time. Contrast that to larger employers who can afford to make multiple offers at once to fill multiple positions and manage the process through historical yield rates.

As often happens with smaller employers, you may receive a job offer when you have one or two more interviews pending in the next week or two, but the employer tendering the offer would like a response sooner than that. The decision becomes even more complicated if the interviews that are pending are with employers you would prefer to work for. There are a number of ways you can address this situation. Explain to the employer making the offer that you have committed to an interview the following week, and you would like to follow through with that commitment and attend the interview. Additionally, the NALP Guidelines offer useful, but not binding, information that such offers from smaller employers should be left open for at least two weeks. Ask if it would be possible to delay the offer response for two weeks in accordance with the NALP Guidelines, or until after your scheduled interview.

If the employer is able to grant you more time, you will have the opportunity to interview with the other employer and explore whether it might be a good fit. Do not be surprised, however, if a small firm that infrequently hires is not persuaded by the NALP Guidelines, and the employer does not feel compelled to give you two full weeks. In that case, contact the second employer with whom you have an interview scheduled, explain that you have a job offer with a short response time, and ask if you can move up the scheduling of your interview. If they are interested in you, they will try to be accommodating. This strategy can also work with employers to whom you have applied but who have not yet called you for an interview.

If you receive an offer and are still waiting to hear from other employers with whom you have interviewed, immediately contact those other employers to alert them that you have an offer. If you have a deadline to respond to the offer, indicate that deadline. If you are contacting an employer with whom you'd rather work, it can be powerful to say, "I have received a job offer that I need to respond to by next Tuesday. You are my first-choice employer, though, so I wanted to let you know about this offer. If I don't hear from you, I will accept this other offer next Tuesday." Employers understand that you need to respond to a viable offer— especially if they are not in a position to make you an offer. If the employer is interested in you, he or she will try to get an offer to you by the deadline, if possible. It is fair and wise for you to explore all your options before you accept the pending offer.

Despite your best efforts to work with all your potential employers, you may be forced to decide about a job offer so quickly that you don't have time to explore other pending options. If that happens, there are many variables to consider. First, conventional wisdom advises, particularly if the current job market is tight, that an actual offer in hand is worth much more than any "potential" offers that may or may not materialize. As such, unless you have some real concerns about the employer, the terms, or the experience you will gain there, the scales tip in favor of accepting the offer you have received. Before you accept or turn down an offer, consider the following factors: your long-term goals; the likelihood of receiving another offer, particularly if this is for summer employment and the start of summer is drawing near; your backup plan if another offer is not forthcoming; the career-development potential of the offer you have received; and any concerns about or drawbacks of the current offer. Even if the offer is not with your first-choice employer, if it is a viable and sound offer, give it due consideration and think hard before turning it down.

Regardless of the type of employer who makes you an offer, your actions throughout the offer and decision process should reflect the highest standards of professionalism and ethics. It is fine to negotiate terms with some employers and to alert other potential employers with whom you have interviewed that you've received an offer. However, you should not play one employer against another or tell more than one employer that they are your first choice.

Regardless of whether or not the NALP Guidelines govern a particular offer you receive, the key to success is to maintain strong communication with all your potential employers. Do not stop communicating with them and do not fail to respond within the offer deadlines you are given. Although offers to which you do not respond by the deadline (either to accept, decline, or request an extension) are considered to have expired, non-response is not a professional way to decline an offer, and most employers will note your lack of follow-up. Professionalism also dictates that you release an offer as soon as you know you do not intend to accept it. Employers need to move on to other viable candidates if you do not intend to accept, so do not keep them waiting any longer than necessary. One of the big complaints that large law firms have had recently is about the number of students who fail to respond to an offer of employment one way or the other. Although it becomes obvious at some point that a student does not intend to accept the offer, employers have to keep the offer open until the deadline expires, absent a student withdrawing. Failing to respond in any way is unprofessional and keeps the employer from making offers to other candidates until the expiration date. It is not something that employers forget—burning such bridges as a law student can come back to haunt you when you are trying to make a lateral move a few years into your career. Don't make that mistake—hiring lawyers and recruiters will remember your lapse in professionalism.

It is good practice and form to reaffirm in writing an offer you receive, to indicate that you are holding the offer open and that you will respond by the expiration date. If you immediately accept an offer of employment, follow a verbal acceptance with a written one. Take the time you need to make a good decision—you are entitled to do that—but once your decision is made, you must notify all other employers who have made offers that you are "off the market." Failing to do so is not only unfair and potentially troublesome for the employers, it may even keep a classmate or colleague of yours from receiving an offer and may impact negatively an employer's hiring. Further, if you have interviewed with other employers that have not yet responded to you, contact them to withdraw from consideration. It is your responsibility to alert anyone with whom you've had contact, beyond the mere mailing of an application, that you are no longer seeking employment.

To Negotiate or Not

If you receive an offer of employment and the terms are less than what you had hoped, it is sometimes acceptable to negotiate. It is not acceptable to ask about offer terms, rate of pay, or benefits in an interview situation—all of that information is appropriately requested at the offer stage. As such, you may discover at the offer stage that the offer is lower than you had anticipated—or than you can afford to consider. If that is the case, decide if this is an employer with whom you can negotiate. Large law firms with set starting salaries and benefit packages are non-negotiable, as are some government positions. Public interest organizations working with very limited funding offer limited negotiation opportunities, as well. Other employers, however, particularly those that do limited, infrequent hiring, may just be a bit out of step with current compensation levels. They may start with a lower offer, expecting that you will negotiate, or they may truly only have a certain amount of funds with which to hire a new lawyer.

The first step in negotiating the terms of an offer of employment is understanding what all the terms are. You need to know more than the salary and basic benefits—take the time to understand all the benefits, including retirement benefits, and the cost of each. Benefits relating to parking, bar expenses, annual fees, CLE-required courses, maternity or paternity leave, health insurance, contributions toward retirement, and vesting provisions, along with which benefits are "pre-tax," all add to the value of the offer you have received.

After you understand everything that is included in the compensation package you have been offered, the next step is to gather as much market information as possible. Your career services office most likely maintains salary information for recent graduates at various types of employers, so that can be a great source of comparable market information. Also check salary information published by NALP. Finally, your state or local bar association may have publications that contain recent salary information for legal employers in your market. If you are able to obtain compelling market data, that can be an effective negotiation tool. Even if you are unable to obtain good market data for your particular offer, you can negotiate effectively.

If you simply cannot or will not accept the position at the salary and benefit level offered to you, it is a little easier to negotiate, and you can be more direct in your communications to the potential employer. If you would like to accept the position anyway, but you feel the salary and benefit package is low, you probably don't want to back yourself into a corner from which you cannot escape as you negotiate. The key to successful negotiating often lies with being creative in your approach in either instance.

When you cannot or will not accept the current offer, you might indicate to the employer that you appreciate the offer, but it is considerably lower than you were expecting, especially given the market information you have gathered. If you have a figure in mind below which you cannot go, present an acceptable salary range to the employer, and add that the final figure will be dependent upon the total package. In the case where you'd like to accept the job, you can indicate that, but say that you need to explore the employer's flexibility with the offer. In either case, the salary figure is not your only negotiating tool, and often you can successfully negotiate on multiple fronts to arrive at a total package with which you and the employer are comfortable. It helps to know what the potential employer's needs are, too, so if he or she provides an explanation about the salary figure, listen carefully. It could be that there are equity issues with current employees, that they are straining to add another person, so the employer wants to be sure this position will pay for itself, or that they simply do not understand what it costs to hire a new lawyer in the current market. Obtain as much information as you can about the circumstances, and use that information to negotiate.

For example, if salary equity issues are a concern with existing employees, you can ask for a number of benefits that the employer possibly hadn't considered. If they're willing to cover your monthly parking fees, CLE expenses, bar dues, and association memberships, for example, these are all items that cost new lawyers money. You will have more money in your pocket without the employer raising the actual salary amount. Another approach, if the employer is unwilling or unable to increase the salary, is to offer to share the risk an employer is taking on an untried junior lawyer by negotiating an annual bonus amount based on specified performance criteria, or an annual retirement contribution. You can also negotiate set income jumps in the short term that result in expanding your income in a shorter period of time, and such increases could be contingent upon you producing certain agreed-upon results.

For example, you might negotiate $10,000 in additional salary from an employer off the top. If that doesn't work, you might negotiate payment of various benefits or expenses that would otherwise total $10,000. You could also negotiate

$4,000 more in salary immediately, with an additional $3,500 raise in six months and another increase of $3,500 at nine months, assuming you are performing at the expected levels. Finally, you could negotiate a performance bonus or a contribution to your retirement account of $10,000 at the end of one year. In any of these scenarios, you have successfully negotiated your salary, although an employer may react much more positively to some requests than others. Your success will depend on meeting the employer's needs as well as your own.

After Acceptance, Reneging Is Not an Option

Plan your negotiations, if applicable, and consider your options carefully before accepting a job offer. Once you accept, you cannot renege, period. Never take a job because it is the only one you have been offered, with the intent of continuing to interview in the hopes that something better will come along. As a professional, you must honor your commitments, including those you make to a potential employer. Unless you have an emergency situation that interferes with your ability to follow through on a job, or other compelling and extenuating circumstances, you should honor your commitments—all of them.

Robert Kaplan, Associate Dean and Director of Externships at William & Mary School of Law, has twenty-two years of experience counseling students through a variety of employment situations. He offers this advice:

> Consider this hypothetical #1: Employer A offers you a job, and you accept. Six weeks later, Employer B, which is your top choice, offers you a job. Is it OK to accept Employer B's offer and notify Employer A that you have changed your mind? Now, consider this hypothetical #2: You accept Employer A's offer. Six weeks later, Employer A calls to tell you that the organization has met a new candidate and will rescind your offer in favor of the new candidate. Is that OK? Of course not. You would, I imagine, be outraged (and justifiably so) that an employer would behave that way. Hypotheticals 1 and 2 are quite similar, however, because both situations involve unprofessional conduct. In the first case, the employer has selected you and, based on your acceptance, likely has released other candidates. In the second situation, Employer A has pulled the rug out from under you after you have turned down other opportunities. The bottom

*line: Always treat employers in the same professional manner
in which you want to be treated.*

Take the time to negotiate the best package you can, and
explore all your options before accepting a job offer. Once you
accept, put other possibilities out of your mind, and plan to
work hard and gain great experience while providing value to
your employer, even if you do not intend to stay with that
employer throughout your career.

Chapter Ten

On the Clock: Your First Summer Internship or Summer Associate Position

Landing your first summer position was a job in and of itself, no doubt about it, but now that you have the job, you want to make a positive impression on your employer. Prior to your start date, you will probably receive employment and preference forms to complete. The paperwork might also include a background check form or security clearance form. Follow all instructions you receive from your new employer to the letter, fill out all paperwork completely and accurately, and respond in advance of any deadlines you are given. Your relationship will not get off to a good start if your employer has to pester you for necessary paperwork.

If your new employer requests a picture of you for its Web site, a publication announcing new interns, or any other reason, submit a photograph in which you are wearing professional business attire and situated against a plain background. It's not good to have a casual, informal, or unprofessional photograph of you circulating before you have even started the job. You need to be taken seriously and respected—it is imperative that you start out on the right note with a strong professional image.

Orientation and Policies

When you arrive at your new job, you will most likely have an orientation—it might be a formal orientation, if the employer has a number of interns or summer associates starting at once, or it might be an informal meeting. Regardless of the type of orientation, the material presented will be rather dry, but it is information you need to know and should retain in a safe place. Learn all your new employer's policies; if the information is not forthcoming in an orientation session, inquire about them. Policies may govern computer/technology use, investments, harassment, conflicts-checking procedures, accepting gifts or items of value, work products, and other items or situations. Any existing policies that govern the behavior of employees should be easily accessible. You need to have a working knowledge of all such policies so you do not inadvertently violate one. Ignorance is not an excuse for a violation, so take the time to learn those policies.

The other part of your orientation will likely include a fair number of introductions to other employees, including your peer interns (if you're at a larger firm or organization) and your supervisor(s), if you haven't met them previously. Approach each introduction as if it was the most important one of the day. Smile, look the person in the eyes, and repeat his or her name. It will take a little while to commit everyone's name to memory, but try hard to remember key people you meet in the first days on your new job. Concentrate on making a professional and friendly first impression with everyone you meet, including mail clerks and cleaning staff. It is a small world, you have a short time to make a lasting impression, and you need all the friends you can get in a new job. Do not squander potential contacts and allies by thinking you are too good to be nice to everyone.

Confidentiality

A lawyer's stock-in-trade is keeping client confidentiality, so when you work for any legal employer, you must keep all such information confidential. Although that seems like a basic concept, it is easy to inadvertently violate this rule. You need to be on guard at all times—particularly in public places. It is all too easy to discuss details of a case with a colleague on an airplane or other public place, not realizing that you are being overheard. You never know who might be listening to a conversation you think is private. As a general rule, avoid discussions of any client issues or other confidential matters when you are in any public place. This is true when you are talking on a cell phone, as well. It's easy to get caught up in a phone conversation and not realize that your side of the dialogue is drawing avid listeners. You must be on guard at all times against inadvertently violating client confidentiality. As one seasoned recruiter advises:

> When it comes to maintaining confidentiality, bear in mind that you never know who is listening or whom they know. Stories of indiscreet conversations on buses, trains, and elevators abound, but don't forget about the dangers in talking about work while running errands, meeting a friend for dinner, or even watching your children play at a park.

Morgan L. Smith, Assistant Director of Attorney Development and Recruitment, Mayer Brown LLP

The same is true in discussions with your classmates, family, or friends. Although it's tempting to tell them the juicy details about an exciting case at work, you should avoid doing so. You may be used to discussing classroom hypotheticals with your peers and calling on them for help when you are stuck, and it may be tempting to do so in a work situation. It's fine to get some input on a research strategy if you talk in generalities, but be careful not to provide any client-identifying or client-specific information.

Work Assignments—A Recipe for Success

Obtaining your first real work assignment is exciting and sometimes daunting. You want to make the most of every opportunity you are given during your internship, and the work assignments you receive are the bread-and-butter of your time with this employer. Whether you are trying to obtain valuable experience and an excellent reference for use in your post-graduate job search, or the summer position you have can actually lead to a post-graduate offer of employment, you do not want to squander any opportunity to learn, to impress, or to polish your legal and professional skills.

When you receive your first assignment, listen carefully, take thorough notes that will help you remember key points later, and ensure that you understand exactly what you are being asked to do. Sometimes, because a summer intern does not want to look confused or seem "stupid," he or she will refrain from asking questions as the assignment is being given. But it's better to ask clarifying questions than to spend a lot of time and energy on a work product that is not what the lawyer requested or wanted. Thus, it is your job to ask appropriate questions as the assignment is being given.

At a minimum, when you are given an assignment, you will want to know what finished work product is required and when it is due. If the lawyer wants you to report your research verbally, you do not want to spend time drafting a full-blown memorandum. On the other hand, if the lawyer wants a section of a brief drafted, you do not want to draft an internal memorandum, and so on. Repeat to the assigning attorney both the deadline and what form the finished product should take. If it's a long-term or very large assignment, ask about interim check-in points—does the assigning attorney want occasional status reports, and if so, in what form? Asking these questions will help you meet the exact needs of the assigning attorney. And, because every lawyer has different work styles and preferences, don't assume that you know this particular attorney's preferences until you have worked together. It is also smart to ask if there are similar work product items that you can review. This way, you can save time and avoid re-creating the wheel with your assignment, and you can get a sense of the form and layout this particular employer or assigning attorney uses and prefers. So, if you are asked to draft a Motion to Dismiss, for example, you can certainly ask if anyone has done something similar that you can review.

Meeting Your Commitments With Your Assignments

Although no intern wants to overextend himself or herself, it is easy to do if multiple people are giving you assignments. If you are having trouble prioritizing, seek help immediately from your mentor or supervising attorney. You absolutely must meet the commitments you make. Too many summer interns view the deadline given as a "soft" deadline, and that is simply not the case. You will be expected to meet or exceed the deadline given, and you should plan accordingly. If you are running into unanticipated difficulties with an assignment, let the assigning attorney know the status and what roadblocks you have hit so that he or she can move you in a new direction or extend the deadline to cover the unexpected delays.

Conversely, if you are low on work or do not feel that you are getting "meaty" assignments, seek more projects—enough to fill your days and to introduce you to a variety of decision-makers within the firm or organization. It is especially important during a summer position that you appear willing to try a variety of assignments in different areas. Although you may think you know exactly what you want to do when you are practicing, it is not unusual for an interesting assignment to open your eyes to a practice area you have not previously considered, or for you to find that you enjoy working in an area even though you disliked the class you took in that subject. Keep your mind and your options open, and show flexibility and a "can-do" attitude toward your summer employer.

Summer Job Quick Tips from an Employer

- Be reliable. Be curious. Meet your deadlines.

- In every office, there are those projects that the staff always wants to do but never get " 'round-to-it." Many of these projects ultimately will help increase the efficiency of some aspect of the office's work. Keep your eyes and ears open for those projects—many are related to how to use the current office technology in ways that allow tasks to be done more efficiently. Show your supervisor a sample of what you can do on such a project, while continuing to do what has been assigned to you. He or she will be impressed with your initiative and you will be using your skills in ways that make your efforts stand out.

- Be aware of and steer clear of office politics. Do not carry office gossip. A summer position is not the time to choose sides on a long-standing office issue. You do not know the full history, and it is not your responsibility. Leave it alone (unless it is discriminatory or otherwise illegal, and then let your supervisor know). There is no win here for your involvement.

- If your work assignments are not challenging, do them well and on time. Then don't be shy about asking for more. Let your supervisor know that you want to learn as much as you can in the time you will be in the position. Supervisors love initiative!

- Work to impress. Do not imitate poor work habits that you observe in others—if everyone tends to come in late and leave early, you come in on time and work your full schedule. Work to impress.

Karen J. Sarjeant, Vice President for Programs and Compliance, Legal Services Corporation

Know Where to Turn for Help

One of the tasks that should be at the top of your list as you start with your new employer is to develop a support network, and learn whom you can turn to for help and advice. Many employers will assign a mentor, buddy, or coach who is different from the supervising attorney to summer interns. The idea is to give you a source of informal advice and assistance and to provide someone to talk with about issues you may not be comfortable raising with your supervising attorney. If you are given such a support mechanism, take advantage of it, and get to know your mentor or coach. However, you need to guard against becoming too vocal or casual with this person. Although he or she is there to help you, that person will most likely weigh in on your evaluations and have a say in whether you should be extended a postgraduate offer, if that is an option. As such, you do not want to appear negative, down on your position, or otherwise ungrateful, nor do you want to appear unprofessional in any way. You can and should use this person to help you better understand the expectations in that environment, the preferences of your supervising attorney, and how to navigate the political currents inherent in any organization.

If your employer does not assign such a coach or mentor, or you do not click well with your assigned mentor, all is not lost. You should work to cultivate a less formally assigned but similarly helpful relationship with anyone with whom you are comfortable in the environment. It might be the person who initially interviewed you, a junior lawyer who remembers what it's like to be in your shoes, or someone with whom you have a lot in common. Whatever the source/s, build and strengthen those helpful relationships, even over a summer.

No matter how long you're at a job, you will benefit greatly from having a strong and helpful network in place to help you navigate the environment.

Feedback—Getting the Information You Need

Unfortunately, many lawyers are so busy that they do not take the time to provide critical and helpful feedback to law clerks and interns. Just as most lawyers are not skilled interviewers, they are also not proficient managers and supervisors. Some of them struggle with giving critical feedback in a constructive way or approaching a difficult conversation at all. The bottom line, though, is that you need feedback—whether it's good, bad, or downright ugly. If you have strayed off-course on a research assignment, you need to know that and understand how and why so you won't repeat that mistake on the next assignment.

If you have a supervising or assigning attorney who is all too eager to provide feedback, to the point that it appears a red pen had a nasty leak on your work product, you should still work to appreciate what they have to say. It's never fun to have your work torn apart, but you need to re-adjust your feelings about such an experience. First, try to remember that it is rare and valuable to obtain unsolicited feedback, and appreciate the time the attorney took to provide the comments. Most busy lawyers won't spend time training someone if they don't like them or aren't interested in them, so view their feedback as a commitment to you and your success. Second, getting defensive will not help you gain anything from the experience. You are a junior law clerk with a lot to learn, so you might as well get used to having your work critiqued. Make every effort to listen openly and with a good attitude to all the feedback you are given. Then try to use that feedback to make your next work product stronger.

When it comes to writing assignments, there are many different styles of writing, and each seasoned lawyer has developed his or her own preferences in that regard. So, it would not be unusual for one lawyer who critiques your work to make a change, only to have the next lawyer who critiques your work change it back. That's a fact of life when you live and work among wordsmiths who make their living parsing out words and phrases. You need to differentiate between mere stylistic changes to your work and substantive suggestions to improve the work product. All are important to consider—you are still developing your own style and can benefit from feedback that helps you better organize and communicate your analysis and conclusions. But the reality is that as you work more frequently with various lawyers, you will begin to understand their style preferences and fashion your work accordingly. The written product you produce for one lawyer may differ from the product you produce for another. You will become adept at meeting the needs of your assigning attorneys over time, and you will strengthen your writing and develop your own personal style preferences in the process.

More troubling than stylistic preferences, however, is any feedback that points out unsupported conclusions you have drawn, faulty analysis, inaccurate or incomplete research, and other such substantive mistakes. If you obtain such feedback, retrace your steps to determine where you went wrong, why you veered off course, and how you can change that. Did you skip an important step in the research process? Did you not read a case closely enough? Did you misunderstand the initial instructions from the supervising attorney? Was the material so complex that you did not understand it, yet you didn't take the time to read some background material to help you better comprehend the issues? Whatever your errors, learn from them, and make sure you don't repeat them.

If you do not receive any feedback on your assignments, conventional wisdom is that "no news is good news." That could be the case, but it won't do you any long-term favors to make that assumption. Try to obtain some feedback from the assigning attorney, even if he or she generally liked your work—ask if you can have a fifteen-minute meeting to get his or her feedback on the assignment, including any suggestions to improve your work for the next time. If the attorney will not meet with you, don't press the issue, but those situations will be rare. Generally, an attorney will take a few minutes to give you feedback, and most will be impressed by your commitment to improve your work. Even if your writing assignment was strong, there are likely a few ways you can enhance and develop your work, and it's good to hear those ideas so you continually strengthen your skills.

Billing and Accounting for Time

Whether you are working in the private sector and have to account for your time in six-, ten-, or fifteen-minute increments for purposes of billing clients, or you are in the public sector and must account for the time you spend on various matters, timekeeping can one of the most annoying, yet necessary, parts of practicing law. As an intern or newer lawyer, everyone understands that it will take you longer to do various tasks than it would for a seasoned lawyer. Supervising lawyers know that you are learning the basics of accounting for your time—it's a very different procedure from any "clocking-in" you might have done at previous jobs.

If your employer offers any training about billing or accounting for your time, be sure to attend. Employers use different systems, procedures, and software to bill and/or account for time, and even if you know how to account for your time, it pays to know your new employer's particular policies. Here's some great advice about billing time:

Listen carefully and take notes during the portion of your orientation that covers time billing procedures. Obtain any written guidelines that are available, including guidelines that certain clients may have provided to the firm. Many clients no longer allow block billing and instead want every separate piece of work delineated on the bill. Talk to the assigning attorney about client preferences (i.e. should you combine all interoffice conferences into "researching motion to compel?"). Some clients will not pay for certain tasks. It's also helpful to talk to your secretary and junior associates to see what they recommend when you have questions.

Sarah Staup, Director of Professional Personnel, Dykema Gossett PLLC

Regardless of where you work, there are some general rules to keep in mind as you keep track of your time. First, ensure that your time entries are accurate. Track your time every day, and if you are billing time in fractional hour increments, it's helpful to take notes throughout the day if you do not have an automatic time-billing software program. Filling time in later will lead to mistakes and inaccuracies. If you don't believe that to be true, try to write down in fifteen-minute increments exactly how you spent your time a week ago today. Although you might remember all the major activities, you will quickly find that there are gaps and won't recall exactly how much time you spent on each item. You cannot afford those gaps and inaccuracies when it comes to accounting for billable time, so keep track each day as you're doing the work.

A second rule of thumb is that you should not under-report the amount of time you spend on a project or matter. Sometimes you will feel like you've spent way too much time on an assignment, but it is important to report all the time you spent. If the time will be billed to a client, the billing attorney will make appropriate adjustments to the amount. If you went in a wrong direction on a project that wasted several hours of time, discuss it with your supervising or assigning attorney; chances are, they will still want you to report the time you spent, even if it was not fruitful.

> *It is a summer associate's or intern's job to accurately record time spent on a matter and the supervising or billing attorney's responsibility to decide how to reflect it on a client bill. Most lawyers will confirm that keeping track of your time on an ongoing basis is the most effective and true way to monitor time spent on a matter. Trying to re-create time afterward leads to under- or over-recording.*

Morgan L. Smith, Assistant Director of Attorney Development and Recruitment, Mayer Brown LLP

A third general rule to follow is to make your entries sufficiently detailed. Even if you are reporting time for your supervisor, not for billing a client, you will want to justify the time you have spent working on a project or assignment. Be specific about the research you undertook, the meetings you attended, the drafting you did, and so on. Detailed entries will help your supervisors understand what you are doing, what kind of support you might need, and, if the time is to be billed to a client, what an appropriate final accounting to the client should be.

Finally, when it comes to recording and accounting for time, professionalism and ethics dictate that you are accurate in your time entries. Do not exaggerate time spent on a client matter, do not round up from five to fifteen minutes, and do not double bill the same time period or task to more than one client or matter. Regardless of the venue in which you work (private or public sector) and whether the time accounting is for a client or for internal purposes, your time entries must be truthful and ethical. Do not make a serious mistake on this important task.

A Word About Summer Social Events

Large law firm summer programs often provide a variety of social activities, including one or more "headline" events, throughout the summer. Other internship opportunities may not have any planned social events, or they may offer a scaled-down version of the events for which large firms are known. It would not be unusual for you to be invited to a dinner, a sports outing, or for drinks after work, even if your employer does not have a formal event calendar. In most cases, attendance at these events is not mandatory, and your job opportunities will not depend on whether or not you go. However, bad behavior at such an event could damage your job prospects.

For most employers, social activities of any kind are offered for the purpose of getting to know you and letting you interact with your colleagues and peers in a less-formal setting than the office. Unfortunately, too many summer interns forget that such events are not the same as a party with friends. As with any business dinner or event, avoid becoming too casual and drinking too much. If you are fortunate enough to be invited to a variety of social events over the summer, make the most of the opportunities to meet people you don't normally interact with during the workday, such as attorneys who may not be able to assign you any work over the summer. Break out of your comfort zone to circulate and talk to different people at these events.

If you are on an overnight trip or retreat with your summer employer, all the same rules apply. Do not show up at events or meals hung over from partying the night before. Social work events are not an invitation to act like professionalism and ethics can be checked at the door. They are still—ultimately—*work* events, and you will be watched closely. Most employers will not take kindly to unprofessional behavior. (The same is true for any workday at the office— never show up suffering from a hangover.)

If you are in an environment in which late-night partying is common and the attorneys drink heavily, do not feel pressured to keep up with them. Nursing a single beverage or switching to nonalcoholic drinks will get you through an event with your professionalism and dignity intact. If people are drinking excessively, and the conversation starts to disintegrate into inappropriate or crude topics, excuse yourself and leave the party. Even if you are not drinking heavily or adding to an inappropriate conversation, you will be associated with the fallout if things go south, and you do not want to have a tainted reputation. Many summer interns have lost respect at best, and their job at worst, after drinking too much at work functions. Respond to any late-night invitations with caution, and select your companions carefully. As one law firm employer says:

> My mother always said, "less is more" and "you are known by the company you keep." These are words to live by. While you don't want to be anti-social, you also don't want to wind up with your hand in the dip up to your elbow or a lampshade on your head. Eat and drink in moderation. Take small portions of food so as not to interfere with talking to others at the gathering, and limit the amount of alcohol consumption to avoid being the subject of conversation over coffee the next morning.

Gayle P. Englert, Director of Human Resources, Cole, Schotz, Meisel, Forman & Leonard P.A.

Don't be a "lemming" and blindly follow a group into a troublesome situation. Think long term, and act accordingly.

Communicating Effectively

Your summer internship will be more successful if you communicate frequently and appropriately with those who need to know about your work and how you are faring in your position. First and foremost, communicate regularly with your supervising attorney as well as any mentors, coaches, or junior attorneys to whom you have been assigned. Regardless of your personal feelings about these people, good or bad, keep them in the loop about the work you are doing, the feedback you have obtained, and any challenges you are facing. Here's some great advice about communicating with other lawyers:

> One of the issues with summer and fall associates I have noticed is premature informality. I don't mean that partners or supervising lawyers need to be addressed as Mr. or Ms., but rather that a certain level of professional formality should be used until a relationship develops and it is clear that a

more casual tone would be appropriate. It is the new lawyer who should adjust to the senior lawyer's style.

Morgan L. Smith, Assistant Director of Attorney Development and Recruitment, Mayer Brown LLP

Another recruiting professional adds this caution about your communication style and attitude during the summer:

> *Be positive in all of your communications during the summer program. While it may be okay to commiserate with alumni of your school about a nutty professor, it is not okay to bemoan the cheapness, unfairness or lack of appreciation experienced at a former employer.*

Sarah Staup, Director of Professional Personnel, Dykema Gossett PLLC

When you begin your internship, find out how your supervising attorney and others prefer to communicate. Some will prefer e-mail, while others will rather have you call or stop by their office. Your job is based on your attorneys' needs, so be sure to learn their preferences. Even if they prefer e-mail, however, you'll still need to have some in-person communication, so ask to schedule a meeting every so often, or drop by to ask a more complicated question, if that's okay. Use the resources available within the firm or organization, and thank everyone who takes the time to show you something, teach you a system, find a case you need to complete a memorandum, or assists you in any way. Support personnel can make or break you, so treat everyone with respect, and take the time to appreciate their efforts.

These words of wisdom from an accomplished practicing attorney are well worth considering:

> *Your first summer job is all about experimenting with an area of law, doing some great work (sometimes for low or no pay), building relationships, and obtaining a strong work recommendation. I think it's very important that, in addition to meeting whatever commitments you make or are asked to make relating to deadlines, projects, and assignments, you should also ask yourself what you can do to make this job better, what unique or creative ideas or opportunities you have to contribute—in short, make sure you are a star. I worked for the Legal Assistance Foundation of Chicago Migrant Legal Assistance Project my first summer, and although I ruled out that area of law pretty quickly, I had an amazing experience. The Labor Camp at which I worked was a complete mess and in disrepair, and in addition to the legal projects I undertook,*

I decided that the workers needed and deserved a nicer, more professional environment in which to meet with me and others. So without being asked, I tackled a small renovation of the "office" space. I painted, carpeted, and repaired items. I created a filing system, organized the place, and generally improved the environment. When my supervisor came to visit (she was located in another location) her jaw dropped when she saw the improvements. We are still in touch today, and she sometimes mentions to me what an impression that made on her.

Christopher A. Snyder, Prosecutor, Montgomery, AL

Chapter Eleven
Putting It All Together: Post–Law School—Your First Legal Job

Graduating from law school, surviving the bar exam, and landing your first legal job are exciting landmarks in your legal career. Your first post–law school position can be an important stepping stone or the start of a long career with your employer. Either way, you'll need to use skills from all three spheres of success: the legal knowledge you learned in law school; the practical skills you obtained through internships, externships, clinics, and summer jobs; and the professionalism skills you built throughout your time in law school. Your first legal job is the culmination of years of hard work, and it is your opportunity to put all three spheres into action, while continuing to hone and perfect your strengths in all three areas, as well.

Your Support System

Identify your support system at a new job early on, and work to continue to strengthen it. Your support should not solely be your peers—although those relationships are important—but also your supervisors, mentors, and other people, including staff and your own assistant, throughout the firm or organization. Much like you built your professional contacts in law school, you will now want to identify and nurture "in-house" contacts to help you navigate what can be tricky political currents or less-than-obvious avenues to success in the organization.

That's not to say you can't make a move without consulting someone, or you should not trust your own judgment and good sense. In most cases, as long as you adhere to high professional standards, you will be fine. Your support system, though, can help you get through a tough assignment, an unexpected change in leadership, a challenging supervisory relationship, or any number of circumstances that can arise in a new position as you are learning the landscape, the expectations, and how to excel in your new environment. If you have always been a student before now and this truly is your first career position, it will be quite a transition from academic life, even if you have worked part-time or throughout every summer. There aren't natural endings, like returning to school at the end of the summer, and for the first time you are planning long-term, not just to the end of the semester. Learn the landscape well, and identify a healthy support system.

Finding and Keeping Mentors

Some mentoring relationships are orchestrated by employers or other organizations such as a local bar association. Others develop naturally from a supervisory relationship, through mutual interests, or if a more experienced person takes an interest in the professional development of a less experienced colleague. Having a mentor can serve you very well in a number of ways. A mentor can be a good sounding board for work product issues, supervisory concerns, and career "next steps". A mentor can also help you see where your career is headed and assist you in developing to your fullest potential. A close mentoring relationship has many benefits, and you need not limit yourself to a single mentor. Always keep an eye out for successful role models who might serve as a mentor to you.

How do you find a mentor if one is not provided to you as part of a formal program, or if your assigned mentor is not that interested in advising you? First, make sure that if you do have an assigned mentor, you treat him or her well, regardless of the relationship. Show him or her respect, and respond promptly to outreach—even if you do not click well with that person or you question his or her ability to mentor you. The key to finding a mentor is to meet as many people as you can; apply the same skills as when building your network and identifying someone with whom you can develop a deeper professional relationship. It is ideal to have a mentor within the ranks of your new employer—that person will understand the politics, challenges, and benefits of working there and can be very useful to you. If your employer is small, however, you may need to go outside your organization to find a mentor, and there are many places to do just that within your community at large.

Identify possible mentors from among the people you meet—select those you admire and respect. Do not assume that a mentor must be just like you to be helpful and valuable. Although it is nice if your mentor can identify with the fact that you have small children, for example, or is the same gender or racial or ethnic minority status that you are, that is not strictly necessary. Many successful mentoring relationships have grown between people who, on the surface, couldn't be more different. What's important is that your mentor takes a sincere interest in you and your professional growth and development, that you are comfortable with him or her, and that he or she is a good role model for you.

Sometimes, a potential mentor may identify you as someone they would like to take under their wing. If that is the case, the hard work has been done for you, and the relationship may develop naturally. If you are surprised by outreach from someone whom you would not have selected as a mentor, you should nonetheless explore the possible mentoring relationship. Mentors can be found in unlikely people—you will not know for sure until you have given the relationship a chance. As long as the person is a solid role model, you have nothing to lose and everything to gain by exploring the relationship. Avoid making snap judgments or assumptions about people based on appearance or initial encounters. Your unlikely mentor may be the best thing that ever happened to your career.

Once you have identified potential mentors, take the next step and invite one of them to coffee or lunch. If the initial meeting goes well, ask to meet again. Although it is a little awkward and forced to ask, "Will you be my mentor?" there is nothing wrong with saying something like, "You have provided me with a lot of great advice that I've found very helpful—would it be okay if we met from time to time to talk?" People who are good mentors are usually busy, but they will make time for mentoring. They understand the value of this relationship, and chances are, they have had a great mentor or two who helped them along the way.

A strong and helpful mentoring relationship should be valued; make the effort to keep that relationship thriving. If you ever have the opportunity to help out your mentor, jump at the chance. Stay in touch, but respect those times when your mentor can't be as responsive as you'd like—everyone gets into crunch periods that force a focus away from such relationships for a short while. Apply the principles of professionalism to your mentoring relationship. As with networking, a successful relationship is more likely to develop with a little effort and outreach from you.

The Golden Rule—Again!

Success in your new job really can't be that simple, can it? To treat others as you would want to be treated? Actually, the Golden Rule goes a long way toward ensuring your success—along with good work product, meeting your deadlines, and behaving with maturity and professionalism. If you are a follower of the Golden Rule, it will contribute to your success in all of these areas. Taking the time to treat everyone as you would want to be treated will ensure that the favor will be returned, again and again. One experienced law firm partner has this to say:

> *Not playing nice in the sandbox with other lawyers is one of the biggest professionalism mistakes I observe. You do not have to be enemies with your opposing counsel outside of court. As Shakespeare wrote—"And do as adversaries do in law,—Strive mightily, but eat and drink as friends." While the gloves may be off in court and the fight furious, you can shake hands afterwards and treat opposing counsel with respect as a member of your profession.*
>
> *Also, if a lawyer on the other side is unprofessional, don't sink to his or her level. Rise above it. And don't be petty with professional courtesies, like extensions of time or date changes. At the end of the day, your reputation is the biggest asset you have. Don't lose it by mimicking others who have poor manners and likely even worse reputations.*

Natalie J. Spears, Partner, Sonnenschein, Nath & Rosenthal LLP

Teamwork, a good attitude, and an upbeat disposition will ensure that you are noticed in a positive way. That's not to encourage you to socialize excessively when you should be working or to encourage you to distract others from their work. You should get to know the staff and attorneys at your organization, be able to call them by name, and remember a few key facts about those with whom you have the most contact. Smile at and greet people you pass in the hall or with whom you ride in the elevator—these are simple ways to illustrate a positive attitude. When someone gives you a deadly assignment at the eleventh hour, accept it with good grace and a "can-do" attitude. No matter how frustrated you are or how rotten your morning was before you came to work, check your attitude at the door, and focus on having a positive demeanor.

Most everyone at your place of employment already knows you are a lawyer, and therefore you need not take steps to announce it or overtly act "lawyerly"! It is easy for new lawyers who are proud of their achievements and new credentials to be overly vocal or even obnoxious about the fact that they are lawyers. Do not become one of those people. You know the type—they act as if they are better than everyone else, just "happen" to mention their credentials in most conversations, and throw their title around to bully others. It is tempting to say you are a lawyer to try to get better customer service, for example, but don't. Use your legal knowledge subtly and without rancor in order to persuade and negotiate—not as a billy club with which to bludgeon people.

Likewise, just as the legal community is small, the firm or organization that employs you is even smaller. Avoid speaking negatively about others, no matter how tempting it might be. You never know who is connected with whom, and you would be ill-advised to take a chance of any kind in that regard. Keep gossip you have heard and your unkind words to yourself, and save the venting of your frustrations for a close family member or partner (while taking care to avoid divulging confidential information, of course). Anything else is just too risky and could damage your career prospects.

Learning Employer Policies—Again

Even if you worked for your new employer while you were a law student—and especially if you did not—carefully review your employer's policies and procedures. Stock-investment, travel, computer-use, and gift policies are all extremely important for you to know and understand. Learn and follow the policies relating to the use of your firm or organization's letterhead, how your credentials should be presented, and what information can and should be disclosed about your bar admission(s). For example, if you are not yet admitted to the bar, that generally must be noted on all items with your name, and you cannot sign any pleadings or official documents requiring a lawyer's signature. Knowing and following all such policies is critical.

In addition to reviewing your employer's policies and ensuring that you understand them, develop your own personal good practices, which may exceed the minimum expectations of written policies. Technology is one area in which this is particularly important. Make no mistake that your employer owns the equipment you are assigned, such as your laptop and BlackBerry, and therefore has an absolute right to access information on them, particularly if it is transmitted over the employer's servers and network. Although most employers do not read an employee's e-mail unless a situation warrants it, they have the right to do so. Other instances that have nothing to do with you may also necessitate accessing your e-mail. Act accordingly, and ensure that all your e-mails follow the best practices discussed in Chapter Seven.

Additionally, keep your personal e-mails separate (even if your employer does not require you to do so) by maintaining a personal e-mail account separate from your work-assigned e-mail. This will ensure that, should your e-mail need to be accessed and read by your employer, your personal messages and information that you might not want your employer to see will be protected. Most employers allow reasonable personal use on work equipment, but many employees mistakenly interpret that to mean that their e-mails are their personal information that can not be accessed. But whatever is done on employer-owned equipment ultimately belongs to the firm or organization—and can be rightfully accessed by them—so keep that in mind.

Surfing, Anyone?

Most employers recognize that lawyers work long hours, may be traveling, and need to access information on company equipment that is not work-related. However, "reasonable personal use" of company-owned electronics requires good judgment on your part to determine what falls within such loosely defined parameters. Some employers will define allowable Internet usage; with others, your prudence and wisdom are crucial to making sound decisions.

An important aspect of reasonable use is keeping your Web surfing to a minimum and doing it only on your own time. A quick break during the workday is fine (during lunch is even better); several hours of Web surfing is not. Steer clear of unprofessional sites, such as anything related to pornography or gambling, as obvious examples. Other sites may not be as obvious—for example, will your employer appreciate your time spent on a social networking site? Your good judgment is key. Most firms and organizations can track the sites you hit, so do not visit inappropriate sites on work equipment. Although some employers have security systems in place that will prevent you from going to such sites, others do not. If you inadvertently land on a questionable or inappropriate site, close out of it immediately and take steps to ensure that it does not happen again.

The usefulness of spam filters and junk mailboxes also varies from employer to employer. If your e-mail works well to filter out unwanted mail, spam, and advertisements, few of these risky messages will land in your in-box. If you do receive a lot of junk mail, take extra care not to open inappropriate or questionable messages, particularly from senders you do not know. Many such e-mails contain viruses (usually in the form of attachments) that will infect your computer and get passed on to others with whom you exchange information, or contain links that will send you to inappropriate Web sites. Unfortunately, viruses can also come from people you know, if their computer has been infected. Check your e-mails and the links within them carefully.

Many new lawyers spend a lot of (hopefully all personal) time on legal career blogs and legal networking sites, which are a great source of information about judicial clerkships, life at various firms, changes in the legal market, compensation, and even news about lawyers and law firms. As a new lawyer, such sites may be entertaining, provide access to current market information about employers, or serve as a networking tool. However, they can also be a career pitfall.

Your time during the workday should not be spent surfing the Web unless you are conducting legitimate legal research for an assignment or client. It may be tempting to post information to a legal blog or networking site. However, it is a violation of professionalism and ethics for you to post confidential information about your employer on such public networking sites. Internal memoranda, salary information, and other business strategies and decisions should remain confidential and not be posted on the Internet. Even if you use an anonymous screen name, such postings can be traced—do not take foolish chances with your career, and do not model the unprofessional behavior of others in this regard. The Internet has been a wonderful source of information and a resource, but it can also lead to information sharing that goes beyond professional. Tempting as it may be, as limited as your chances of being discovered may be, do not fall into that pitfall. If you are so unhappy with your job or career choice that you do not care about the harm you might cause your employer and your profession by such unprofessional conduct, then it is time to refocus your energy and attention on finding a new job or career that will inspire such enjoyment and loyalty.

This is not to say that you shouldn't participate at all in legal networking and information sites. Far from it—they can provide valuable learning and networking opportunities. Just be sure that your posts and information-sharing are professional and ethical and not done on your employer's time.

What Are the Resources?

As when you started your first summer internship, you will want to learn about the resources available at your new firm or organization (or review them if you have worked there previously). Your first post-graduate employer has a host of resources that can help you become successful within the organization and the profession. Although resources vary widely from firm to firm and from government venues to corporate environments to public interest organizations, each employer will have a variety of resources you should learn about and use at appropriate times.

First, investigate the research and library resources available to you. If you are at a small firm that does not have a library or extensive research tools, develop these resources through other mechanisms. A bar or court library or a college library might offer free resources. Although books aren't used for research purposes as much as they used to be, the expertise of legal librarians may be a helpful resource in your first few years of practice. Whether the library and experts you use are in-house or external, build strong relationships with these research experts. They can save you time on projects and assignments and help you avoid going down the wrong path on a tricky research question.

When it comes to on-line research, you may be at a real disadvantage when you first start practicing. Even if on-line research resources are available, they are probably not free for unlimited use, as they were in the academic environment. As such, efficiency and accuracy count when using these services now paid for by your employer and, in many cases, ultimately the client. You do not want to be the person who racked up a huge bill with the unapproved or inefficient use of subscriber-based research services. It is important that you take the time to learn appropriate use of such research tools—hopefully before you graduate, but certainly immediately upon graduation if you have not already. Obtaining help from the experts and consultants available to you is essential.

Explore other technology resources with your employer, as well, such as remote connectivity options for traveling and working from home, technology tools you can request for free or a small charge (such as BlackBerries and work cell phones), and software options that may simplify your life. Regardless of whether such options are offered by your employer or not, technology options are worth learning about. You may decide it is worth a personal investment for something that will save you time or make you more efficient if your firm or employer does not offer it. You might also convince your employer to purchase it on your behalf, possibly on a trial basis. It is also smart to stay in touch with the technology staff at your workplace. They can alert you to new technology options as they become available, to pending software changes, and to other items of interest that will help you develop your practice and expertise.

If you are in the private sector, check out the resources and people in your employer's marketing, communication, and business-development departments, if your employer is large enough to have such departments. They are a staple at mid-and large-sized firms. If you are in private practice, learning business-development skills will be an important part of your growth and progression at a firm. If resources are available to help you learn such essential skills, take advantage of them early and often. And in addition to your business cards, the communications and marketing department no doubt has a plethora of snazzy marketing materials available for your networking efforts outside the office.

The networking skills you honed in law school will now have a new purpose—developing future business contacts. The principles are the same, but the tools may be much slicker if you have access to high-end marketing materials. Explore these services, learn what is available to you, and use them whenever possible to expand your network.

Staff resources are critically important in all employment venues. Learn early on who and what is available to help you do your job most efficiently and effectively. In addition to your assistant, do you have access to paralegals, floaters, additional assistants, document-processing services, couriers, in-house or external copy services, and overnight shipping services? Do you know your employer's policies governing the use of such services? Explore what approvals might be necessary to ask your assistant or others to work overtime, if necessary to meet a deadline. What staff and other resources are available, for example, if you have an early morning deadline that will require you to work throughout the night? Do you have technology resources available for after-hours glitches?

Any number of issues can come up that will require your leadership and judgment when using the staff resources available to you. Learning what those resources are and the policies governing their use ahead of a critical deadline is an important piece to planning ahead and ultimately to your success in dealing with a crisis. And how you treat the staff and people available to you will determine how effective they are in helping you. If you are consistently pleasant, reasonable, and appreciative of people's efforts, you will be rewarded by those with whom you work going the extra mile for you when necessary. On the other hand, if you are always in a bad mood, act as if the world owes you a favor, and never bother to thank the people around you for the good work they do on your behalf, you will quickly learn that you'll receive the minimally acceptable results from those with whom you work, and they will be the first to find reasons why they cannot stay late or put your work ahead of someone else's.

Working to Achieve

Perhaps the most important aspect of your professional work ethic to take with you from law school to your new employer (or to develop if you did not have this mentality in law school) is "working to achieve." Every task you undertake should be completed with your full concentration and best effort. And every project must be completed on or before the deadline. This is especially important when you are doing a first assignment for someone. He or she has no reason to trust your work or respect your professionalism, so it is your job to impress them. You will have to earn the trust and respect of the attorneys with whom you work, and you will have to do it again and again as you obtain work from additional lawyers.

Maximize Your Ability to Achieve

You, like most law students and new graduates, no doubt aspire to be an outstanding, not merely good, attorney. However, you may have realized that, while learning the law is relatively straightforward, it is much harder to cultivate other, more loosely defined, qualities and skills that lead to success. While employers do provide training, they expect you to take ultimate responsibility for your own professional development. What exactly does this mean? In part, it involves reaping the maximum value from every learning opportunity. Here are a few suggestions to illustrate how you can make that happen:

- Find a balance between asking for help and taking initiative. This can be a bit tricky in the beginning. However, make it a practice never to ask a question that you can answer for yourself with more research or analysis. In those situations where you legitimately do need guidance, review your notes and prepare a list of well-reasoned questions before meeting with your supervising attorney.

- Ask for the experiences you want to have. The skills and abilities that you develop during the first years on the job are actually building blocks upon which you will grow into an accomplished lawyer. Thus, every project, experience, and interaction adds to your knowledge and adds value to your career. What do you hope to see, do, and learn in the next six months? In the next year? With whom would you like to work? Your employer is committed to your professional growth, but ultimately your career is your own responsibility. Make your interests known, and ask for the experiences you want to have.

- Stay engaged. As a "newbie," your assignments will be in line with your experience (translation: basic, possibly repetitive, and perhaps ranging from mildly boring to mind-numbing). Hang in there and resist the urge to mentally tune out. Your project (or piece of the project) is important to the client, to your supervising attorney, to the firm ... and hopefully to you. While there is nothing exciting about review-ing box after box of discovery documents, the out-come of the case could hinge on your discovering a single fact or piece of paper. Give every project your full attention. Your supervisors will notice, and the quality of your learning will increase exponentially.

- Be proactive in processing feedback. At a basic level, feedback provides reassurance that what you pro-duced is what the attorney expected, and it also gives you an indication of the quality of your per-formance. With reflection, you can learn more im-portant information. For example, did you learn new ways of thinking about a legal issue, conducting research, organizing the document, or organizing your work habits that you can apply to future pro-jects? Did you learn anything about your supervi-sor's personal preferences, idiosyncrasies, or com-municating style? Are there aspects of your legal analysis or writing that need correction or improve-ment?

- In addition to mastering their craft, most new law-yers look forward to having more control over their daily schedules and, in the long term, over their careers. By your attitude and approach to work, you can send a signal that you are serious about your professional growth. This is the first step to developing a satisfying career and gaining the control over your professional life that you seek.

Paula Nailon, Esq., Assistant Dean for Professional Development, University of Arizona Rogers College of Law and Coauthor of *Excellence in the Workplace: Legal and Life Skills*[9]

Once you have developed a good reputation among the more senior lawyers, word of your competence will spread, and you will find that it affects the work assignments you receive as well as how "in demand" you are. But initially you must prove your worth and learn from more seasoned practicing lawyers. No one expects you to be perfect or to know what to do each and every time. It is understood that you are learning. At the same time, however, you will be expected to put forth a tremendous effort to overcome the large learning curve that exists between law school and law practice.

Working to achieve means that you pay attention to the big picture while not losing sight of the details. Ask questions when you are given an assignment to ensure that you understand what is being asked of you and that you do not go off-track. Clarify and then stay within time and budget constraints as you work on an assignment. Communicate with the assigning attorney if you run into problems or challenges. Explore the research, and apply sound legal analysis. Make creative arguments, if necessary. Save enough time so you can proof your work before turning it in, and then proof it again. Complete your work product in the format requested and by the deadline. Work hard, and give each project your full attention. Doing all this will ensure that your end product is the best it can be. Although that may seem overwhelming, if you approach each project or assignment with your full attention and effort, working to achieve will flow naturally from your desire to succeed. Kari Anne Tuohy provides this caution:

9. Kay Kavanagh and Paula Nailon, *Excellence in the Workplace: Legal and* *Life Skills* (Thomson/West, MN, 2007).

Nothing suggests that you are not interested in succeeding more than being unprepared. It is very easy to write off otherwise brilliant people if they are unprepared for an opportunity.

She provides this additional insight:

Quite simply, to be accountable, do what you are supposed to do. Fulfill your role and your responsibilities. If you do, people will want to work with you. You will have choices about what you do and with whom you work. When you make mistakes (and you will if you are challenging yourself and developing professionally!) fess up, look for solutions and learn from the mistakes.

Kari Anne Tuohy, Principal, KAT Consulting and former Director of Lawyer Personnel at a large international law firm with oversight for recruitment and professional development

Chris Snyder, a former judicial clerk who has practiced in several venues, including a large firm, has worked with many new lawyers. He notes the following common mistakes:

There are three common mistakes that I observe among new lawyers, and each one can be extremely detrimental to the lawyer's reputation. First, the most common error is not meeting deadlines that are given. Such deadlines are generally not flexible, although many new lawyers do not realize they are hard deadlines. In practice, the flexibility that students may have experienced in school does not exist. The deadlines are usually client-or Court-imposed deadlines, and with junior lawyers there are a number of people who will need to review that work and a number of approvals that will need to be obtained before the work is finalized. As such, the deadlines are set to allow time for those additional reviews before the work must be submitted to the client or Court. If someone is running into problems with their work, they should immediately take the initiative to talk to the assigning lawyer—I was always willing to help or provide a reasonable extension in light of unexpected challenges in the research. On the other hand, nothing stops me from giving a new lawyer work or selecting someone else for a project faster than a missed deadline without communication.

A second common problem that new lawyers encounter is not doing what was asked in an assignment. They often fail to ask critical questions about the assignment and to record the expectations for the project. When they are given an assignment, they need to ensure they know exactly what the finished product should be, have a general idea of how much time should be spent on the project, and how detailed it should be. If in doubt, they need to ask.

Finally, I think new lawyers tend to have a failure of imagination in their work product. In addition to the traditional arguments they need to make, they should be creative and think outside of the box. They should learn to make creative arguments—not to replace the standard arguments, but to supplement them and add to their work. Such creativity and initiative will serve them well, and it always impresses me.

Christopher A. Snyder, Prosecutor, Montgomery, AL

Developing Expertise

As a new lawyer, you will be inexperienced at almost everything you are assigned or that you attempt to do. That is perfectly normal, so your job is to learn as you go and to work to perfect your efficiency and skills. In short order, though, you will probably develop some kind of expertise, and when you do you will quickly become the "go-to" person for issues of that kind. Developing any kind of expertise, no matter how small, should be a goal for you. Although it is not necessary to be the only person with such expertise, if you can identify areas in which you will be the only expert, your stock will rise even higher.

There are a number of ways to develop such a niche or expertise. At times it happens fortuitously through drawing a research assignment on a new issue or a recent change in law or administrative rules. In other cases, it can happen by design as you see a need and seek to fill it. As one experienced practitioner advises:

If you want to be a "go to" person, you have to earn a reputation and work at it. Once you've developed an area of expertise—or decided on one for yourself—get involved in one of the professional development groups, like the ABA Sections and Forums or state and local bar associations, that are devoted to the area. But don't dabble. And don't just join so you can put it on your resume. That will really do very little for you. Pick one or two groups at most and get involved substantively. Have a plan of eventually holding a leadership position in the organization within a few years. Come up with new ideas for the organization and offer to implement them; ask the current leaders what they need help with and then help them—and make them look good; volunteer for the jobs that no one wants to do. These efforts will allow you to get to know key players and will give you an opportunity to learn more about the area of law. You'll also earn some capital with the group's current leaders, and in due time you can spend that capital by asking to be responsible for more high profile positions, events and activities.

Natalie J. Spears, Partner, Sonnenschein, Nath & Rosenthal LLP

Whatever method you employ, developing useful expertise is a sound way to contribute to your new employer. While you develop expertise with one specific area or issue, you will still be very junior and need to take direction in other areas. That will be a common juxtaposition throughout your career, so become comfortable with it. Lawyers often seek help from lawyers with different areas of specialty or expertise.

If you are in private practice, learn the client-development skills that will ultimately sustain your business. Even if you are not in private practice, strive to differentiate yourself, first among your supervisors and then among your clients. Just as you will want to impress your clients eventually, your first "client" is really your supervising attorney(s), and your job is to impress him or her at every turn. This advice from Karen Hough, the former improvisational performer who uses the concepts of improv as she works with lawyers and other businesspeople to improve performance, applies to differentiating yourself to your supervising attorney as well as to your clients:

We base some of our workshops on the concept that one of the few differentiators among lawyers is client service. Want to stand out in a sea of lawyers? Provide excellent client service at all times, regardless of where you work. Show people you care about them as an individual and they will be loyal. It's not always easy for clients to distinguish average legal work from superior legal work, but they can tell if you are prompt, responsive, attentive, and caring—that's what can differentiate you.

Karen Hough, Founder and CEO, ImprovEdge

Training, or Trial by Fire?

The work that you turn in to the Court, your supervisors, clients, and assigning attorneys should be properly documented and cited. Do not take credit for work or work product that is not your own, and ensure that all law and precedent you are citing is current and valid. These are basic ethical considerations of practicing law and developing work product on behalf of clients; if you violate them, there will likely be consequences that extend far beyond your employer's purview, in the form of Court sanctions, disciplinary action, and the inability to continue to practice law or become admitted to the Bar. Beyond these basic principles, though, how do you actually learn to be a lawyer?

You will learn a lot through the research you do for assignments, the drafting you do for senior lawyers, the clients with whom you meet, and even the small hearings you observe or cover. The reality in most places of employment is that your legal career training is often "trial by fire." Lawyers learn by doing, and even at large firms with elaborate training programs, you may still find that your best learning occurs working side by side with a talented lawyer on a complex deal, an interesting litigation matter, or an administrative proceeding. Thus, even your training and development will benefit from the relationships you develop with the other lawyers at your firm or organization.

If you show enthusiasm for a lawyer's practice and let him or her know that you would like to observe or help with a case he or she is working on, you are much more likely to get the invite than someone who doesn't take the time to show interest. Sitting in your office waiting for the phone to ring is not the way to get interesting work. Relationship-building has so many uses and advantages, even your own training and development can benefit greatly from practicing and mastering these skills.

As Nancy B. Rapoport, Gordon & Silver, Ltd. Professor of Law at the William S. Boyd School of Law, UNLV, advises:

Your employer will mentor you, but only up to a point. You have to mentor yourself, by making opportunities happen. Volunteer for tough assignments. Tell assigning attorneys and other lawyers that you want to do work for them. Repeat as necessary. If you're not getting experience in a certain area, sure, your employer or supervising attorney should be looking out for you, but you are (by definition) your single biggest fan, and if you're not looking out for yourself, then you can't expect others to do your outreach for you. Figure out what the lawyers a few years ahead of you are doing that you want to do, then roll up your sleeves and work extra hours to get experience alongside them.

Professor Rapoport adds:

> *I ended up being a bankruptcy lawyer because I did a single project for a bankruptcy partner—back in the days when I was working as a securities associate—and he was willing to explain the way that my project fit into his overall client matter. I figured out that this partner would mentor me better than anyone else, so I told him that I'd love to do more projects for him whenever he had any. He gave me a few more, and my instinct about him was right: He kept teaching me how what I was doing fit into the overall scheme of things with his clients' needs. I finally cornered him one evening and told him that, as soon as there was an opening in his group, I wanted "in". Considering that I took bankruptcy pass/fail in law school, and that I had been reluctant to do that first project for him because it had involved (ick) bankruptcy law, this was a real about-face for me. But I wasn't getting mentored in my current group the way that he was mentoring me, and I knew that I would learn how to be a better lawyer faster with more hands-on mentoring. I made the switch, learned to love bankruptcy law, and never looked back.*

Professor Rapoport is a prolific author, teacher, lecturer, and expert in the field of bankruptcy law. Creating and taking advantage of the opportunities you see for training and mentoring can lead not only to developing expertise, but eventually to tremendous career achievement, as it did for Professor Rapoport.

You can supplement your on the job training in a number of meaningful ways. Take advantage of any in-house training opportunities that are offered to you. Some employers offer sophisticated negotiation or litigation skills programs, for example, and such programs and seminars are a great way to obtain skills practice and training. Continuing Legal Education seminars (CLE) are another terrific way to learn the ins and outs of specific practice topics and to expand the resources available to you. Some firms have membership in services that provide on-line CLE Webinars, so that may be a possibility as well.

It's also a good idea to join the local and state bar associations and the practice sections or divisions relevant to your practice. Networking opportunities are abundant through bar association events, and you usually receive law and case updates relevant to your area through the divisions or practice sections. Also, don't forget to join the "Young Lawyers" sections of various bar associations as a way to build your network with colleagues across the city or state.

Feedback and Performance Evaluations

Your work habits and skills will be subject to evaluation by your new employer. Some employers have a formal system of evaluation; for others, it is informal and "off-the cuff." Whatever system your employer uses, you should learn about and understand the process, timing, and details early on.

Beyond formal evaluations, though, and just as with your summer position, get in the habit of actively seeking feedback and ideas to improve your work, as discussed in Chapter Ten. This is even more critical in your career position. Judith Finer Freedman offers these thoughts about establishing good communication patterns with your supervising lawyers:

> *It is imperative that new lawyers take the onus upon themselves to set up the appropriate channels of communication. A question such as, "How have you provided feedback in the past to new lawyers?" is a good place to begin. This way the new lawyer will learn if the feedback is via e-mail or in person, how often it takes place, or if feedback took place at all. A new attorney does not have to accept how it has been done in the past. Senior attorneys are open to new ideas, particularly those that will save them time. You can also provide a framework for how you would like feedback. For example, "It is helpful to me to understand where I am exceeding expectations so I can continue to do that. However, at the same time, I need clear examples of how I may be falling short of expectations so I can remedy that and move on in my career development." This statement demonstrates a strong work ethic through the desire to provide a high-quality work product to your employer.*

Judith Finer Freedman, Founder, The Balanced Worker Project ™ whose clients are based in the U.S. and Canada

Kari Anne Tuohy adds this advice:

> *It is your responsibility to seek out feedback; don't wait for it to happen to you. Ask for feedback respectfully–it will show that you care about your career and are willing to take responsibility for your own professional growth. When receiving feedback, keep an open mind and don't be defensive. Try*

to understand the reviewer's perspective, to see the situation from an objective standpoint and to learn something new.

Kari Anne Tuohy, Principal, KAT Consulting, formerly in charge of lawyer recruitment and professional development at a large international law firm

Remember, great lawyers are not necessarily strong managers and supervisors, and they may not be good at making time to give feedback, or at delivering feedback. Nonetheless, you need critical feedback in order to better your performance. Even if you are in an environment in which "no news is good news," meaning, if you do not receive feedback, you are doing fine, you still owe it to yourself to seek out feedback about your work product and performance. Regardless of how wonderfully you are performing as a new lawyer, you are not perfect—even seasoned lawyers are not perfect. Thus, you can improve, and to do that you will need feedback.

If you are not comfortable receiving constructive criticism, work on your reaction so that you are able to receive critical feedback without appearing uneasy or distressed. Without becoming defensive, you should process the feedback you are given, determine if and how you can address any noted deficiencies, and put a plan in action to do just that. If the feedback you are provided is general or vague, ask for specific examples, ask clarifying questions, and to try to understand exactly what the perceived deficiency is. Find out if your supervising attorney has suggestions to improve your performance deficiencies. If you are told you have weak writing skills, find out exactly why your writing is perceived to be weak. Is it the organization of your work, your persuasive writing skills, the analysis, or are typos and grammar issues obscuring otherwise sound analysis? General feedback like "weak writing skills" does not help you hone in on the area on which you really need to focus in order to improve. It's more helpful to hear that your writing is poorly organized so you can focus on bettering that.

You may have a different perception of your performance than your supervising attorney—if in doubt, seek feedback from additional sources. But remember that someone's perception, even if different from your own, is their reality. As such, it is to your benefit to address that perceived performance gap if you can.

Courtney Lynch is a former practicing lawyer and former Marine who is the co-founder of Lead Star LLC, a leadership consulting firm. Courtney offers these thoughts about seeking feedback:

> Soliciting feedback is critical to your success. You won't be able to identify successfully areas for improvement without having a full view of your performance. If you aren't receiving the feedback you need from your supervisor, you can do one of two things: Ask for very specific feedback from your supervisor, or identify a professional close enough to you who would be able to give you guidance. The latter step is more along the lines of seeking out a mentor, which can also allow you to receive ongoing feedback as well as a clearer view of your career path.
>
> Whenever you ask for feedback, it's important to treat the information you receive as a gift you're given. This isn't your time to be defensive. You don't always have to act on the feedback that you receive, but it's important to consider all feedback as useful information that can help you develop professionally.

Strive for continual improvement and constant feedback throughout your career, but particularly as a new lawyer. You will be amazed at the progress you make in your first short year on the job—and that progress will be enhanced greatly if you receive helpful feedback along the way.

Stepping Stones and Milestones

Some employers use a competency-based model of professional development and evaluation. Within this model, you will be expected to do certain items or master specific "competencies" at various points in time. Typically, competencies are developed for each year in practice, and there may be overarching competencies as well as competencies particular to your practice area. If your employer uses a competency model of training and development, familiarize yourself with the components and expectations so you can proactively work to meet the milestones set for you and gain the experience expected of you.

Even if your employer does not use a competency model or does not have a formal training and development program, you should work to enhance your own development using the various resources discussed earlier in this chapter. You can set your own interim or short-term goals as well as annual goals to ensure that you learn the skills that will help you progress in your area and with your employer. Explore what skills and competencies those with whom you work deem important for you to focus on the first year, the second year, and thereafter. Regularly assess your progress toward these goals, and reassess them as necessary.

A strong supervisor will help you set such goals without prompting. Lawyers, however, are often not trained to provide such guidance. If help is not forthcoming from your supervisor, schedule a lunch with him or her to talk about what he or she thinks are important goals for you to consider for the upcoming six months or year. Schedule follow-up conversations to assess your progress. Even if the burden falls on you to make sure these meetings happen, chances are they will be well worth the effort of scheduling them, obtaining the input, and working to incorporate the goals and experiences into your professional life.

Coping With a "Less Than Perfect" Supervisor

There are some less-than-stellar supervising attorneys out there, and you could be unlucky enough to land one. If you are working with a difficult person, there are a couple approaches you can take to make the situation tolerable, if not ideal. First, recognize the difference between a supervisor that is difficult or hard to please and one who is harassing or abusive. The former is difficult to tolerate, the latter should not be tolerated. If you are in the latter situation, follow your employer's policies for reporting such behavior immediately. You do not have to work under such conditions, and your employer should have the necessary policies in place to protect you.

If you are dealing with someone who is difficult to please, first of all, it can help to develop a thicker skin and not take everything personally. Although that is difficult as a new lawyer, this skill will serve you well in many situations throughout your career. Take the criticism you receive as a work-related comment and use it to try to improve. Next, try to figure out which attorney *does* please the difficult supervisor—and why. Observe the successful person, and maybe even ask them for tips about meeting the expectations of your supervisor.

Another technique, if you have the flexibility, is to get assignments from various supervisors or attorneys. A broader range of feedback will help your personal growth and improvement as well as your satisfaction with your employer, and will ensure that your ultimate evaluation is not based solely on the feedback of someone who is difficult to please.

If you strive to please a difficult person and your efforts are completely unrewarded, you may need to have a direct conversation with your supervisor. You might want to bring along various work assignments on which you have received feedback from that supervisor and ask to discuss your progression—specifically, what improvements he or she is able to acknowledge. If he or she is unable to acknowledge any improvement at all over time, it is best that you know that, and why. Ask for specific feedback—if he or she makes general comments that "your writing is weak," for example, ask what, specifically, you can do to improve your writing, and ask the supervisor to provide a specific example of such weakness and how he or she would have improved it. Every time a general statement is made, seek a specific example and an exact clarification of what is meant. Do not let it rest at general feedback—that will not give you the information you need to address any perceived problems. At the conclusion of this meeting, ask for a follow-up session in the near future to assess your additional work product in the interim. Frequent follow-ups and proactively seeking to address the perceived problems will help ensure that you are seen as a hard worker who wants to improve. Sometimes attorneys are hardest on those for whom they have the highest hopes, expectations, and sense of future growth, so it could be that you are actually valued beyond what the constant criticism would suggest.

Chris Snyder, former judicial clerk and practicing attorney, remembers a difficult supervisor he encountered early in his career at a law firm. He offers this advice:

> *If you have a difficult supervising attorney, there are really two approaches you might take to handle the situation. First, if you have a choice, try to get as busy as possible doing assignments for other lawyers you like and respect. Seek out opportunities, and impress people with your initiative. Sometimes the lawyer you ask for work might not have any projects to give you at the moment, but he or she may follow up with you in the future. If that's the case, seize the opportunity when*

*it comes your way, no matter how busy you are. Just do it, do
an amazing job, and you'll be surprised at how quickly that
relationship develops. Second, if you don't have the option to
seek out work from other people, or you really want to learn
the practice area and the difficult supervisor is really the only
option, be as proactive as possible in your relationship with
him or her. When you are given an assignment from your
supervising attorney, do not leave without an extremely clear
understanding of what you have been asked to do. Find out
what the finished product should be, approximately how
much time you should spend, when it is due, and then follow
up those understandings with a confirming e-mail to your
supervisor. I found that this method worked really well to
avoid negative reviews when I was faced with working closely
with a difficult attorney.*

**Christopher A. Snyder, Prosecutor, Montgomery, AL,
and former Judicial Clerk to Judge Jose A. Gonzalez,
Jr., U.S. District Judge, Southern District of Florida,
and Judge Lavenski R. Smith, U.S. Circuit Court
Judge, Eighth Circuit Court of Appeals**

Despite your best efforts, you cannot always please everyone. If your work is generally well received with the exception of a difficult supervisor, you may just have to accept that
you aren't going to be able to please that person. On the
other hand, if this supervisor makes your day-to-day existence at work so miserable that you are contemplating leaving the job, it's definitely worth exploring what options may
exist within your employer. A good rule of thumb is to give a
rough situation six months to a year before trying to make a
drastic change. Sometimes a rough start can lead to a strong
mentoring relationship that endures for an entire career. You
are adjusting to a lot of new transitions, and your supervisor
is adjusting to you. No one is perfect, but you may eventually
find common ground that paves the way for a smooth working relationship going forward. If you've tried to make it
work every way you can, you've given it plenty of time, and
the relationship is still not working, talk with someone you
trust. Sometimes junior attorneys can be reassigned to a
different supervisor, department, or practice area, or there
might be other workable resolutions. You won't know until
you explore the possibilities, and you owe it to yourself and
your employer to at least give your firm or organization a
chance to develop a workable solution for everyone.

Working With Support Staff—Especially Your Assistant

If you have never had your own support staff before, it can be odd to be a brand-new attorney and also someone's supervisor immediately! Typically, your assistant will have many more years of experience working with your new employer than you do. Even though you have a law degree, you can learn a lot from your assistant. Rather than being uncomfortable with that situation, use it to your advantage. As one consultant advises:

> *Treat the professionals with whom you work as essential members of your team. In most cases, they are incredibly knowledgeable, they can create efficiencies and superior work product that you cannot achieve alone, and they will go the extra mile for you in times of need if they feel their contributions are valued.*

Kari Anne Tuohy, Principal, KAT Consulting, Former Director of Lawyer Personnel at a large international law firm with oversight for recruitment and professional development

If you develop a strong relationship with your assistant, he or she will be your support, watch out for you, and often save you from making serious faux pas in the course of your transition from law school to lawyer. Professor Rapoport of UNLV advises law students to learn early on how to work well with support staff; she knows how critical these relationships are to career success. Her advice:

> *Your assistant is your partner, and you should treat him or her as such: Filling that person in on why you're asking him to do something is key to your own success, and respecting his knowledge and ability to carry out his part of your projects with the right understanding of why you're doing those projects will go a long way toward having a good working relationship. Thinking of your assistant as somehow less than a full partner is flat-out dumb: It demeans your relationship with him, and it deprives you of getting as much out of your relationship as would respecting his knowledge and experience.*

Nancy B. Rapoport, Gordon & Silver, Ltd. Professor of Law, William S. Boyd School of Law, UNLV

Just as you appreciate when your supervising lawyer fills you in on how your sometimes less-than-scintillating work fits into the bigger picture, project, case, or trial, so will your assistant be glad to know how what he or she is doing contributes to your work, or to the work of the firm or organization.

Take the time to get to know your new assistant early on, and ask questions about how he or she prefers to work with lawyers. Attorneys use assistants to varying degrees—some draft documents entirely and just ask their assistants to "pretty them up," while others go through endless drafts of handwritten edits on hardcopy that they have their assistant incorporate into documents. Although there is not really a right or wrong method to use an assistant, your goal should be to avoid spending time on matters your assistant can do, and to focus on using your time for the highest and best uses.

Angie Morgan is a former Marine and a co-founder of Lead Star LLC, a leadership consulting firm. She works with professionals in a variety of contexts and often helps them learn how to work effectively with their colleagues and support staff. She has this advice for new lawyers:

When you find yourself in the position as a supervisor (especially to someone who has more experience at the firm or organization than you do) it's critical that you take the time necessary to develop that relationship. Always look for opportunities to learn about your assistant. Ask him or her questions about their experiences, tenure, background, etc. The more you know about your assistant, the better able you are to understand their professional strengths and how to utilize them to the best of their ability. Your assistant will only be a valuable resource if you invest time in your relationship. It would be disastrous to think that your assistant is only there to serve you and your needs. Your assistant needs to feel empowered, which will allow him or her to fulfill their role to the best of their ability.

Learning to delegate can be tricky. It may be easier to do a task yourself than to ask someone else to do it for you, but delegation is a necessary skill for success. If you have an assistant with strong skills and a desire to learn more, many day-to-day work items can likely be delegated to him or her. In order to succeed at delegating and at working well with your support staff, you must have strong and frequent communication. Do not assume that your assistant knows what you want. Don't hesitate to have a frank and open discussion with your assistant about your needs and preferred work style, but listen and obtain ideas from him or her, as well.

You can learn a lot from your assistant, and you should make your expectations clear, without being demanding or mean. Your goal is to have an open working relationship in which both of you feel free to communicate.

Do not, however, expect your assistant to do personal work or run errands for you. Nothing will mark you as an egotistical lawyer faster than such inappropriate requests. Your assistant is there to do the business of the firm or organization for which you were hired. Although some attorneys may argue that having their assistant take care of personal duties frees them up for more client work, that is not an appropriate use of your assistant's time, and you should not make such requests.

Just as you appreciate feedback and praise, so, too, will your assistant. Recognize a job well done, and do not be afraid to surprise him or her every once in a while with a small token of appreciation (such as movie tickets, a plant, or a lunch certificate). This is a particularly nice gesture if he or she goes above and beyond, stays late at a moment's notice, or otherwise shows his or her dedication. Likewise, if there is something your assistant did not do correctly, or a project did not meet your expectations, address it directly and immediately in a non-threatening manner. Do not wait until once-a-year performance evaluations to give positive or negative feedback. Your assistant deserves contemporaneous feedback, just as you do. Too many attorneys hide behind annual performance evaluations to tear apart the performance of their assistants, relying on the office manager as the mouthpiece to provide such feedback. Take time each day to recognize the work of your assistant and give direct and immediate feedback, if necessary.

If your expectations are reasonable and you work well with your assistant, you will be amazed at how much more you can accomplish. Every once in a while, however, a challenging assistant issue may arise. One common issue junior associates in law firms encounter is having an assistant who also serves a busy senior partner. Although talented assistants can juggle several demanding attorneys with ease, it is not unheard of to have an assistant who gives the partners the majority of his or her time and attention and makes your work their lowest priority. As a new lawyer, you are definitely lower in the hierarchy, so do not be surprised if your work gets bumped from time to time by someone more senior. But if this is a constant issue, discuss it with your assistant to see if there is a resolution on which you can both agree. Sometimes the assistant is truly overburdened, in which case you both may need to seek help from another source to resolve the problem. If you and your assistant are united in this endeavor, it will be much easier to make headway.

On the other hand, if your assistant is unwilling to work with you to resolve an issue like this, you definitely should not suffer in silence and you should seek assistance elsewhere. Always try to work it out directly with your assistant first. If that does not work, consult with your mentor, supervising attorney, office manager, or human resources personnel to determine your best course of action.

If you have an assistant whose performance does not meet your standards and those of your employer, consult with your human resources staff as you work to resolve the problem. Human resources can advise you as to their disciplinary policy—often progressive discipline—and the steps and documentation required to effect change. Do not try to handle such issues on your own. Improper documentation or missteps on your part will only exacerbate the problem.

Finally, avoid blaming your assistant for mistakes that are found in your work by others. Despite the help your assistant provides, the final work product that you submit to supervising attorneys, partners, clients, or the Court is your responsibility. Do not blame your assistant or anyone else with whom you work for mistakes that are your responsibility, and definitely do not throw any of your support staff under the bus to save your own skin. If you don't catch your assistant's mistakes before you turn in a project or assignment, then the mistakes remaining in the work product are your fault. You should work overtime to protect the people who help you. Immediately discuss any mistakes with your assistant or other support staff. An overabundance of mistakes should be addressed through the appropriate channels at your employer. But a mistake that remains because you did not take the time to proof the work, or you just missed it, is *your* mistake, so accept responsibility for it.

Organizational Issues

One of the most important tasks when you start a new job is to find and use an organizational system that works for you. As soon as (or before) you begin to receive assignments and work, talk to your assistant about filing options, and learn the record-retention policies of your employer. You will need good organizational techniques to tackle paper files and documents as well as e-mails, attachments, and electronic documents. The software and programs offered will vary from employer to employer, but whatever technological capabilities are available to you, be sure to learn them and the best practices for using them.

As we discussed in Chapter Four, having a neat and organized workspace will save you time and hassle every day. You will not have to spend valuable time searching for the document that you know is there but you just cannot seem to locate. There are many organizational techniques—some people prefer a blank workspace in which everything is filed away, while others like a workspace in which there are neat piles of projects. Whether you are a "piles" or "files" person is not important. The critical factor is being able to find what you need when you need it—not just today or tomorrow, but a year from now when you need to refer back to a document or some notes you took.

Your assistant, if he or she has been around for any length of time, will likely have invaluable advice for you in this regard. Use his or her ideas to help you get and keep your workload and documents under control. If you have already been working for a while and you find that you are wasting time searching for items and that you do not feel like you have a good organizational system, it's time to get help. Seek help from your assistant or someone else before you get too buried. There are many books and resources about organizational techniques, but it is also smart to talk to a few attorneys who are seemingly successful in their organizational techniques to find out how they do it, what systems and supplies they use, and if you might replicate their system for yourself.

In addition to getting your paper and electronic documents in order, your calendar of appointments, meetings, and critical deadlines also needs to be well-organized. If you are late or missing from meetings, if you miss deadlines, or if you fail to respond in a timely fashion to e-mails and other communications, you are destined to fail in your new job. Work out a system with your assistant about who is responsible for calendaring what types of deadlines. Maintain a prioritized "to-do" list of all of the tasks you must accomplish, the phone calls you must return, and the e-mail or written responses you must send, in addition to assignments and other deadlines. Review the list each day, make prioritization adjustments as needed, and seek help or advice if you are approaching overload. Your ability to manage your workload is critical to your success as a lawyer. Know the danger signs: If you find that you are missing items, you narrowly make a deadline, or you happen to remember a meeting at the last minute, you are probably in need of a new organizational system. If your employer does not have your preferred software program, explore ways of making your own investment in the program. It may be money well spent.

It's important that you spend the initial time to get organized, and then take the time, as necessary, to *stay* organized. Try new ways to keep your tasks and life running smoothly, stay on top of your meetings and assignments, and learn to prioritize. It will make life much easier for you and everyone with whom you work.

Mistakes—Everyone Makes Them; Not Everyone Recovers

Mistakes are a natural part of life and learning, and if your goal is to avoid making any mistakes, you will be sadly disappointed. In fact, if you never make mistakes, you're probably not learning, taking risks, or developing. There are small mistakes, not-so-small mistakes, really big mistakes, and mistakes that jeopardize your job and/or career. Mistakes can be made on the work product you produce, actions you take, research you conduct, and decisions you make (or fail to make). Mistakes can also take the form of a lack of good judgment or common sense, however momentary. The worst mistakes, however, are those that call into question your ethics and professional reputation, so take particular care to guard against making mistakes of that type.

It is not uncommon for a junior lawyer to make a mistake that appears to be of disastrous proportions. You might be working on something, only to get a sinking feeling that you've messed up in a big way. Or a mistake you made might be discovered by someone else, and you may not realize you have made it until the other person brings it to your attention. Whether discovered by you or someone else, mistakes can be learning experiences. How you handle the mistake can be the difference between career-saving and career-limiting.

If you have discovered a mistake that no one else knows about, take steps to remedy the situation immediately. Do not suffer in silence, hoping that the mistake won't be discovered or that it will be blamed on someone else. You need to go to the relevant, affected person immediately (a supervising attorney if a client is affected) and explain exactly what happened, why the mistake was made, what you suggest to remedy the mistake, and how you will ensure it does not happen again. If it can be remedied immediately, take whatever steps necessary to do so. Take full responsibility for the mistake you have made—offer a sincere apology, and work to rectify the situation in whatever manner you can, with the guidance and input of your supervising attorney, if the mistake is a really big one. Tracy LaLonde, a training and coaching consultant, agrees:

> The key to handling a situation when you've made a mistake is to take ownership of the mistake and state what actions you will take to prevent the mistake from happening again in the future. The conversation could go something like, "I apologize for missing the deadline for the Acme Company research. It was not my intention to cause a delay in the schedule. I had intended to have the research memo prepared for you by yesterday, and I underestimated how long it would take me to write the memo. I will allow myself more time in the future and will be sure to communicate my progress to you along the way. I hope that we will be able to put this behind us and continue working together."

Tracy LaLonde, Partner, Akina, a national sales coaching and consulting firm

If someone else discovers a mistake you have made, and you are brought in to discuss it or answer for the mistake, obtain as many relevant facts as you can. If you are not sure what happened or how the mistake was made, ask questions so that you can learn the circumstances. Develop a plan to ensure that the mistake is not repeated. Take full responsibility for your actions, and offer a sincere apology. Do not make excuses, try to blame a colleague or staff member, or dodge the truth. Being forthright and candid about what happened will not save you from the consequences of the mistake you made, but it can increase others' respect for you and your approach, and may make the sting of a big mistake diminish more quickly.

Don't beat yourself up about mistakes—they *will* happen—but work to minimize the impact of your mistakes through a checks-and-balances system. If you're worried about missing a deadline, ensure that you, your assistant, and maybe even a third pair of eyes are tracking critical deadlines. If your research skills are lacking, work to improve them with the experts available to you. If you exercised bad judgment, study the situation to determine what caused you to act unprofessionally. If alcohol was involved, limit or completely stop drinking at business functions. If you inadvertently broke a confidence, work to ensure that you do not discuss any professional matters outside of a "need-to-know" basis. Junior lawyers can encounter many possible pitfalls, and some lessons will be learned the hard way. Work to minimize the potential impact of your mistakes by acting professionally, reliably, and above reproach the rest of the time.

Consequences to a Lack of Professionalism on the Job

There can be no doubt in your mind by this point that your professional behavior on the job and off has consequences—good if you exercise the highest standards of professionalism, and bad if you do not. There are costs to acting irresponsibility and unprofessionally, and if they are not immediately apparent, they will be over time. The key is to recognize lost opportunities or costs while the long-term results can still be modified.

One of the main consequences of a lack of professionalism on the job is the potential loss of career-advancement opportunities. Those who are trusted to act professionally and responsibly and who have proven themselves in this regard typically obtain the choicest assignments—working the bigger cases with the sexier clients or the more interesting matters. Those lawyers are typically given more responsibility, which in turn jump-starts their learning curve. Over a short time, the difference in work assignments can have a large impact on professional development, training, and advancement. Mentors will seek out mentees who demonstrate strong professionalism traits—and may avoid those who do not. Give yourself every opportunity to succeed by being a model of professionalism.

Beyond career-advancement opportunities, there are also relationship consequences to a lack of professional behavior. If you are unprofessional, those who are striving to be professional will not want to be associated with you. As such, you may lose the opportunity for collaborative working relationships, team-building opportunities, and the chance to learn from strong lawyers and colleagues. Something as seemingly minor as constantly complaining about anything work-related can cause people to reevaluate if they want to work on projects with you. And if your work product is questionable, there is even more potential for avoidance.

Finally, you may experience social consequences for exhibiting unprofessional behavior. Others may avoid socializing with you at the lunch hour, after work, or even during short breaks in the day. Although you are not at work to socialize, having strong relationships with your colleagues and the staff can only help your overall success. If people avoid you, do not want to be seen with you, or are concerned about tainting their own reputation because of yours, you are suffering social consequences in addition to the penalties relating to work assignments and collaborative relationship-building.

These types of consequences probably won't appear overnight. They may begin gradually, bit by bit. First, you are passed over for an assignment you really wanted, you are not selected to work on a new initiative as part of a team, or you were the only one not invited for a round of drinks after work. A single instance is not cause for concern—you don't need to be a part of everything that goes on at your employer. But if you begin to see any type of pattern—either in one type of consequence, or across the board—chances are you are exhibiting (or failing to exhibit) behaviors that need to be corrected immediately. Pay attention to the warning signs, and make any necessary changes before it is too late.

Chapter Twelve
Putting It All Together: Pro Bono and Community Service

One of the best parts of being a law student and a new lawyer may be the time you spend on pro bono matters. The ABA Model Rules of Professional Conduct expect that lawyers will provide legal services to those otherwise unable to pay. Rule 6.1 specifically states, "A lawyer should aspire to render at least (50) hours of pro bono publico legal services per year."[10] These legal services should be provided without expectation of a fee to persons of limited means or organizations designed to address the needs of such persons.

As a law student and new lawyer, your obligation to provide such services is no less real and you should get in the habit of doing fifty hours or more of pro bono work every year. But pro bono should not be viewed as just an obligation—it can be one of the best parts of your career. Pro bono work and community service are excellent opportunities to give back to the community in which you live and work, and are fulfilling in ways that your paying job may never be. You can learn excellent lessons from helping those who are less fortunate, you will meet people that you wouldn't otherwise work with, and you may find a niche area of law that really excites you in the process.

Karen J. Sarjeant, Vice President for Programs and Compliance, Legal Services Corporation, has spent her career in

10. Available at: http://www.abanet.org/cpr/mrpc/rule_6_1.html.

public interest work. She says this about your time in law school:

> Do not participate in pro bono activities in law school just because they will look good on your resumé. Participate in pro bono activities in law school because:
>
> • You should develop a public interest ethic—helping those who are unable to afford legal assistance is a responsibility of membership in the legal profession;
>
> • No matter where your law degree takes you professionally, you will continue to have that same responsibility;
>
> • You will learn a lot about the barriers to justice that confront millions of people and the role that your voice and support can play in breaking those barriers down; and
>
> • Your involvement will require you to think about the circumstances of someone other than yourself.
>
> Further, be a pro bono leader in law school. There are still too many law schools that do not do enough to inculcate a pro bono ethic in students. Your voice is important, and your law school administration will be more responsive to you than to anyone else. They want happy and supportive alumni.

If you still aren't convinced of the merits of fulfilling your pro bono obligation, you will be once you start. And you can work on pro bono matters in any area of law that seems interesting to you—it need not be your primary area of specialty. However, you don't want to do your pro bono clients a disservice, so if you're working in unfamiliar areas, training is essential. Your help might be needed in a particular specialty, and there are often training and CLE opportunities for pro bono attorneys to help them get up to speed in areas about which they are not as familiar. Support is available as you enter the world of pro bono—all you need to do is take the first step. Although you and your fellow students or colleagues are very busy, you can and should make time for pro bono. Melanie Kushnir offers these encouraging words:

> Making time to participate in pro bono is a challenge for law students and lawyers. Fortunately, pro bono opportunities vary in length and time commitment, and some even offer weekend and evening work. Some pro bono work must be performed at an organization's office or elsewhere in the field, while other assignments can be done at the office, library, or even at home. This flexibility allows you to do pro bono on

your own terms, in whatever way works best with your schedule. Whatever your circumstances, you should evaluate your workload and your personal capacity. Exercise caution before making a commitment so you do not shortchange yourself, the organization for which you are volunteering, or your clients.

Melanie Kushnir, Assistant Staff Counsel, ABA Center for Pro Bono

If you work at a large firm, corporation, or agency in which your contact with clients is minimal for the first couple years, you will be meeting with, interviewing, and representing your pro bono clients in short order. It's a win-win situation in which you can offer your legal skills, willingness to learn a new area, and commitment to helping others by working with clients who cannot afford legal representation and who desperately need your help.

You can get started in pro bono in any number of ways. Your community may have a pro bono organization that will match lawyers to clients who need help in specific areas of interest. You might also volunteer for a specific project—be it death penalty cases, landlord/tenant disputes, family law, or immigration matters, or you can volunteer to work with a particular agency or organization that has a mission of interest to you. The world of pro bono is wide open to you. This is your opportunity to select the exact work you would like to do.

Understand Your Employer's Commitment to Pro Bono

Most employers wholeheartedly support the commitment of their employees to pro bono work. Some employers provide work credit and/or billable hour credit for a certain amount of pro bono work each year. In fact, some employers actually require their employees to give a minimum number of hours per year to pro bono efforts. As you are weighing the pros and cons of various employers, consider their commitment to pro bono work. If you have already committed to an employer without understanding its pro bono policies, you should take the time to learn about them as soon as you can. If your employer has pro bono expectations, you should understand what those are, but even if they don't, you have a duty to perform pro bono work, regardless.

Additionally, you should know what you will need to do to track your pro bono hours, receive billable credit for them (if that is the norm), and what other procedures you might need to follow to accept pro bono cases. You may need to be screened for conflicts of interest, explore malpractice insurance issues, and learn how to log the time spent on pro bono matters in accordance with your employer's policies and best practices. Your employer may have fairly loose policies, or they may be very structured, with a pro bono coordinator or a committee in charge of approving such work. Whatever the situation at your firm or organization, learn the policies and practices, and follow them closely.

Pro Bono Challenge©

Law firms with fifty or more attorneys have the opportunity to become part of the Law Firm Pro Bono Challenge©, which is designed to tie pro bono performance to a percentage of the firm's business goals. The Law Firm Pro Bono Challenge© is offered through the Pro Bono Institute at Georgetown University Law Center: "The Pro Bono Institute's Law Firm Pro Bono Challenge[SM] is a unique global aspirational pro bono standard. Developed by law firm leaders and corporate general counsel, the Challenge articulates a single, unitary standard for one key segment of the legal profession— the world's largest law firms. Major law firms that become Signatories to the Challenge acknowledge their institutional, firm-wide commitment to provide pro bono legal services to low-income and disadvantaged individuals and families and non-profit groups."[11]

Signatory firms agree to an institutional commitment that either three or five percent of the firm's billable hours will be in pro bono work. If you are seeking employment at a large law firm, check to see if they have become involved in and met the goals of the pro bono challenge. If your firm has fifty or more attorneys and has not participated in the Pro Bono Challenge, perhaps you can spearhead such an effort.

Split Summer Opportunities

A number of law firms will sponsor a split summer pro bono/public interest opportunity. If you are able to land such

---

11. The Pro Bono Institute at Georgetown University Law Center Web site: http://www.probonoinst.org /challenge.php, August 2008.

a split public interest summer opportunity, you will generally work at the firm for half the summer and at a pro bono project of your choice (sometime with geographic or other limitations) the rest of the summer. Yale Law School publishes a list each year of the law firms that offer such opportunities. See the resource section at the end of this chapter for information on accessing the list.

The participating firm will typically pay your entire summer salary, including the time spent at the public interest organization. Such split summers are an excellent way to gain valuable experience, earn a fairly large amount of money in a single summer, and provide much-needed services to an organization. Students who are bound for either public service or private practice participate in such split public interest summers. The number of such opportunities are limited—typically one per participating firm—so the competition can be intense. If this particular opportunity is not available to you and you are bound for private practice, you can still volunteer for a week or two at the end of the summer (and throughout the school year) at the public service organization of your choice. If you are with a firm that does not currently offer a split public interest summer, perhaps you can initiate such participation on behalf of your firm.

Jump In and Do It!

You have everything to gain by meeting your pro bono obligation as a new lawyer and even as a law student. It may seem daunting to get started, especially if you are with an employer for which there is not a lot of institutional support. You can, however, change that—your enthusiasm for public service and pro bono work is likely to inspire others. The good you can do for someone who cannot afford legal representation is enormous. The good you and three of your colleagues can do is outstanding. Set a good example on the pro bono front, and as you progress through the ranks, mentor junior lawyers and expose them to opportunities to give back and do good.

Listen to this strong and helpful advice from an experienced practitioner:

> Pro bono is an important part of your future career. It will
> provide you excellent training and an opportunity for front
> line experience that may be more difficult to realize in other

cases. You will also achieve the professional satisfaction of actually making a difference in the life of an individual, a family, or even a community, by being the last hope of the least fortunate among us. And, there are networking and mentoring benefits, in addition to the opportunity to work in different practice areas and skills development.

Even if you are graduating soon and have been unable to find time for pro bono, it is not too late. Many recent law graduates find the period following law school graduation while waiting for bar results and searching for a job to be an excellent time to do pro bono work. They not only gain practical legal experience but can also use the opportunity to network with lawyers and establish contacts in the community.

The more legal experience you obtain during your law school years, the more you will be in a position to market yourself to prospective employers. Participation in pro bono enables you to gain relevant legal experience, explore a variety of career paths, and network with practicing lawyers. While performing a much-needed community service, you will enhance your professional development and ultimately become a better lawyer.

Melanie Kushnir, Assistant Staff Counsel, ABA Center for Pro Bono

Resources

There are a variety of resources available to help you assess an employer's commitment to pro bono, to assist you in beginning pro bono work, and to locate opportunities in your community to contribute.

- **Harvard Pro Bono Guide:** http://www.law. harvard.edu/students/opia/docs/guide-pro-bono.pdf (Information and resources about pro bono opportunities in law firm settings.)

- **ABA National Pro Bono Opportunities Guide:** http://www.probono.net/aba_oppsguide/ (A state-by-state guide of pro bono opportunities for which you can volunteer.)

- **ABA Directory of Pro Bono Programs:** http:// www.abanet.org/legalservices/probono/directory.html

(By state and by city, a guide to pro bono programs for which you can volunteer.)

- **ABA Standing Committee on Pro Bono and Public Service:** http://www.abanet.org/legal services/probono/ (A comprehensive list of resources to assist in all facets of pro bono and public service—articles, projects, CLE programs, model rules, and more.)

- **ABA State-by-State Pro Bono Service Rules:** http://www.abanet.org/legalservices/probono/stateet hicsrules.html (A compilation of the pro bono rules of each state, how the state rule compares to ABA Model Rule 6.1, and a link to the state rule.)

- **Firms Sponsoring Split Public Interest Summers:** http://www.law.yale.edu/documents/pdf/cdo-firmsSponsSplitSummers.pdf (Contains a summary of firms that will sponsor a split public interest summer.)

- **NALP Online Directory of Law Firms (and Workplace Questionnaires):** www.nalpdirectory. com (Provides self-reported employer information in both the directory and workplace questionnaires about pro bono policies and work.)

- **The Path to Pro Bono: An Interviewing Tool for Law Students:** http://www.abanet.org/legal services/downloads/probono/path.pdf (A pamphlet with sample interview questions and information about assessing pro bono opportunities at a law firm.)

- **The Pro Bono Institute at Georgetown:** http:// www.probonoinst.org/(Resources, articles, and information for law firms, corporations, and public interest organizations interested in expanding pro bono work.)

- **The Vault Guide to Law Firm Pro Bono Programs:** Available for purchase in Vault Bookstore at www.vault.com. (Published each year, the Vault Guide summarizes the in-house pro bono programs of the top one hundred law firms.)

Chapter Thirteen
Putting It All Together: In Pursuit of Happiness and Well–Being

You have landed your first legal job. You have done everything you can to prepare for your career. You are working hard to become successful. Yet sometime in your first year of practice you cannot help but feeling a bit let down. Is this all there is? Is this really what you worked so hard for—to spend long days reviewing documents, obtaining minimal feedback on your work, and feeling tired a lot of the time?

Although some new lawyers take to their profession like a duck to water, for others the transition from student to lawyer and from academia to practice can be overwhelming, daunting, and downright depressing at times. If you fall into that second camp, all is not lost. It takes a while to work through those transition issues, to get accustomed to the professional working world, and, particularly, to adjust to the legal profession.

There are a number of ways you can work to ease your transition, but recognize that sometimes it just takes time. Realize that your ambivalent feelings about your career are normal, and give yourself ample time and space to adjust to your new career. Only by giving your position the full benefit of time and experience can you truly judge if this is a longer-term position for you or if it will be a stepping stone to greener pastures. Either way, you probably won't be satisfied immediately—you are building a path to your future, which takes time and effort and probably some sweat and anxiety. Although you may feel that you have spent your undergraduate and law school years building such a path—and you have—you need to continue building. Being a junior lawyer means learning, growing, and adjusting to the legal profession. It means exploring your options and opportunities and making the most of the prospects that present themselves. Being a junior lawyer means learning how to be a better lawyer every day.

Obtaining and Maintaining Balance

One of the most common stressors for new lawyers is the time commitment their career demands. Time demands are huge in law school, and if you worked part-time and had other commitments as well, it probably felt like you were burning the candle at both ends. Most new lawyers quickly learn, however, that the practice of law takes even more time and effort than being a law student. Regardless of their employer, new lawyers tend to work long hours and struggle to make time for any other aspect of their life—in short, they rapidly lose balance and even perspective.

If you find that you are approaching burnout, are constantly stressed, rarely get enough sleep, are eating too much fast food and other unhealthy meals, are fighting illness, and often feel more cranky than happy, you are lacking balance in your life. No matter how busy you are at work, no matter how committed you are to becoming a success at your job and your career, you absolutely *must* protect some time each week to spend with your family and friends and on pursuits you enjoy away from the legal profession. If you are barely getting your work done, it seems counterintuitive to preserve time for family and fun. Amazingly, though, that is exactly what you need to do. Working long hours is necessary at times, no doubt about it, but you are less productive after twelve hours of work than you are after two. As such, you are not at your best or most efficient when you are always working long hours.

If you must work late into the night, build in a half-hour break, if possible, to do something completely unrelated to work. Taking a walk, working out (even an abbreviated workout) or catching a catnap are all quick ways to rejuvenate your mind and body and to obtain a bit more efficiency. The thirty minutes you lose by taking a break will be made up for in your renewed efficiency when you return to the task at hand.

Even though your schedule may be unpredictable, you can still preserve time to spend with family and friends each week, as well as to pursue your hobbies and interests. If you have to return to work after a rousing sporting event, so be it, but do not miss the chance to do something outside of work for a few hours. The tasks at hand often seem less daunting and more manageable when you build in some mandatory downtime and return to work with a fresh eye and new perspective.

In addition to scheduling downtime to give yourself mental breaks, also take care of your physical health. Get plenty of rest, eat healthy foods, and drink lots of fluids. Whether your workouts are tame or intense, make exercise a regular part of your schedule. Walking, biking, lifting weights, spinning, yoga—whatever your preference, get active on a regular basis. By taking care of yourself, you will handle work and the stress that comes with it much better and more efficiently.

Although you will struggle to find balance in your new career, remember that this is a common challenge—you are not alone in your quest to keep work from dominating your life, particularly with today's technology that keeps us in constant communication with the office, even when we are not there physically. One expert on finding balance offers this advice for managing technology and working toward balance:

> What attorneys don't realize is that they have the power to control the boundaries between technology and its ability to control one's time clock. Part of learning how to achieve a balance in one's life is to create time slots within the rubric of work and life. It is appropriate to turn one's cell phone or BlackBerry on the "silent" mode from the time one leaves the office until she/he feels the commitment to life outside of work has been met. This could mean turning a cell phone back on once the kids have gone to bed or once a workout or social event is over. This way, it puts control in the hands of the person, not in the hands of the caller or e-mail sender. It is appropriate to let others know at work that you will not be reachable during these hours but that you will check back in at a certain time. By doing so, you are demonstrating your commitment. It may be a type of commitment that is different

*in the realm of your employer's cultural norms, but it is
commitment nevertheless.*

**Judith Finer Freedman, Founder, The Balanced Work-
er Project ™ whose clients are based in the U.S. and
Canada**

As you progress through the ranks, however, you will find
that balance is easier to achieve—as long as you always make
it your goal. There are plenty of senior lawyers who never
find balance. . .and the costs to them personally are likely
very high. But there are many senior lawyers who have found
balance throughout their career, and you can, too.

In the first few years of practice, the scales will tip more
heavily toward work, and this may be the case at other points
in your career, as well—as you work toward a promotion,
take on a particularly challenging leadership position, or
undertake the training and mentoring of others. But as you
start a family, care for aging parents, face a health crisis, or
pursue a dream like writing a book or traveling the world,
you will necessarily have periods in your career when the
scales dip more toward your personal life. Trust that these
phases will occur—and understand that how the scales are
currently tipped is not how they will always be tipped. This
will help you go with the flow a bit more as you are navigating these ebbs and flows—they are a normal part of the
intersection of your career progression and the rest of your
life.

You need to be committed to balance, regardless of which
direction the scales are currently tipping in your life. Balance
is essential to your overall health and well-being and to your
satisfaction with your career and your life. It is not hard to
make that commitment—you simply need to preserve time
for pursuits besides work at regular intervals. Take a vacation each year—and do not work during your time away from
the office. When you are doing something other than work—
attending a family event, for example—do not spend that
time worrying about work, checking in with the office, or
talking on your cell phone. Be present, and give your full
attention to those with whom you are spending time. Do not
skimp on time for pursuing your interests, either. You will be
more focused, less resentful, and more productive at work if
you have some downtime to yourself, as well. Finding balance
is essential. It becomes easier with time and practice, but you

need to commit to seeking balance from your first day on the job.

The Flexibility Quotient: Flex-Time and Part-Time Options

For some people, there are times in their career when the scales of balance tip so heavily in favor of personal concerns or pursuits that they cannot give their career their full attention, at least for the time being. If that happens to you, it is important to know that part-time and flex-time options are becoming more common and acceptable in a variety of employment venues—for both women and men.

With many legal employers, part-time and flex-time options become more viable after you have a few years of experience under your belt. Because the first few years of law practice are spent overcoming a huge learning curve, many, but not all, legal employers require a full-time commitment at first. Law school prepares you and gives you a strong foundation, but it does not really teach you how to practice law. As such, many employers feel that your full-time presence is important at first. Over time, after you have learned the basics of your practice area and established a record of professionalism, dependability, and reliability, employers become more comfortable offering different work options. Judith Finer Freedman offers these thoughts on flexibility:

> When new law graduates begin their careers, they will need to weigh the quest for balance against the quest to establish themselves as committed and respected attorneys in the field. To accomplish this, they need to assess what type of reputation they want to establish and then work backwards to decide what steps they will need to take to achieve that end. Their quest for balance may need to be put aside in the short term in order to achieve the longer-term goal of being known as a reputable attorney. Once this is accomplished, they will have the equity they need to be able to negotiate balance on their terms. Without the equity piece, it is difficult to assess the cost/benefit ratio of granting requests for a more open and flexible work schedule, especially considering where the profession is today. The good news for associates is that the profession is now open to dialogue on flexibility and the need for balance. The bad news is that the profession still has a

long way to go to translate these needs into norms in the day-
to-day culture.

**Judith Finer Freedman, Founder, The Balanced Work-
er Project ™ whose clients are based in the U.S. and
Canada**

It is also true that certain practice areas are more conducive to a part-time or flex-time schedule than others. Some
are more predictable, which allows for more regular hour
parameters. Unfortunately, some legal employers still find it
easier to let a valued lawyer go than to work at developing a
part-time or flex-time work option to retain that lawyer. Such
employers are becoming less common, but they're still
around.

Many part-time and flex-time options exist within legal
employment venues. Some are called reduced-hour arrangements, whereby the lawyer works a reduced number of billable hours for a salary that has been adjusted downward on a
pro rata basis, or a pro rata basis that is also adjusted for
overhead costs. If the employer is a law firm with a partnership opportunity, the time working on a reduced-hour arrangement may or may not count toward partnership progress. There are also arrangements in which a lawyer is paid
an agreed-upon salary to work in the office on a regular (less
than full-time) schedule each week.

Some employers offer project employment on a part-time
and/or as-needed basis to cover certain client projects or
needs. Often such arrangements do not offer benefits, and if
the work slows down, so do the hours. Flex-time options may
include telecommuting for a set amount of time in addition to
time spent in the office. Flex time may also encompass
working a full week, but doing it on your own terms—a
compressed schedule of four days a week, or fewer hours each
day, including some weekends. Some creative legal employers
have experimented with job-sharing arrangements, whereby
two lawyers share a single position including the salary and
resources, such as a single office and computer.

For most legal employers, the practice workload, client
and business needs, and nature of the work in that practice
(Can the work be performed remotely? Does someone need to
be available when the stock market is open?) drive what part-
time and flex-time options may be available. If you are
interested in exploring such options, first familiarize yourself
with your employer's existing policies relating to part time
and flex time options for lawyers. If you are in private

practice, are you still on the partnership track? Are you still eligible for a bonus? If you are in another context, can you still be promoted? What are your benefit options and costs if you are working less than full time? What are the implications to your employer's retirement contributions? These and other questions should all be explored thoroughly.

Next, find out if there are lawyers already successfully working on a part-time or flex-time schedule, preferably in your division or practice area, if you are with a larger employer. If you are in a group for which there have not been any successful arrangements like this, explore whether it has been attempted before, if the work is conducive to something other than a full-time commitment, or if there is a distinct lack of support for flexible options. If it has not been tried before, there is no reason you cannot be the first successful part-time lawyer at your firm, organization, or practice group. If it is due to the work not being conducive or to a lack of support, you could still explore the options, knowing the challenges and taking great care to address the concerns that will arise. You may even want to explore your options in another group.

A successful part-time or flex-time arrangement depends upon having accurately expressed expectations and accountability upon which both the lawyer and employer agree. The more specific the terms of the arrangement, the better. Strong communication is key to navigating these situations, so it is good to know who will be monitoring the success of the arrangement from the lawyer's and the employer's perspective. Think through scenarios that could arise under such an arrangement and how they will be handled. For example, if a lawyer is on a reduced-hour arrangement and finds that he or she is working more hours than were agreed upon, how will that be handled from a salary perspective and from the lawyer's perspective? Presumably she or he wanted a reduced-hour schedule for a reason. Although there may be projects that require an increased presence at work, how will expectations on both sides be managed, and how can the lawyer ensure that he or she will be back to reduced hours once the intense project is done?

When you are requesting a part-time or flex-time option, acknowledge the need for your availability and responsiveness at key or critical times. You must also set some boundaries. Too many part-time lawyers complain that they work a full-time schedule. Keep in mind, though, that many full-time lawyers work schedules that are far in excess of full time. In this high-performance profession, making flex-time and part-time arrangements work requires commitment and professionalism on both sides of the equation. Successfully negotiating an arrangement that works for you and your employer is key—be creative to meet the employer's needs while meeting your own.

It can be scary or uncomfortable to approach the subject of working less than full time with your employer. After working so hard for so long, you might fear that you will seem uncommitted or unable to handle the demands of the job. The reality is that most (though not all) employers will be open to this discussion if you are a valued employee. Because so many people have successfully navigated the part-time pitfalls before you (and because so many employers have lost valued employees due to their previous inflexibility on this topic), you may not have to advocate too hard for your arrangement. After researching your options and other lawyers who are working part time, think about what arrangements might work for you. Also think about your employer's potential concerns with such an arrangement, and develop ways to address them.

You won't know what your employer's reaction will be until you ask. It is always better to know, than to guess at what you might or might not be able to arrange. If the answer is not what you were hoping for, you will have to make a decision—either to continue to work as you are, if that is possible, or to seek a new position that can accommodate your current needs. At least you will know your options with certainty and you can plan accordingly.

With a strong commitment from both you and the employer, good communication at all times on both sides, and a healthy dose of professionalism, a part-time or flex-time arrangement can work very well. Alert your employer to any snags that you hit. Address them head-on, communicate with your supervisor, and navigate through them to better the relationship and keep the arrangement workable for everyone.

Know the Risks: Substance Abuse and Depression

Lawyers are at higher risk than the general population for both substance abuse and depression.[12] Law school and law practice are demanding and challenging under the best of circumstances, and students and lawyers are at risk for developing a host of addiction or mental health issues.[13] Law students and lawyers need to understand these risks and know where to seek help for themselves or for a fellow student or colleague, when necessary.

There is a strong movement in legal education to publicize and de-stigmatize the negative implications that legal education and law practice can have on students, including mental health and substance abuse issues. A growing body of scholarship addresses the negative impact law school can have on students and argues for transformation and improvement in teaching and classroom methods and a greater availability of resources for students and lawyers who fall victim to these issues.[14] Law students are also getting involved—the ABA Law Student Division is launching a mental health initiative that will include resources for students, as well as a National Mental Health Day to be observed at law schools.[15]

There are an increasing number of resources available to assist students in understanding and resisting the pressures inherent in the legal environment. The Humanizing Law School Web site (http://www.law.fsu.edu/academic_programs/humanizing_lawschool/humanizing_lawschool.html) has a full section devoted to resources for students. However, there is no substitute for (or shame in) seeking assistance that goes beyond printed material, and most mental health and substance abuse issues cannot be overcome single-handedly. One primary resource of which to be aware are lawyer assistance programs, which are also available to law students. All states now have lawyer assistance programs, in concert with the

---

12. See Lawrence S. Krieger, *Institutional Denial About the Dark Side of Law School, and Fresh Empirical Guidance for Constructively Breaking the Silence*, 52 J. LEGAL EDUC. 112 (2002); the ABA Commission on Lawyer Assistance Programs, available at: http://www.abanet.org/legalservices/colap/ (2008).

13. Id.

14. See, for example, Krieger, *supra*, note 11; Susan Grover, *Personal Integration and Outsider Status as Factors*

in Law Student Well–Being, 47 Wash L. J. 101 (2008); Humanizing Legal Education Web site, which contains links to a number of helpful resources and scholarship for students and law faculty: http://www.law.fsu.edu/academic_programs/humanizing_lawschool/humanizing_lawschool.html.

15. Leigh Jones, *ABA Law Student Group Tackles Depression*, The National Law Journal, March 13, 2008.

state bar, which can be accessed by both lawyers and law
students. According to the ABA Commission on Lawyer Assistance Programs, "These programs employ the use of inter-
vention, peer counseling, and referral to 12–Step Programs to
assist in the lawyer's recovery process."[16]

A law professor who volunteers with her state's lawyer
assistance program offers this advice:

> For law students and lawyers having any sort of mental
> health issue (including depression, substance abuse and oth-
> ers), help is readily available. Simply make an anonymous
> call to your state's lawyer assistance program (LAP). LAPs
> are operated by attorneys and health care practitioners who
> understand the stresses that law students and lawyers con-
> front. LAP professionals also understand that maintaining
> the strictest confidentiality is absolutely essential to protect
> the individual's reputation in the legal community. Most
> LAPs have a confidential hot line; you can obtain the hotline
> number for your state on the ABA website.
>
> A confidential telephone call to the LAP will give you an
> opportunity to confide the problems being experienced and to
> obtain moral support and suggestions for how to proceed to
> address the problem. An important thing you need to know
> about the LAPs: The whole reason for their existence is to
> offer help to law students and lawyers. Many LAP directors
> and other personnel have been in your shoes and will under-
> stand exactly what you are talking about. They WANT to hear
> from you! The LAPs would rather have a call where no help
> is really needed than not get a call in a case where someone
> could have been helped. If you feel reluctant to call, that may
> just be a sign that you should take a deep breath, pick up the
> phone and make the call. Set your fear and self consciousness
> aside. Calling does not mean that you are committed to
> taking any action, that you are admitting to a problem or
> anything else. You can use the call as an opportunity to list a
> few symptoms and ask the LAP professional whether they
> think you need to be concerned about them.
>
> If your conversation persuades you that you need help, the
> LAP professional can guide you in appropriate directions to
> obtain that help. It might be a recommendation that you get
> counseling, that you attend meetings, or that you have a more
> formal assessment, all depending on the circumstances.
>
> If you believe that a friend or colleague may be experiencing
> such difficulties, the exact same hotline is a good place to

16. ABA Commission on Lawyer Assistance Programs, *supra* note 11.

begin. The LAP professional can help you understand whether the individual may be in need of help, and, if so, how best to help them obtain that help. When in doubt, make the call.

Susan Grover, Associate Professor of Law, William & Mary School of Law; Volunteer and Board Member, Virginia's Lawyers Helping Lawyers; Member, ABA Commission on Lawyer Assistance Programs, Law School Assistance Committee

The purpose of the lawyer assistance program is to identify the problem and assist the law student or lawyer confidentially and without formal discipline. If lawyers do not seek such assistance, and their ability to practice becomes impaired to the point of disciplinary action, it may be too late to avoid repercussions. These programs are accessible long before that point, however, so please be aware of them and, if necessary, place a confidential call to seek help for yourself or on behalf of someone who needs it. The ABA provides a state-by-state listing of all such assistance programs, which can be found at: http://www.abanet.org/legal services/colap/lapdirectory.html.

If you are a law student at risk, you may be concerned about seeking assistance for fear that it will keep you from becoming admitted to the bar. Recently, the ABA adopted a new model rule allowing for conditional admission to the bar for candidates who have sought help and are in recovery for past substance abuse.[17] Seek help before you become part of a disciplinary proceeding or are kept from admission to the bar.

It is helpful to know the warning signs of addiction and what to do to seek help for yourself or on behalf of someone else. George Hettrick has written a strong piece about recognizing the signs of lawyer impairment that can serve as a good resource.[18] There is no shame in seeking assistance, and

17. Full text of the model rule is available at: http://www.abanet.org/legal services/downloads/colap/ABAModel Rule_ Conditional Admission_Feb2008.-pdf. The ABA Commission Web site states, "On February 11, 2008 the ABA House of Delegates adopted as ABA policy a new Model Rule on Conditional Admission to Practice Law. This rule is offered to the states as a model to guide states in coping with situations where candidates for admission to practice who have sought treatment for problems with substance abuse or mental health and appear to be in recovery, but where admission authorities wish to monitor such individuals for a period of time to insure that recovery is successful. The model rule provides for confidentiality so that such individuals will feel free to seek treatment without suffering stigma or denial of admission."

18. See George Hettrick, "Addiction to Alcohol and Other Drugs: Recognizing the Signs of Lawyer Impairment," *The Bar Examiner*, October 1999.

doing so can save your career and even your life, or that of a close colleague or friend.

Taking Control of Your Career

We started this journey by discussing the three spheres that comprise your successful career as a lawyer:

1. Sphere One: Legal knowledge and skills gained through your legal education

2. Sphere Two: Legal experience gained through clinics, internships, and legal jobs

3. Sphere Three: Professionalism skills, including respect, courtesy, etiquette, strong communication, leadership, debt management, good judgment, maturity, management aptitude, networking, ethical standards, timekeeping, and organizational skills

In order to maximize your lawyer potential, you need to develop your skills across all three spheres. Lacking knowledge or skill in any one of the three can quickly lead to problems. This book has focused on those skills in Sphere Three—professionalism skills. This is the sphere that is given the least amount of attention during and after law school, but these skills are no less important than those in the other two spheres. A critical aspect of professionalism, although it has not been named directly yet, is personal responsibility. This is a key component to every aspect of professionalism discussed in this book. No one besides you has as much investment and stake in the outcome of your career. It is incumbent on you to take charge of your career and land on the path that inspires and excites you.

Taking charge of your career is not difficult, but it is not always easy, either. When you set goals, be deliberate about the career moves you make. If you begin your career in a high-paying job, it is natural to adjust your lifestyle accordingly and make financial commitments that are difficult to support at lower income levels. If you decide that you do not like the work you are doing, you may find it difficult to make a move financially. Sometimes referred to as "golden handcuffs," these constraints can limit your options. Thus, if you do start your career in a high-paying job, guard against such commitments. Pay down any debt you have and bank the rest, in case you decide to change jobs. If it turns out you love where you're at, then you will be that much further ahead. Conversely, if you begin your career in a lower-paying position, be sure to manage your finances carefully, and explore options that may be available to help repay your loans if you are in the public interest sector.

Your income level should not be the measure of your worth or career success. Your passion, development, career progression, career satisfaction, and overall life satisfaction are the factors that really matter—but, certainly, your ability to live comfortably and repay your debt is never irrelevant. Taking charge of your career presumes that you know what is important to you and that you can plan your career path in accordance with your strengths, assets, and passions. If you don't yet know what is important to you, focus on figuring that out through trying various positions, becoming involved in bar and community activities to help discern your passions, assessments, or even through the assistance of a career coach.

Life will throw you career curveballs and unexpected setbacks that you cannot control. How you handle such stumbling blocks is within your control, however, and professionalism will be more important than ever in the face of adversity and obstacles. You can recover from setbacks, whether a mistake you made on the job, a funding cut that leaves you jobless, losing a big client, or simply deciding that you are not happy in your current position or practice area. Whatever situations you encounter, follow the principles in this book. Use your networking contacts, exercise leadership and professionalism, take initiative, meet your commitments, and maintain the highest of ethical standards.

Karen Sarjeant offers the following wisdom:

Align your personal life with your professional goals—if these are constantly at odds, you will never be happy. In The Measure of Our Success *by Marian Wright Edelman, the CEO and Founder of The Children's Defense Fund, her Life Lesson #4 is, "Never work just for money or for power. They won't save your soul or build a decent family or help you sleep at night." There is no better advice.*

It is a privilege to do work that you love. Develop self-mastery and self-reflection skills, listen to your inner voice, set goals, know where you are trying to go, and be realistic about what it will take to get there. Be happy with the decisions that you make. Trust your instincts; they are usually right.

And, remember, most legal careers are not linear. Seize those moments of opportunity and change as they occur, even if they do not seem to be a natural fit to what you think your career path should be. Be willing to take a risk. It will usually turn out better than you think!

Karen J. Sarjeant, Vice President for Programs and Compliance, Legal Services Corporation

In the end, you are the only one who can determine what career path is best for you. Pay attention to your career, your development, and your satisfaction. Build and maintain your network, and constantly seek to improve the many "soft skills" we have discussed throughout this book. These skills are really anything but "soft"—they will provide the sturdy foundation and infrastructure for your legal career, and they are necessary and attainable, with work, practice, and commitment. Armed with all three spheres—legal skills, legal experience, and professionalism—you truly can maximize your lawyer potential.

Index

References are to Pages

251

INDEX

INDEX

INDEX

INDEX

INDEX

†